SYMBOLS OF FREEDOM

SYMBOLS

—— *of* ——

FREEDOM

Slavery and Resistance Before the Civil War

—

MATTHEW J. CLAVIN

NEW YORK UNIVERSITY PRESS

New York

NEW YORK UNIVERSITY PRESS
New York
www.nyupress.org

Library of Congress Cataloging-in-Publication Data
Names: Clavin, Matthew J., author.
Title: Symbols of freedom : slavery and resistance before the Civil War / Matthew J. Clavin.
Description: New York : New York University Press, [2023] |
Includes bibliographical references and index.
Identifiers: LCCN 2022050017 | ISBN 9781479823246 (hardback) |
ISBN 9781479823253 (ebook) | ISBN 9781479823260 (ebook other)
Subjects: LCSH: Antislavery movements—United States—History—19th century. |
Signs and symbols—United States—History. | Rhetoric—Political aspects—
United States—History. | National characteristics, American—History. |
United States—History—1815–1861.
Classification: LCC E441 .C593 2023 | DDC 973.7/114—dc23/eng/20230105
LC record available at https://lccn.loc.gov/2022050017

New York University Press books are printed on acid-free paper, and their binding
materials are chosen for strength and durability. We strive to use environmentally
responsible suppliers and materials to the greatest extent possible in publishing our books.

Manufactured in the United States of America

10 9 8 7 6 5 4 3 2 1

Also available as an ebook

For the loves of my life, Gladys, Madeline, Joseph, and Joshua

Any critic of the American present must have profoundly mixed feelings about our country's past. On the one hand, he will feel shame and distrust toward Founding Fathers who tolerated slavery, exterminated Indians, and blandly assumed that a good society must be based on private property. On the other hand, he is likely to find himself articulating his own demands in the Revolutionary language of inalienable rights, a natural higher law, and the right to revolution.

—Staughton Lynd,
Intellectual Origins of American Radicalism
(1968)

CONTENTS

LIST OF FIGURES

INTRODUCTION

Hail Columbia

Shortly after the War of 1812, members of the House of Representatives who had gathered near the United States Capitol in Washington, DC, saw something truly extraordinary. For years, slave traders had forced African Americans to walk in chains through the streets of the nation's capital and politicians rarely took notice, but on this day one of the captives drew lawmakers' attention by raising his hands and lifting his voice in opposition to his enslavement. "Elevating his manacles as high as he could reach," a congressional eyewitness recalled, the captive "commenced singing the favorite national song, '*Hail Columbia! Happy land.*'"[1]

Despite its spectacle, the impromptu performance seems to have had no effect on slave traders or political representatives in the capital city. Indeed, the enslaved soloist completed the chain-bound journey to a local slave pen or auction house where he and his companions were ostensibly sold to the highest bidder. Still, the story did not end here, for a small but growing group of antislavery activists seized upon the incident to highlight the hypocrisy of slavery in a nation nominally dedicated to freedom.

Decades later, the American Anti-Slavery Society issued a broadside entitled, SLAVE MARKET OF AMERICA. The oversized handbill, which included nine artfully crafted illustrations, reveals the long and disturbing history of slavery in and around the nation's capital. In the placard's upper right-hand corner under the heading "THE HOME OF THE OPPRESSED," a black-and-white engraving offers a compelling representation of the event that took place in front of the Capitol. At the center of the scene, American flags fly on both sides of the building's rooftop dome, while congressmen amble on the steps below the iconic semicircular structure. At ground level in the picture's forefront, a dozen Black men chained in pairs walk behind a White man with a whip at the ready. A slave toward the front of the coffle holds an unidentified flag in his one unchained hand as those behind him gesture—and most assuredly sing—in the direction of both the congressmen and the Capitol. Underneath the rectangular image the caption reads: "CAPITOL OF THE UNITED STATES. 'Hail Columbia.'"[2]

Though inspired by the actual event, the image is full of inaccuracies. Several captives sing the national anthem with their arms raised, when only one brave vocalist had committed the defiant act. That many of these bondmen wear hats, shoes, jackets, and long pants, while carrying their personal belongings in small bags, suggests the engraver had never seen this or any other slave coffle in person—despite claims that the illustration was made "by an artist on the spot."[3] Another glaring error is the depiction of the Capitol, which at that time was in ruins. British forces had burned the so-called Temple of Liberty to the ground months earlier, forcing Congress to meet in a modest three-story brick building nearby for years.[4]

What the iconic engraving most notably failed to capture was the revolutionary nature of the public protest. Though little-known today, "Hail Columbia" was the first song the American people considered a national anthem. Written in honor of George Washington and the other patriots who "fought and bled in freedom's cause," the hymn was a musical tribute to those who were willing to fight and die for their nation's liberation. It was also a repudiation of slavery that prayed "truth and justice will prevail, / And every scheme of bondage fail." The song's subversiveness makes its performance by an enslaved Black man in front of powerful White politicians against the backdrop of the Capitol truly astonishing—even more so when considering the song's last line, which repeated the Revolutionary War-era mantra, "death or Liberty."[5]

FIGURE I.I. "*THE HOME OF THE OPPRESSED*," from William S. Dorr, *SLAVE MARKET OF AMERICA* (New York: American Anti-Slavery Society, 1836). Courtesy of the Library of Congress.

Like any public protest, the shackled singer's rendition of "Hail Columbia" can only be understood in the context of the time and place in which it occurred. Since winning independence from Great Britain in 1783, the American people had begun inventing a series of rituals, customs, and traditions to secure the foundation of the "imagined community" they were building out of the materials of disparate people, interests, and ideas.[6] A decade-long surge of nationalism following the War of 1812 that became known as the "Era of Good Feelings" accelerated the process of nation-building.[7] Within several years, citizens adopted several unofficial national anthems and standardized a national flag. They also began observing national holidays, including the anniversaries of George Washington's birth on February 22nd and the Declaration of Independence on July 4th.[8]

As powerful symbols of an American identity, anthems, flags, and holidays helped unify a divided people. So too did a commemorative landscape of monuments and memorials that recalled the brave sacrifice of the nation's founders as well as their philosophy of freedom.

From Boston's Bunker Hill to Independence Hall in Philadelphia and St. John's Church in Richmond, Virginia, where Patrick Henry offered his life for liberty, the signs of an emerging nation were everywhere. This was especially the case in Washington, DC, where a national capital seemed to appear out of the Potomac River's swamplands overnight.[9]

In addition to these iconic symbols, a national language of freedom, which derived from the natural rights philosophy of the Enlightenment, also served as a source of American identity. The Declaration of Independence's assertion "that all men are created equal," Patrick Henry's cry of liberty or death, and Francis Scott Key's "star-spangled banner" waving over "the land of the free and the home of the brave," were widely repeated words and phrases that fostered a collective consciousness. Resonating across the country, they reinforced individuals' determination to build a new nation where the right to "life, liberty, and the pursuit of happiness" was universal, natural, and inalienable.

There was every reason to expect the establishment of such a truly exceptional society but for slavery. With state, local, and federal laws regarding African-descended people as property, the language and symbols that served as national touchstones made a mockery of freedom. They encouraged an empty American culture that accepted the abstract notion of equality rather than the concrete idea. For millions of enslaved people and their allies, these rhetorical expressions rang hollow. Nevertheless, as the performance of "Hail Columbia" by the shackled bondman before the Capitol suggests, they continued to offer inspiration.

An analysis of the role that the language and symbols of American freedom played in the conflict over slavery illuminates how enslaved people and their allies rejected the rhetorical nationalism of their proslavery counterparts.[10] Interpreting both the language and symbols of freedom literally, they embraced a revolutionary nationalism that not only justified but generated forceful and even violent resistance to slavery. Mindful and proud that theirs was a nation born in blood, these disparate patriots—Black and White, male and female, northern and southern, rich and poor—fought to fulfill the radical promises of the republic and its founders by waging a real and revolutionary war against slavery.

———————

Interrogating the impact of national language and symbols comes with some risk. Long before the "global turn" of early American history, when wounds wrought by fascist governments in Europe and Asia in the mid-twentieth century remained open, scholars started rejecting the nation-state as a conceptual framework of analysis, choosing instead to adopt a less provincial and more cosmopolitan worldview in their research and writing.[11] As a result, nationalism, which can briefly be defined as a strong attachment to, and identification with, the nation-state, its interests, and its people, received tremendous academic scrutiny. In the twenty-first century, a resurgence of authoritarian and repressive regimes in the United States, Russia, and across the globe has further damaged nationalism's reputation among scholars and students of history.[12] Today, Yuval Noah Harari writes in his bestselling *Sapiens: A Brief History of Humankind*, academics see "nationalism as a deadly plague that spread throughout the world in the nineteenth and twentieth centuries, causing wars, oppression, hate and genocide. The moment people in one country were infected with it, those in neighboring countries were also likely to catch the virus."[13]

The aversion to nationalism derives largely from its relationship with racism. The two historical phenomena, which appeared at the same time, share a great deal in common—so much so that "The difference between racism and nationalism is sometimes difficult to determine."[14] From the late eighteenth century, Europeans and their descendants built nation-states on the bedrock of White supremacy. The result was revoltingly contradictory. While White people enjoyed an unprecedented expansion of rights and liberties, non-White people faced enslavement, dispossession, and, to use historian Kay Wright Lewis's term, "extermination."[15]

Even so, African-descended people often identified with, and fought for inclusion in, these transatlantic polities. Olaudah Equiano's story is an oft-cited example. Enslaved as a child in West Africa, the Igbo captive spent his formative years traversing the Anglo-Atlantic world until buying his own freedom and settling permanently in London. In a popular antislavery tract describing his experiences, Equiano admitted a strong affinity for the English people and their culture. Though subjected to unthinkable emotional and physical trauma by years of captivity on English ships and in English colonies, the native African proudly considered himself "almost an Englishman."[16]

That Equiano and other Black people played a pivotal role in national freedom movements is unsurprising, for nationalist policies that targeted racial minorities often had unanticipated results. In the United States and South Africa, for example, these plans, programs, and procedures "had the unintended consequence of consolidating and legitimating subordinated racial identity into a potential basis for resistance." According to historian Anthony Marx, efforts to codify racism that intended to unite White people unintentionally brought Black people together. They moreover emboldened them to challenge their oppressors.[17] For African-descended people seeking inclusion in nation-states that repressed and persecuted them, the fight for freedom was about much more than ending enslavement. It was also an effort to redefine the nation-state. By challenging existing racial paradigms, they endeavored to create egalitarian communities, governments, and societies that not only rejected slavery but racism as well. Alas, doing so proved almost impossible.

In response, racial resistance often took the form of force and violence. The reason is easy to explain. Reflecting on a life full of opposition, Nelson Mandela remarked that freedom fighters quickly learn that oppressors determine the "nature of the struggle," leaving the former no alternative but to copy the methods of the latter. "If the oppressor uses violence, the oppressed have no alternative but to respond violently."[18] History confirms these words. In the early United States where racial violence was widespread, peaceful and passive resistance to slavery and White supremacy proved futile.[19] Fortunately, for enslaved people and their allies, the republic's revolutionary birth offered a powerful model for forcefully challenging the status quo. Buoyed by this historical example, they subsequently fought not only to redeem their nation, but the idea of a nation as well.

Despite nationalism's racist roots, it still matters. Indeed, it is a powerful and persistent global force, which historians ignore at their peril. "We can write history that implicitly denies or ignores the nation-state," the Pulitzer-Prize winning historian Carl Degler declared decades ago, "but it would be a history that flew in the face of what people who live in a nation-state require and demand." Encouraging historians to continue to write a national history of the United States, Degler urged, "This pursuit will gain for us a history that is distinctly American, not simply because it happened to us, but because it did not happen to others."[20]

Symbols of Freedom acknowledges nationalism's significance in the early United States; therefore, it is important to briefly consider the closely related concept of patriotism. While there is no entry for *nationalism* in the first edition of Noah Webster's *American Dictionary*, the 1828 work defines *national* as being "Attached or unduly attached to one's own country." *Patriotism*, by contrast, is described favorably as the "Love of one's country."[21] Since then, nationalism has become a negative term, meaning an aversion to, or even hatred of, foreign nations and people, while patriotism has also taken on a pejorative connotation. This study contextualizes these terms in the time when the United States and the very idea of a nation-state were in their infancy. As such, it takes its cues from new and important histories of the early American republic, which show that "nationalism and patriotism once carried more positive meanings."[22]

Highlighting nationalism's influence on slave and antislavery resistance in the early United States requires a significant departure from the historical literature, which has deemphasized national identity. While slavery alone was always enough to spark slave opposition, enslaved people drew added inspiration from various sources. Since the late twentieth century, Black nationalist scholars have highlighted the significance of race consciousness and racial solidarity in stimulating slave resistance among African-descended people. Exposing the pursuit of Black people throughout the Atlantic world to establish race-based communities and societies, they downplay the attachment of these men and women to traditional Western nation-states.[23] More recently, historians of the Atlantic world have established numerous instances of enslaved Americans forcefully opposing their bondage after learning of the measures adopted by foreign nations, namely Haiti, France, and Great Britain, on the behalf of freedom.[24] Still, it is important to remember that the United States had its own revolutionary tradition, which similarly inspired captive people. As this study reveals, resistance was a natural response to enslavement that only increased and intensified in a nation birthed in freedom.

Like the enslaved people they advocated and fought for, American abolitionists also took inspiration from both foreign and domestic sources. The movement's transcendence of regional and national boundaries is well documented.[25] It is epitomized in the international endeavors of William Wells Brown, William Lloyd Garrison, Frederick Douglass, and Maria Weston Chapman. Scholarly emphasis on the overseas adventures of American abolitionists has tended to obscure the fact that while earning their reputations as "transatlantic agitators and transatlantic *thinkers*," they remained deeply devoted to their native country. In truth, they obsessed over its shortcomings, which derived from slavery, and dedicated their lives to eliminating them.[26]

As historians of northern nationalism have demonstrated, abolitionists' attachment to the United States did not impede their sectional identification. To the contrary, the hatred of the South and its peculiar institution encouraged a devotion to the North that increased and intensified over time. Across the antebellum era, abolitionists came to believe that as a geographic region rooted in the principles of freedom and equality, the northern states were far superior to the southern states, which suffered from slavery and the attendant vices of racism and violence. The North's comparatively egalitarian institutions and ideals unified abolitionists and fortified their movement. At the same time, they served as a model for the entire nation to both aspire to and achieve.[27]

For free Black northerners, who were in the vanguard of American abolitionism, race trumped region. Demonstrating what W. E. B. Du Bois called "double consciousness," they identified primarily with their people and their nation.[28] In a society blighted by both slavery and White supremacy, these collective identifications reinforced each other and at times became indistinguishable. "More than any other facet of antebellum African American thought," writes historian Patrick Rael, "black takes on American nationalism constructed the African-descended as a people, united in purpose and destiny."[29] Not surprisingly, then, Black abolitionists were both Black nationalists and United States nationalists who displayed a revolutionary commitment to liberating their enslaved countrymen and women that was both racial and national in nature.[30]

Evidence of this commitment came in the rejection of colonization, a policy that sought the permanent removal of all Black people from beyond the nation's borders. While some free African Americans supported voluntary emigration to Haiti, Africa, or other destinations abroad to escape persecution at home, the vast majority condemned colonization as a racist conspiracy to deprive them of their rights as natural-born citizens. In articles published in Black-owned newspapers like *Freedom's Journal* and *The North Star*, and in speeches delivered at regional, state, and national Colored Conventions, Black men and women vowed to stay in the land of their nativity and fight. In historian Jacqueline Bacon's words, "Declaring themselves unwilling to leave their enslaved brethren and asserting their rights as Americans, African Americans continued their militant stand in pursuit of freedom."[31]

For enslaved people and their allies, the language and symbols of American freedom both justified and inspired revolutionary violence in the pursuit of two interconnected objectives—the death of slavery and the birth of a new and truly egalitarian nation. The result was a decades-long effort that explodes the idea that in the early United States slave and antislavery resistance was passive and peaceful. On cotton farms and sugar plantations across the South, and in smalls towns and large cities throughout the North, enslaved people and their allies took great solace in the United States' revolutionary tradition. Like the republic's Founding Fathers, who against almost insurmountable odds took up arms against their oppressors, they eagerly embraced the dangerous and deadly fight for freedom.

To prove this, the chapters that follow are divided into two parts. The first examines the sectional contest over the meaning of the language and symbols of freedom, while the second investigates violent slave and antislavery resistance through the lens of early American nationalism. Chapters are arranged thematically, though chronological ordering is employed whenever possible. The first and second chapters offer a snapshot of the half-century between the War of 1812 and the Civil War, when slavery's opponents openly contested the appropriation of the US flag and the Fourth of July by the institution's supporters. The third considers Frederick Douglass's most illustrious oration, in which he contemplated the significance of Independence Day and the Declaration of Independence for enslaved people. Chapters 4 and 5 focus on enslaved people who forcefully and in some cases violently resisted their oppressors. The final two chapters consider violent abolitionism in the decade before the Civil War, culminating in John Brown's raid at Harpers Ferry, Virginia, in 1859. A brief coda on Black soldiers' fidelity to the American flag suggests how far the United States has come in the fight for racial equality and the distance that remains to be traveled.

PART I
CONTESTING

1

THE FLAG

Few lines in American history are as well-known as those comprising the first verse of Francis Scott Key's "Star-Spangled Banner." Written on a ship floating in Baltimore Harbor after American forces survived a bombardment from British ships during the War of 1812, the opening stanza can still be heard emanating from the sites of political rallies, military exercises, and athletic contests across the United States. Key's colorful description of the national flag flying high above Fort McHenry is a triumphant expression of American patriotism. It holds a special place in the minds of the nation's citizens, even if many of them are unable to recite its lyrics accurately.[1] While the most famous line of the National Anthem is the opening exclamation, "O! say can you see by the dawn's early light," the most infamous line appears in the third of the song's four original sections. Assailing the enslaved people who had absconded from their American owners and volunteered for the British armed forces during the war, it surmises these traitorous bondmen had either fled in fear before the Battle of Baltimore or lost their lives in the process of betraying the pro-slavery republic: "No refuge could save the hireling and slave / From the terror of flight or the gloom of the grave." After reveling in the alleged demise of these formerly captive people, the song repeats its inspiring crescendo, "the star-spangled banner in triumph doth wave / O'er the land of the free and the home of the brave."[2]

Key's lyrics did not go unchallenged. Years later, the Quaker abolitionist Dr. Edwin Atlee parodied the "National Song" to illuminate the plight of the fugitive slaves who fought alongside the British against the United States in the hope of becoming free. Unlike Key's original poem, this revision depicts the plight of all enslaved people whose blood daily streamed under the lash of their American oppressors, while the national banner, "With its stars, mocking freedom, is fitfully gleaming." Instead of a land of liberty, the United States was a shelter for slavery: "No refuge is found on our unhallowed ground / For the wretched in Slavery's manacles bound." Should the nation fail to achieve its boasted ideals, "our star-spangled banner at half mast shall wave / O'er the death-bed of Freedom—the home of the slave."[3]

As the two contrasting compositions demonstrate, the American flag was from its inception a controversial and contested symbol. Its history is familiar. In the Revolutionary War era, colonists across Great Britain's thirteen rebellious colonies flew a variety of colors to rally support against British tyranny. But it was a red-and-white striped flag adopted by the Sons of Liberty in Boston that served as a model for many of the republic's earliest flags. In 1818, after several decades of confusion over the proper design of the national standard, the federal government passed a law requiring the flag of the United States to include thirteen alternating red-and-white stripes in honor of the original states. The upper-left quarter of the banner was to consist of a blue field with twenty white stars, corresponding with the numbers of states in the Union at the time of the law's adoption. Additional stars were to be added upon the admission of new states. While the flag's dimensions and the pattern of the growing constellation of stars went unmentioned, the result was a standardized banner that remains recognizable today.[4]

Though universally regarded as a national emblem, the American flag meant different things to different people in the early United States. There were a variety of reasons for these disparate views, with attitudes toward slavery being among the most prominent. For slavery's defenders, the flag represented countless liberties, including the right of White citizens to buy, sell, and own Black people. For slavery's opponents, it symbolized the American republic's failed promise of freedom. In a nation shamed by slavery, its flag was a blot that invited and deserved condemnation both at home and abroad.

To be sure, abolitionists and their antislavery predecessors' feelings toward the flag stemmed from a love—rather than hate—of their nation. Despite the growing interest of historians in the organized effort to end slavery, there is a dearth of scholarship on the influence of United States nationalism on the movement and its culture. Important analyses of antislavery texts and images often embrace an international perspective, as it demonstrates the dynamic and sophisticated nature of these materials and the people who produced them.[5] At other times, these studies see the development of a strong sectional identity among antebellum northerners as the impetus behind increased slave opposition.[6] As a result, American nationalism's impact on abolitionism has largely gone unnoticed.

This chapter offers a corrective. Through an analysis of antislavery and abolitionist culture in the decades before the Civil War, it reveals the existence of a sectional skirmish over the meaning of the American flag that fed the much larger national conflict over slavery. When southern slave owners and traders flew the Stars and Stripes over plantations, pens, and auction houses, they provoked a strong reaction from northern speakers, writers, and illustrators who rejected the standard's use as a pro-slavery icon—and endeavored to reclaim it.

Driven by an intense love of country, slavery's opponents made the reclamation of the American flag as a symbol of freedom an important part of their crusade. By abolishing the South's peculiar and unpatriotic institution, they strove to redeem both the republic and its most recognizable symbol in their own eyes and those of the world as well. Though proud and patriotic people, these American activists valued the opinions of their international counterparts and continually looked to them for validation.

In the summer of 1822, while traveling through Paris, Kentucky, James Dickey's heart leapt when he heard music in the distance, which he interpreted as the approach of a military pageant or parade. The minister's anticipation quickly turned to terror when instead of witnessing a patriotic procession, he saw dozens of enslaved people walking together in pairs, dragging a forty-foot-long chain between them. Even more revolting than the sight of as many as seventy captive people being led through the woods like animals was the fact that one of them carried a flag bearing the distinctive stars and stripes of the American standard. "My soul was sick," Dickey wrote of the disturbing scene. "As a man, I sympathized with suffering humanity, as a Christian, I mourned over the transgressions of God's holy law, and as a *republican* I felt indignant, to see the flag of my beloved country thus insulted."[7]

A flag-carrying coffle could have been spotted at almost any time and place in the antebellum South and few, if anyone, outside the local area would have noticed; in this case, however, the story spread nationwide because of the efforts of the offended eyewitness. No ordinary observer, James Dickey was one of the United States' earliest and most influential abolitionists west of the Appalachian Mountains. Born in Virginia and raised in South Carolina and Kentucky, he identified with southern people and traditions. But the "abominations of slavery" caused him to forsake the land of his "childhood and youth" and move to the opposite side of the Ohio River.[8]

After witnessing the coffle, Dickey fired off an angry letter to the local *Paris Western Citizen*. While proud of "Columbia's free born sons" for turning the Kentucky wilderness into a commercial emporium, he decried the traffic in human beings, "a business commenced at first on a moderate scale, in Kentucky, but now grown so enormously as to be become truly alarming." He also denounced the use of the American flag as a symbol of the nefarious trade. It was hard to imagine a greater insult to the republic and its founders than "to hoist the 'Star-Spangled Banner' the flag of freedom, the Eagle of proud America, over a set of poor unhappy slaves, fettered to misery, to despair, who never knew Liberty, save in dreams of the night, or the airy visions of the day." It was, Dickey concluded, a "shameful prostitution."[9] Others agreed.

In the *Genius of Universal Emancipation*, the United States' first significant antislavery newspaper, editor Benjamin Lundy addressed the incident as soon as he became aware of it.[10] Besides reprinting Dickey's

FIGURE I.I. "UNITED STATES' INTERNAL SLAVE TRADE," *Genius of Universal Emancipation* (January 1823), 97. Courtesy of Proquest American Periodical Series.

letter and calling the Kentucky slave coffle "a shame and foul dishonor to the flag of my country," he published a front-page visual aid to fully convey his revulsion.[11] The crude woodcut centers on a well-dressed White man on horseback, who while holding a whip in his outstretched arm menacingly, leads a coffle of bowing Black bondpeople across a field. In front of the slave driver, a horse-drawn cart full of enslaved children moves forward, while behind it follow seven captive men, women, and children on foot and in various states of dress and undress. Nearly all the distinguishing characteristics of the ambulatory figures are lost in the amateurish engraving—yet the star-spangled banner that is held aloft by one of the captives and flies above them is impossible to miss.[12]

Exclamatory text frames the image's four sides. The title proclaims, "UNITED STATES' INTERNAL SLAVE TRADE. '*Hail Columbia. Happy Land!*' while the left and right margins read respectively, "TO THE SOUTH-WESTWARD" and "A GLORIOUS SPECTACLE!!!" The caption beneath the image inquires of the American flag, "SHALL THY FAIR BANNERS O'ER OPPRESSION WAVE?" A short description of the engraving demands readers consider the illustration in light of the last line of Francis Scott Key's anthem: "LOOK AT IT, *again and again*; and then say whether you will permit so disgraceful, so inhuman, and so wicked a practice to continue in our country, which has been emphatically termed THE HOME OF THE FREE."[13]

The engraving's resonance among readers, which is indicated by its reproduction in the newspaper's very next issue, lies in its appeal to both nation and religion. For Lundy, the domestic slave trade violated both "the founding principles of our government" as well as "the maxims and precepts of Christianity." Accordingly, a closer look at the engraving reveals a metaphorical Station of the Cross as a shirtless and dark-skinned Jesus carries his own cross—in this case the flag of the United States—toward the place of his American crucifixion.[14]

The image was not the last to juxtapose slavery with the American flag on the pages of Lundy's paper. Shortly after publishing the engraving of the Kentucky slave coffle, the editor disseminated the first visualization of the now familiar scene of a manacled bondman singing "Hail Columbia, happy land" in front of the beflagged US Capitol. The quality of the engravings in Lundy's paper left much to be desired, so much so that the editor apologized to readers for utilizing the talents of "some of Nature's unskillful workmen." But despite their "imperfections," the images marked a growing commitment of antislavery activists to literally illustrate the misappropriation of the symbols of American freedom by slavery's defenders.[15]

After the publication of Lundy's various illustrations, antislavery artists and editors amplified and improved on his pioneering efforts. In 1835

FIGURE I.2. "BEHOLD, BEHOLD THIS CRUEL CHAIN!!!" *Genius of Universal Emancipation* (November 1823), 68. Courtesy of Proquest American Periodical Series.

the American Anti-Slavery Society (AASS) reimagined the Kentucky coffle on the front page of its illustrated monthly, the *Anti-Slavery Record*. In this vastly improved picture, a large American flag with easily distinguishable stars and stripes is the clear focal point. It waves high above a long procession of Black captives who number in the dozens. They, along with a whip-cracking White slave trader on horseback, remain silhouetted, but their bodies and the surrounding scenery are perceptible. As a work of art, it is superior to Lundy's engraving, though it delivers the same message. The caption reads: "HOW SLAVERY HONORS OUR COUNTRY'S FLAG." Like other popular antislavery iconography, the *Anti-Slavery Record*'s graphic remained in print for years. Appearing on the pages of a variety of the society's publications, it became one of the movement's most recognizable visual tropes.[16]

HOW SLAVERY HONORS OUR COUNTRY'S FLAG.

FIGURE 1.3. "HOW SLAVERY HONORS OUR COUNTRY'S FLAG," *Anti-Slavery Record* (February 1835), 1. Courtesy of the Library Company of Philadelphia.

THE COFFLE GANG. (*See page 164.*)

FIGURE 1.4. Prepared for publication in 1857, this engraving improves upon all earlier depictions of the antebellum slave coffle by detailing the possessions, facial expressions, and genders of the Black and White figures. While the specifics of the US flag are obscure, its service as a proslavery symbol is clear. "The Coffle Gang," from George Washington Carleton, *The Suppressed Book About Slavery!* (New York: Carleton, 1864), 48–49. Courtesy of the Library of Congress.

For slavery's opponents, the proliferation of the slave trade in front of the flag-topped US Capitol was the ultimate symbolical betrayal of American freedom. "The District of Columbia is the grand mart for the sale of men," David Lee Child declared before the New England Anti-Society. "Kofle after Kofle are collected in that wretched space, and driven, under the flourish of whips and the foldings of the flag, by the very doors of Congress." The clanking of slaves' chains made "fine harmony with the voices of pretty orators, who are up, praising liberty."[17] Joshua Danforth considered the traffic in Black people a republican tragedy, especially since the federal government had already outlawed the slave trade internationally. "It is still carried on, to the disgrace of the nation," the son of a Revolutionary War officer railed in a published letter, "even in the District of Columbia, within sight of this Capitol, and of 'freedom's banner,' that streams from its summit, and plays in the breezes of heaven, as if in mockery of the chains of the poor slave."[18]

When abolitionists witnessed the Washington slave trade in person, the experience was often epiphanic. In May 1836, a prolonged illness prompted New England's Henry Wilson to visit the warmer climate of the South to recover his health. While traveling through Maryland in a railroad car, the twenty-four-year-old shoemaker witnessed "slaves of both sexes toiling half-naked in the fields," but what he observed in Washington, DC, over the course of the next several weeks, was even more revolting: "I saw slavery beneath the shadow of the flag that waved over the Capitol," as merchants and traders drove enslaved men, women, and children to the markets of the Deep South. "I left the capital of my country with the unalterable resolution to give all that I had, and all that I hoped to have, of power, to the cause of emancipation in America." This was not just talk, as Wilson spent the next three decades of his life crusading against slavery.[19]

Vermont's William Slade was moderate on the issue of antislavery when first elected to the US House of Representatives in 1831. Several years of residency in the nation's capital, however, convinced him to join a group of northern politicians who made the abolition of slavery and the slave trade in the District a legislative priority. In a speech before the Congress in 1835, he entreated "that measures may be taken to put an end to slavery *here*, and especially that here, where the flag of freedom floats over the Capitol of this great Republic, and where the authority of that Republic is supreme, the trade in human flesh may be abolished." The "*Character of the country*" was at stake, Slade insisted, leading him to decry the turning of men into merchandise "within sight of the Capitol in which their Representatives are assembled, and on whose summit wave the stripes and stars of freedom?" Fortunately, there were those across the nation who "as Americans" were reaching out "their hands to wipe out the stain from the escutcheon of their country."[20]

When Congress ignored Slade's advice, he persisted. In January 1839, the sight of a slave coffle near the Capitol sent him to the office of Joshua Giddings, the freshman representative from Ohio and noted abolitionist. To "arouse Mr. Giddings's indignation and inspire him with renewed courage and zeal in the fight upon which he had entered," Slade detailed the scene: "This day a coffle of about sixty slaves, male and female, passed through the streets of Washington, chained together, on their way South." The captives trudged alongside a wagon that carried women and children who because of injury, sickness, or age, were unable to walk. Guiding the coffle was a "*being* in the shape of a man" who continually chastised the group with a large lash. "This was done in the day time, in public view of all who happened to be so situated as to see the barbarous spectacle."[21]

Slade was furious. Several days later, despite the notorious "gag rule," which since 1836 barred the introduction of any antislavery petitions in the House of Representatives, he convinced the chamber's clerk to read the opening portion of a series of resolutions, demanding information on the men responsible for the coffle.[22] Representatives stopped the clerk before he could finish and tabled the resolutions indefinitely. Undeterred, Slade alerted antislavery writers and editors, who immediately commented on the incident. A correspondent for the *Boston Courier* undoubtedly spoke for many of the paper's readers when he protested,

"Here, at mid-day, under the eaves of the capitol of the oldest republic in the world, the capitol of a country boasting to be the advocate of liberty and human rights, over whose walls the star-spangled banner was then floating in majesty, a band of men, chained together, were driven by, in the presence of the American people! Shame! shame!"[23]

While Slade continued to work toward the relatively conservative goal of eliminating slavery and the slave trade in Washington, Giddings became the most radical abolitionist US Congressman in history. To convince the unconverted of the righteousness of his cause, he regularly cited the trafficking of enslaved people in the nation's capital. In one instance, after publishing an account of a slave coffle that he had personally witnessed in the city, the American and Foreign Anti-Slavery Society produced a visual aid to advertise the incident. Though appearing almost as an exact replica of the AASS's "THE HOME OF THE OPPRESSED," this engraving depicts a more diverse group of Black captives, consisting of eight men, four women, and two children. Their proximity to each other, as they pass the Capitol and its star-spangled banners behind a whip-wielding White slave trader, suggests that some of them are related. The introduction of a gendered element into the familiar scene is significant, as it illuminates the nation's complicity in the deliberate destruction of enslaved families.[24]

Giddings reserved some of his greatest scorn for the slave owners and dealers who plied their trade under the national standard. In a speech before the US Congress, he blasted his colleagues for allowing city residents to traffic in "the bodies of men, women, and children." Addressing the Speaker of the House of Representatives directly, Giddings railed, "Here, sir, in view of this hall, under the shadow of the 'star spangled banner' which floats over this edifice, consecrated to freedom, to the maintenance of the undying truth that 'governments are instituted to secure all men in the enjoyment of life, liberty, and the pursuit of happiness,' these hucksters in human flesh critically examined the bodies and limbs" of these mothers, fathers, brothers, and sisters, whom they considered only as property. "I doubt whether any slave market in

SLAVERY

AND THE

SLAVE TRADE

AT THE

NATION'S CAPITAL.

NEW YORK:
PUBLISHED BY WILLIAM HARNED,
FOR THE
AMERICAN AND FOREIGN ANTI-SLAVERY SOCIETY,
5 Spruce Street.
$1 PER 100, $8 PER 1000.

FIGURE 1.5. US Congressmen Joshua Giddings described a slave coffle that he saw pass through Washington, following the US Congress' adoption of several proslavery resolutions in 1838: "Nine days after the adoption of these resolutions a coffle of thirty slaves chained together, and followed by about the same number of females, who were permitted to travel unchained, were driven past the Capitol, on their way to a southern market." Title page of *Slavery and the Slave Trade at the Nation's Capital* (New York: American and Foreign Anti-Slavery Society, 1846), 1. Courtesy of the Samuel J. May Collection, Cornell University.

Africa was ever attended by more expert dealers in human chattels, than was the market of this city, which profanes the name of Washington."[25]

Though he did not mention it specifically in his speech, Giddings was well aware of the notorious slave pen operated by William H. Williams, who flew an American flag at the corner of 7th and B Streets, just a few blocks from the Capitol. For more than twenty years, the distinctive yellow structure was a local institution. "In an era before the memorials to Washington or Jefferson (much less the yet-unknown Lincoln) had been erected," notes historian Jeff Forret, "D.C. travelers oriented themselves based on the Yellow House, which stood as a prominent landmark within the nation's capital." For slavery's enemies, there was no greater symbol of the failure of American freedom.[26]

In the *Boston Emancipator*, Henry Stanton and Joseph Lovejoy wondered how slave markets like Williams's could exist in the capital city of a nation that proclaimed all men were created equal. In the federal district, "under the very shadow of the capitol," the slave trader yoked, branded, chained, and scourged his "human cattle." He advertised his "flesh" products in the local papers, hung his sign in open public, "as boldly as if he were a dealer in dry goods or groceries." If that were not enough, he flew "the flag of his country over his den of despair" while letting "its stars and stripes steam in the breeze of heaven."[27]

After learning of William's slave pen, AASS founder James Miller McKim traveled from Philadelphia to Washington to see the facility himself. Upon entering the "*Slave-factory*," his heart sank. In front of him were "about 30 slaves of all ages, sizes, and colors," crammed into a small room in the building's basement, where they awaited being sold at auction. "The *hypocrisy* of this nation!" McKim exclaimed. "These are some of the abominations that exist in the District of *Columbia!* the national domain of the American REPUBLIC! within sight of the Capitol and under the stars and stripes of our national flag!"[28]

Of course, the irony of a slave pen standing in the capital of a nation conceived in liberty was most evident to the people held captive inside the compound. Though evidence of what they thought is wanting, at least one extant record offers some insight. In 1841, while working in Washington as a musician, Solomon Northup, a free Black man from upstate New York, awoke in a jail cell inside the pen after being incapacitated by his employers the previous evening. Twelve hellish years later, after being transported to Louisiana and enslaved, he managed to secure his freedom. Upon returning to New York, Northup published his autobiography. In the wildly successful *Twelve Years a Slave*, he described his brief stay in the slave prison in graphic detail.[29] "Strange as it may seem, within plain sight of this house, looking down from its commanding height upon it, was the Capitol," he recalled. "The voices of patriotic representatives boasting of freedom and equality, and the rattling of the poor slave's chains almost commingled. A slave pen within the very shadow of the Capitol!" How hypocritical![30]

The appropriation of the American flag by slave owners and traders in Washington convinced some abolitionists to stop flying the standard at movement events. After Maria Weston Chapman and the other organizers of the Twelfth Annual Anti-Slavery Bazaar secured the use of Boston's famed Faneuil Hall for the occasion, their attention turned to choosing the appropriate decorations. When considering what, if any, flags, ensigns, or banners should stream above the fair, the group "all felt the inconsistency of acting under the stripes and stars that float over the slave-auction, and the Capitol that sanctions the slave-auction." Consequently, throughout the duration of the ten-day bazaar that attracted thousands of paying customers, "not a United States flag or pennon was to be seen." Only the white flags of the various antislavery societies, imprinted with biblical passages or the AASS's new motto—"No union with Slaveholders"—graced the walls of the Great Hall.[31]

The refusal of the racially integrated all-female Bazaar Committee to fly the national standard in Faneuil Hall was a symbolic act rife with political meaning. In literature promoting the event, the committee members divulged that their motivation to hold the bazaar was "to inspire the American people" to abolish slavery. While this was unremarkable, their rebuke of male leaders for failing to accomplish abolition was quite notable: "Our object is to arouse those whose office it *should* have been to bear the truth to *us*: those whom all confess to be, by their prudence, mildness, judiciousness and position, right qualified for the work we have undertaken, if they could but be induced to undertake it." Committee members intended the bazaar to inspire a new generation of men whose efforts to end slavery would "put to shame" those of their predecessors.[32]

Antislavery fairs and bazaars have attracted historians' attention for good reason. Hypotheses about the significance of women's roles in these important fundraising, promotional, and organizational events vary, though the consensus is that male abolitionists who enjoyed the right to vote and hold elected office willingly deferred to their female counterparts on such ostensibly apolitical affairs. Rather than exercising real power, female event organizers were "adjuncts to the male-dominated" abolitionist associations, which protected them from the public sphere.[33] That may be, but by granting women power over the choice and displays of the symbols of freedom, the potential for subversion remained. Unwilling to accept the presence of slavery and the slave trade in the nation's capital any longer, the Bazaar Committee took a powerful political stance when it refused to fly the American flag over its annual showcase event.

And they were not alone. Several years earlier, a racially diverse group of teachers, students, and parents gathered on the Fourth of July inside New York City's Chatham Street Chapel to observe the holiday. When reporting the event for the *Colored American*, William Johnson of the First Colored Presbyterian Church described the extraordinary banner that organizers hung in the church that day: "Instead of having a star-spangled banner unfurled, waving in the air, an emblem of liberty and equal rights, we had a more appropriate one, a large *slave ship*, which I thought ought to be hung in place of flags throughout our country." Johnson thought it would be appropriate to place "a pair of slave *hand cuffs*" atop these flagstaffs instead of liberty caps and keep them there until slavery was abolished and freedom and equality reigned through-out the land.[34]

Johnson was not the only person to imagine a revised American flag. Abolitionists on the opposite side of the Atlantic Ocean had creative ideas for the new standard. This was no surprise, given their long and ambivalent relationship with the United States' foremost symbol of freedom. In 1804, the Irish lyricist Thomas Moore traveled to Washington, DC, as a part of a North American tour. Like so many visitors to the mosquito-infested swamp that the American people had only recently christened their capital, the "Bard of Erin" was unimpressed. After visiting several plantations nearby in Maryland and Virginia, he composed a long poem that later became known as "American Slavery."[35] For Moore, Americans' cries of "freedom! freedom!" were meaningless cants that muffled the sounds

> Of whips and charters, manacles, and rights
> Of slaving blacks and democratic whites.

The hollow boasts of "perfect liberty" convinced the poet to depart the shores of the hypocritical republic at once:

> Away, away—I'd rather hold my neck
> By doubtful tenure from a sultan's beck,
> In climes where liberty has scarce been named,
> Than thus to live, where bastard freedom waves
> Her fustian flag in mockery over slaves;

While the word *fustian* has since fallen out of favor, it was once a familiar term, meaning bombastic, pretentious, or inflated speech. By attaching the pejorative to the star-spangled banner, Moore affronted the United States and its people; nevertheless, for American abolitionists, his *fustian flag* became a mantra, appearing on the pages of antislavery and abolitionist books, pamphlets, and newspapers for decades.

From the 1830s, an abbreviated American version of Moore's lines became popular in these same media. The "contemptuous couplet" read:

> The fustian flag that proudly waves,
> In splendid mockery, o'er a land of slaves

It was a short and simple rebuke of the United States and its flag. "The lines would be harmless enough, if they were false," Lydia Maria Child wrote in a popular antislavery essay: "the sting lies in their truth."[36]

Over time, other foreign critics joined Moore in profaning the American flag because of slavery. In 1838, Scotland's Thomas Campbell composed a short poem after seeing the Stars and Stripes on an American ship in English waters. In "To the United States of North America," he wrote:

> UNITED STATES, your banner wears
> Two emblems—one of fame;
> Alas, the other that it bears
> Reminds us of your shame,
> Your standard's constellation types
> White freedom by its stars;
> But what's the meaning of the stripes?
> They mean your negroes' scars.[37]

The epigram resonated across the Atlantic. They were, one AASS agent reveled, "a specimen of scorching sarcasm, which we have rarely seen equaled."[38]

Daniel O'Connell's comments on the American flag several years earlier were equally critical.[39] Known worldwide for championing the civil rights of Roman Catholics living under British rule, the Irish nationalist was an avowed enemy of slavery who repeatedly denounced the United States for its hypocrisy. In one oratorical assault, O'Connell howled, "Let America, in the fulness of her pride, wave on high her banner of freedom and its blazing stars. I point to her, and say, there is one foul blot upon it—'*You have Negro Slavery*.'" Americans' shouts for liberty rang hollow, for they stifled the sounds of "negro children" who were daily torn from the arms of their mothers. That the people responsible for these scenes had only recently secured their own freedom from oppression was "doubly unjust." O'Connell thought that if the citizens of the United States insisted on flying a "flag of liberty," they should adorn it with "the whip and rack on one side, and the stars of freedom upon the other." Far more than the star-spangled banner, it would epitomize their concurrent commitment to slavery and freedom.[40]

The renowned British preacher and writer John Angell James imagined another alternative emblem of the United States. At a meeting of the London Missionary Society, he marveled at how American citizens could boast of freedom while holding more than two million people in captivity. James prayed for the United States that the day would come "when her noble bird, her *Eagle* should be soaring in the air of liberty— not with the helpless children of Africa, writhing and shrieking in her talons, followed by the philanthropic to scare her from her prey—but when, having washed her beak from gore, and her talons from blood, she should soar in mid-heaven without one cloud to obscure her flight, without a stain upon her plumage." It was only recently, he recalled of the recent abolition of slavery in the British colonies, "that the British lion himself was seen with the helpless child in his jaws," but the philanthropists in England rose in unison and induced the beast to drop the child from his mouth. "Now that very lion had placed himself, in all the majesty of his nature, over that very child for his protection, and is prepared to flash his eye, to bristle his mane, to lash his sides with his tail, and utter his growl in menace of the wretch, that should dare again to lay a cruel hand upon the child." James prayed the American people would soon know how the British felt when they finally washed their hands of the blood of slavery and saw "the stain wiped from their escutchion [*sic*]."[41]

James was not finished. In the *Evangelical Magazine and Missionary Chronicle*, he reiterated his impression of the United States as a "moral and political enigma." He considered it a "monstrosity" that the same people who seized their own freedom while declaring "'that all men are created equal; that they are endowed with certain unalienable rights, that among them are life, liberty, and the pursuit of happiness," deprived others "of two of these 'unalienable rights,' and often directly or indirectly the third." Given the contradiction, he believed "the national emblem of the American states" required alteration. "The eagle with liberty on his wings should," he suggested, "clutch in his talons the manacled and writhing form of the coloured man."[42]

Rather than reject James's criticisms, American abolitionists internalized and embraced them. "Let every American read this, and confess, that the rebuke is just," a correspondent of the *New York Observer*, who heard James's London speech in person, admitted. "That it ought first to humble us, and then rouse the nation, *as one man*, to imitate the people of our father-land."[43] Oswego, New York's James Brown described the embarrassment he and other American patriots felt every time they saw "that *last hope of liberty*, the STAR SPANGLED BANNER, floating in its one appropriate citadel, over its enchained and imbruted fellowmen" in the nation's capital. Equally discomforting was seeing, "as I have lately seen, the American eagle described with sarcastic bitterness, in a British periodical, as bearing aloft in his talons the lacerated and gasping body of a kidnapped child of Africa."[44]

In 1840, John Whittier undoubtedly had James's vision on his mind when he dedicated a poem to the hundreds of delegates attending an antislavery convention in London. The Massachusetts Quaker urged these international crusaders to summon all the earth's philanthropy until the "bugle-blast of Freedom" could be heard across Europe, Africa, Asia, and the Americas. The sound needed to reach the United States at once, for even in the nation's capital, "where my country's flag is flowing," the gavel of the slave auctioneer could still be heard. Heartened by the

London assembly, Whittier imagined the time when his country would renounce its hypocritical ways:

> Her Regal Emblem, now no longer
> A bird of prey, with talons reeking,
> Above the dying captive shrieking,
> But, spreading out her ample wing—
> A broad, impartial covering—
> The weaker sheltered by the stronger!—[45]

American abolitionists followed Whittier's lead by continually invoked James's aquiline image. In one memorable instance, Francis Gillette argued before the US Senate that abolishing slavery in the nation's capital would vindicate "our national character" around the world. "American liberty is understood abroad to mean the liberty to oppress, the liberty to enslave, the liberty to imbrute our fellow-men," the Connecticut senator informed his colleagues. "One foreign writer has even suggested that our national emblem should be made truly emblematic of our real character, by picturing the eagle with liberty on his wings, and with a negro chained and writhing in his talons, and his heart's blood dripping from his beak."[46]

Visual interpretations of Reverend James's predatory American eagle mangling its enslaved human prey ensured its survival among slavery's American opponents. At a meeting of the New England Anti-Slavery Society in 1844, an abolitionist artist ascended a platform inside Boston's Marlboro Chapel carrying a banner he had created for the occasion. One of the society founders, Charles Burleigh, then presented the standard to William Lloyd Garrison, the AASS President and editor of the Boston-based *Liberator*—the first newspaper in the United States committed to slavery's immediate abolition—who proudly accepted it. The flag was, Garrison proclaimed, superior to the American flags, which so often served as "Emblems of division."[47]

For those unable to see the new banner in person, Garrison provided a description: "The principal object which strikes the eye is the American eagle, trampling upon prostrate humanity, with one foot upon the Constitution and the Right of Petition, which also helped to keep down the slave, who is chained to the earth by the neck and ankle, with his head upon a pillow of thorns." An American flag, on which is inscribed "PROTECTION," partially covers the sufferer, who looks toward the eagle as if to say, "What infamous hypocrisy!" Protruding from the bird's beak a streamer reads, "*All men are created free and equal*,' and the English of the national motto, '*We many are one*.'" Underneath one of the eagle's wings, a racetrack circles the Capitol, "implying that horse-racing is there a matter of more consequence than the wants and rights of the people." A flag on which is written "Equality" flies from the Capitol dome, while underneath it a slave auction ensues. The American church appears beneath the eagle's other wing, "with whipping and branding going on in front of it." Smoke from the fire of a branding iron pours into the church's front door but congregants fail to take notice. A frowning "*Eye of the Supreme*" looks down upon the entire scene whose background is painted red "as emblematic of the bloody character of the scene."[48]

Two months later, Elizabeth Delly of Hanover, Massachusetts, presented a similar standard to Robert L. Killam, a Universalist minister and recent abolitionist convert. "In that bird, you will recognize the American Eagle," she began her description of the creature on the flag's face. "It is a bird of prey—fit emblem of the American people." Though a noble creature, it had for seventy years "been preying on the vitals of humanity, amid the shoutings and rejoicings of the American people, who love to have it so." The time had come to bring this eagle down, "that it should no longer strike its talons into the quivering flesh of the bondman." Delly implored Killam to hold the banner high before the "nation and the world" to expose the hypocrisy of American slavery. He accepted the invitation, vowing in response, "We shall never strike this

Banner while there is an arm to bear it, or until victory is won, and oppression and slavery shall be banished from the earth."[49]

The evocative images that began circulating among abolitionists amplified the efforts of the AASS to imagine James's aquiline scene on the cover of its annual *American Anti-Slavery Almanac*. The black-and-white engraving, which stretches horizontally across the front page of the 1843 issue, shows a rapacious bird sinking its sharp talons into the body of a young Black woman who has fallen to the ground. While staring at the predator in terror, the enslaved mother tries to protect her small child, whom she clutches desperately in her arms. Behind the bloodthirsty bald eagle and its intended victims are the familiar dome and façade of the US Capitol with the Stars and Stripes streaming high above the structure.[50]

To underscore the shame brought upon the flag by the vivid tableau, the caption copies several lines from Ireland's Dr. Richard Robert Madden:

> Oh, hail Columbia! Happy land!
>   The cradle land of Liberty!
> Where none but negroes bear the brand,
>   Or feel the lash of slavery.
> Then let the glorious anthem peal!
>   And drown, "Britannia rule the waves"—
> Strike up the song that men can feel
>   "Columbia rules three million slaves!"[51]

While it is difficult to imagine a more powerful visual protest against slavery in the United States, the image on the back cover of the almanac was similarly effective because of its ingenious exploitation of the American flag. This black-and-white engraving centers on a bearded Black man whose wrists and ankles are bound to a liberty pole more than twice his height. A conical liberty cap rests atop the vertical post, while an oversized American flag streams above the head of the shirtless and shoeless

FIGURE 1.6. Front cover of *American Anti-Slavery Almanac, for 1843* (New York: American Anti-Slavery Society, 1842). Courtesy of the Library Company of Philadelphia.

United States! Your banner wears
    Two emblems—one of fame;
Alas, the other that it bears
    Reminds us of your shame.

The *white* man's liberty in types
    Stands blazoned by your *stars ;*
But what's the meaning of your *stripes ?*
    They mean your *negro's scars.*   THOMAS CAMPBELL.

FIGURE 1.7. Back cover of *American Anti-Slavery Almanac, for 1843* (New York: American Anti-Slavery Society, 1842). Courtesy of the Library Company of Philadelphia.

sufferer. A version of Thomas Campbell's epigram appears beneath the image, underscoring its irony.[52]

The images on the almanac's front and back covers enthralled Garrison, who dedicated nearly an entire column in the *Liberator* to promote their circulation. He reported the sale of the publication at the AASS's New York and Boston offices while emphasizing the inclusion of two extraordinary illustrations. The front cover displayed an engraving depicting "the U.S. Capitol, and in front of it a female slave lying prostrate on the ground, with the American eagle on her body, ready to tear out her eyes and otherwise mutilate her person with his beak and talons." The back cover showed a "Liberty pole, *from* which is floating 'the star-spangled banner,' and *to* which is chained a negro slave, with his back bared for the lash!" Garrison continued, "none who profess to be abolitionists can object to giving it the widest circulation, but all should feel willing and anxious to 'scatter it as the seed-wheat of humanity' all over the land."[53]

As one of the most important purveyors of abolitionist texts and images in the antebellum era, Garrison's story is worth considering. Though attracted to antislavery from an early age, it was a short stint in the slave state of Maryland that converted him to abolitionism. While in Baltimore, the New England native assisted Benjamin Lundy in the production of the *Genius of Universal Emancipation* and saw the evils of the South's peculiar institution firsthand. The experience inspired Garrison to seek the immediate abolition of slavery throughout the United States. A conviction by a southern jury on the charge of slandering a slave owner, followed by a nearly two-month-long stay in a Baltimore jail, convinced Garrison to return to New England, where he began publishing the *Liberator* in January 1831. A new edition of Garrison's abolitionist publication rolled off the presses of Isaac Knapp's Congress Street print shop in Boston every week for the next three-and-a-half decades.[54]

While the impact of the *Liberator*'s text is widely acknowledged, its visual content was also a powerful shaper of public opinion. The masthead was special in this regard, as it served two essential purposes: first, attracting readers' attention amidst a sea of mass-produced, popular, and inexpensive periodicals; and second, encouraging these readers to support the radical movement to immediately abolish slavery throughout the nation. Toward both ends, the *Liberator*'s masthead made a creative and effective use some of the most recognizable symbols of American freedom.

Beginning in April 1831, three different graphics adorned the header of the paper's front page. The first depicts the auction of an enslaved family in the nation's capital. In the foreground, a gavel-wielding White auctioneer, four White slave buyers, and signs reading "HORSE MARKET" and "SLAVES HORSES & OTHER CATTLE TO BE SOLD AT 12:00," encircle a Black family. For this man, woman, and their two children, there is no escaping their impending sale and separation. Another Black man sits beneath the auctioneer's stand. With his face and head hidden under a cloth, he is desperate and forlorn. The background shows a slave owner whipping a Black man, who is bound to a post. The two men are positioned directly in front of the US Capitol, whose waving flag proclaims, "LIBERTY."

The second masthead revises the original scene, while adding an additional illustration. In the tableau to the left, which takes place on "FREEDOM ST.," a diminutive Black child stands on a table for prospective White buyers to determine her value. Behind her are several dark-skinned adults and another child—undoubtedly, some are family members. An indistinguishable white flag waves above the auction, while in the background a White man lashes a Black man in front of the Capitol. To the right of this tableau, the new engraving imagines the potential impact of freedom on enslaved people. Underneath a banner reading "EMANCIPATION," a Black mother and her small children look up to the family's esteemed patriarch. Behind them, one group of free Black men work diligently at a saw, demonstrating their belief in the benefits of hard work. Another group celebrates their freedom, which they see appearing over the horizon underneath a nondescript dark flag. Far off in the distance, the US Capitol is barely discernible.

FIGURE 1.8. First illustrated masthead of the *Liberator*. Courtesy of the Library Company of Philadelphia.

FIGURE 1.9. Second illustrated masthead of the *Liberator*. Courtesy of the Library Company of Philadelphia.

FIGURE 1.10. Third illustrated masthead of the *Liberator*. Courtesy of the Boston Public Library.

The third and longest-running image on the *Liberator*'s masthead shared much in common with its predecessors, though it offered much greater detail and complexity. Lest anyone miss its symbolism, Garrison elaborated: "The idea represented is the same as in the former head, the contrast of slavery with freedom, with the addition of a central medallion representing Jesus, the Liberator, around whose head is this inscription: 'I COME TO BREAK THE BONDS OF THE OPPRESSOR.'" Beneath the Messiah are two figures: a Black man on bended knee pleading for his freedom, and a White slave owner, who after dropping his whip, "shrinks from his rebuke." The day of judgment has arrived.[55]

While the medallic scene resonates with common Christian themes, the two accompanying images invoke national icons exclusively. To the viewer's left, a large American flag—this time with stars and stripes clearly visible—hovers over a slave auction. A smaller standard inscribed "Slavery" floats over the distant Capitol while underneath it, a slave coffle embarks on the "middle passage" from the upper to the lower South. A large, rectangular sign broadcasts the sale of "SLAVES, HORSES, AND OTHER CATTLE." Nearly a dozen finely dressed White men watch and listen attentively as an auctioneer announces the price of a small Black boy who, standing alone and terrified, cries into his hands. Nearby, several enslaved men, women, and children, similarly await their fate. To the viewer's right, former slaves rejoice before "a triumphal arch, decorated with flags, and bearing the word 'EMANCIPATION.'" Through this structure, a long procession of free Black people passes towards their ultimate destination—the Capitol, which now proudly "floats the flag of FREEDOM."[56]

In the nearly two thousand issues of the *Liberator* that displayed one of the three illustrated mastheads, Garrison printed a slogan that has since come to epitomize his cosmopolitanism: "OUR COUNTRY IS THE WORLD—OUR COUNTRYMEN, ALL MANKIND." Early in his publishing career, while attending an anti-colonization conference in London, Garrison explained his reason for adopting the maxim, which he had crafted from Thomas' Paine's revolutionary treatise, *The Rights of Man*: "It is long since I sacrificed all my national, complexional and local prejudices upon the altar of Christian love, and breaking down the narrow boundaries of selfish patriotism, inscribed upon my banner this motto:—*My country is the world; my countrymen are all mankind.*"[57]

Notwithstanding Garrison's self-identification as a citizen of the world, he was and always remained an American.[58] Indeed, in the same speech in which he explained the reasoning behind the choice of his universalist motto, he confessed an abundance of pride for, and attachment to, the United States: "*I cherish as strong a love for the land of my nativity as any man living. I am proud of her civil, political and religious institutions—of her high advancement in science, literature and the arts—of her general prosperity and grandeur.*" Still, there was a problem. Because of slavery, Garrison's cherished nation made a mockery of the idea that "all men are created equal; that they are endowed by their creator with certain inalienable rights; that among these are life, liberty, and the pursuit of happiness."[59]

Garrison's love for his nation and its flag was conditional, as he demonstrated at a large abolitionist gathering in Framingham, Massachusetts, on the eve of the Civil War. Held on the Fifth of July to highlight the hypocrisy of annual freedom celebrations in a slave nation, the rally began when Garrison stepped to the podium and addressed the "friends of the slave." For these men and women, he began, the Fourth of July was not a day for "proud exultation, for ostentatious parade, for extravagant vain-glorying, for revelry and dissipation, for the ringing of bells and the firing of cannon." It was rather a day of sadness and humiliation, "in view of the hypocrisy and blood-guiltiness of the nation." Accordingly, the star-spangled banner did not wave over the outdoor event.[60]

Garrison appreciated the gesture. "Wherever else the American flag is unfurled to the breeze," he proclaimed, "I thank God it is not waving over our heads, and that it would not be tolerated on an occasion like this." After reciting Thomas Campbell's epigram, Garrison affirmed the significance of the flag's red stripes: "Yes, they mean—at least they

symbolize, the stripes continually inflicted on the bodies of the manacled slaves—and, therefore, away with that flag forever!" As long as "four
millions of men are driven with impunity to their unrequited toil, like
brute beasts" beneath it, "let the true friends of freedom discard it with
indignation and horror."[61]

As the assembly at Harmony Grove in Framingham, Massachusetts,
illustrates, the American flag was not the only symbol of freedom challenged by slavery's opponents. In the decades before the Civil War, the
annual celebration of national independence every Fourth of July also
prompted a dynamic response. When slavery's supporters bought and
sold Black people on Independence Day or used the occasion to deny
the radicalism of the Declaration of Independence, their antislavery
and abolitionist adversaries responded in various ways. From refusing
to observe the Fourth of July to publicly celebrating the end of slavery
in Great Britain's Caribbean colonies on the First of August, they determined to contest the annual celebration of the nation's birth until the
egalitarian principles of the nation's founding document prevailed and
slavery ceased to exist.

2

THE FOURTH

On the Fourth of July in 1815, the residents of Savannah, Georgia, cele-brated the anniversary of Declaration of Independence with great pomp and circumstance. The day began with the sounds of cannon blasts and ringing bells, and the familiar sight of the unfurling of the American flag. Volunteer corps paraded through the city's streets, while citizens walked in procession from the public Exchange Building to the local Presbyterian Church. Inside the crowded house of worship, men and women heard a reading of the Declaration of Independence by a local judge and a formal oration by the city's mayor. Following these for-mal proceedings, celebrants retired to their preferred places for dinner and drinks. At the Coffee House located inside the Exchange, revelers toasted the nation, its principles, and its people.[1]

Most symbolic of the events that occurred that Independence Day in Savannah was the raising of a liberty pole in the town center—a re-publican tradition dating to ancient Rome. In this case, the ninety-foot-tall wooden totem "was erected in front of the Exchange, from which proudly waved the striped Standard and Spread Eagle of America." In yet another nod to the Roman Republic, a conical-shaped liberty cap, which in the ancient world signified the emancipation of an en-slaved person, rested atop the iconic pole, "ornamented with wreathes and branches of Laurel."[2] By using the passive voice, the *Savannah Republican* concealed the identity of the individuals who raised the lib-erty pole to a standing position.

Years later, a local resident offered clarification. The Revolutionary War veteran recalled being awoken on the Fourth of July by the noise of a raucous crowd. After following the sounds, he saw a group of revelers bearing a liberty pole with a liberty cap. The sight was unremarkable, but when the throng reached the public square, "there was not an individual employed in setting up the pole, and crowning it with the cap, except *slaves*." The veteran openly voiced his revulsion at seeing enslaved people forced to raise a liberty pole on the anniversary of the Declaration of Independence. This earned him a quick rebuke from a "friend," who cautioned, "You had better take care how you say such things in this place."[3]

It is a striking scene, opening a window to a time and place where the Fourth of July was a divisive and at times even dangerous day. Across the antebellum South, the holiday became a bulwark for slavery and White supremacy. Fearing the nefarious influence of the egalitarian ideals of the Declaration of Independence on the region's enslaved population, slave owners and their supporters distanced the holiday from the historic text. "Instead," in historian Michael Conlin words, "they emphasized the Constitution (with its protections of property held in humans) as the iconic document of the day."[4] In this manner, White southerners stripped Independence Day of any potentially subversive political meaning and transformed the holiday into a conservator of the proslavery status quo.

The situation in the antebellum North was quite different and complicated. Here, most citizens looked favorably upon the annual celebration of the Declaration of Independence and its egalitarian ideals, yet racism made many of them ambivalent over the tradition. As the decades passed, antislavery and abolitionist activists increasingly used the Fourth of July to highlight the failure of American freedom. By boycotting the nation's preeminent holiday and in some cases observing alternative anniversaries, they demonstrated their commitment to both destroying slavery and redeeming the republic. Rather than producing widespread and systemic change, this peaceful effort to appropriate Independence Day for egalitarian purposes prompted violent reprisals. Across the northern states, White supremacist mobs unleashed their fury on those who used the annual celebration of national independence to oppose slavery.

Offering a brief history of the controversial and contested nature of the Fourth of July, and by extension the Declaration of Independence, in the antebellum era, this chapter reveals the critical role that race and slavery played in shaping northern and southern variations of the pre-eminent national holiday. Narrowing the lens on the staunchest proponents of both slavery and antislavery, it reveals the Fourth of July as much more than a public celebration of the republic's birth. It was a fiercely and even violently contested tradition that inspired and galvanized both the supporters and opponents of slavery.

From the earliest days of the American republic, there was little disagreement over how to annually celebrate the nation's birth. In 1776, John Adams predicted that the event would "be celebrated by succeeding generations, as the great Anniversary Festival." As the creation of the United States was a divine act, "It ought to be solemnized with pomp and parade, with shows, games, sports, guns, bells, bonfires, and illuminations, from one end of the continent to the other, from this time forward forevermore." Though the founder referred to July 2nd—rather than July 4th—as the historic day, the point was clear: the anniversary of American Independence deserved annual remembrance.[5]

By the early nineteenth century, the Fourth of July had developed into a tradition much as Adams had imagined. Across the country, citizens assembled in town centers and city squares where they viewed local soldiers parading through the streets, and then listened to prayers, speeches, and a reading of the Declaration of Independence. At the conclusion of these scheduled events, revelers consumed copious amounts of food and drink late into the night, while firing guns, cannons, and other artillery into the air. As a symbol of national unity among an often deeply divided people, the holiday was unequaled.

For all of Adams's foresight, he failed to mention where enslaved people figured in these Fourth of July fêtes. With every northern state passing abolitionist legislation by the turn of the nineteenth century, the question became an exclusively southern one. Because of the holiday's association with the Declaration of Independence, some in the slave states tried to make it a segregated one by barring Black people from the festivities.

White southerners' fears of an integrated Independence Day revealed themselves in a proslavery pamphlet published by Frederick Dalcho in 1823. "The celebration of the *Fourth of July*, belongs, *exclusively* to the white population of the United States," the esteemed Charleston, South Carolina, minister, medical doctor, and author proclaimed. As "*Negroes*" had nothing more to do with the nation's birth than with the Pilgrim's landing at Plymouth Rock, their presence at its annual observation was unwarranted. In fact, it posed a serious threat to the established order. "In our speeches and orations, much, and sometimes more than is politically necessary, is said about personal liberty, which Negro auditors know not how to apply, except by running the parallel with their own condition." Consequently, by joining in Independence Day celebrations, they could "imbibe false notions of their personal rights."[6]

Dalcho was not alone in recognizing the potential subversiveness of the Fourth of July; nevertheless, the region's substantial slave population made excluding enslaved people from the holiday difficult and at times even impossible. Consequently, southern slave owners allowed and even encouraged the men and women they held captive to participate in Independence Day festivities. Even so, as historian Len Travers has shown, they "could never quite dispel their fears of what their enslaved servants might do while their masters celebrated liberty."[7]

To eliminate this fear, White southerners tried to strip the Fourth of July of its political meaning. Making the holiday a carnival of food, drink, and entertainment, rather than a celebration of revolutionary people, events, and ideas, they fashioned a southern version of the tradition that preserved and protected their peculiar institution. No longer simply a ritualistic commemoration of the republic's birth, Independence Day in the antebellum South became another opportunity for slave owners and their supporters to reinforce their authority over enslaved people.

The influential *American Cotton Planter* elucidated. It encouraged the celebration of the Fourth of July across the South because "this festival may be made a powerful controlling power in the management of negroes." As for the type of celebrations to be held, "we do not mean political assemblages where the platitudes of the Declaration of Independence are read" or abolitionist doctrines proclaimed. As enslaved people might become convinced that they were "*white* men with black skins, as their friends would have them to think, and that all men are really 'born free and equal,'" Fourth of July activities needed to be carefully planned and executed. "Instead of singing 'Hail Columbia,' let them sing 'Walk-jaw-bone'; instead of marching to the strains of martial music, let them engage in the more congenial employment of patting 'Juber,' and instead of listening to the rehearsal of the victories over the British, let them rejoice in their well-earned triumph in their long, hard contest with 'General Green'—that is with the crab-grass."[8]

The effort to depoliticize the Fourth of July seems to have met with some success. Decades after the Civil War, the autobiographer and formerly enslaved Mississippian Louis Hughes recalled of the Fourth of July barbecues held on Edward McGee's antebellum plantation, "the anticipation of it acted as a stimulant through the entire year." In the days leading up to the holiday, enslaved people worked harder than ever before, with the expectation they would be rewarded with a feast of roasted hogs and sheep, peach cobbler, apple dumplings, buttermilk, and a variety of "temperance drinks." Once the meal was prepared, they graciously sent some of the finest cuts of meat to the plantation house for the master and his family. "It was a day of harmless riot for all the slaves," who for many months following "would rejoice in the memory of the day and its festivities, and 'bless' Boss for this ray of sunlight in their darkened lives."[9]

In interviews recorded during the 1930s as part of the Works Progress Administration (WPA), other formerly enslaved people echoed Hughes's sentiments.[10] Mose Davis, who resided on a large plantation outside of Perry, Georgia, recalled that his owner, Colonel Davis, yearly hosted an Independence Day "festival" in which "Barbecue was served and there was much singing and dancing." Most memorable of these "frolics" was the presence of visitors from other plantations and the music provided by "some of the slaves."[11] Emma Blalock, once a slave on John Griffith's Auburn plantation in Wake County, North Carolina, recollected similarly, "Dat wus a big day to ever'body, de Fourth of July." The day began with the slaves singing at Auburn and then proceeded nine miles to Raleigh, where "Dere wus a lot of lemonade. Dey made light bread in big ovens an' had cheese to eat wid it. Some said just goin' on de fofe to git lemonade an' cheese."[12]

More than music, food, or drink, it was the footraces Douglas Parish participated in—and normally won—that he most remembered about the Fourth of July in antebellum Florida. The former field hand "was a very good runner, and as it was a custom in those days for one planter to match his 'nigger' against that of his neighbor," his owner prepared his athletes for the big race. In the days leading up to the holiday, Parish trained alongside other enslaved sprinters by racing "to the boundary of his plantation and back again," with the winner receiving "a jack-knife or a bag of marbles" as a reward. On July 4th, the fastest runners from all the local plantations competed in a championship race, "and the winner earned a bag of silver for his master." Parish tried desperately to win every race. When he failed, "he was hard to get along with for several days, but gradually he would accept his defeat with resolution."[13]

Enslaved people's understanding of the Fourth of July as an inane jubilee shorn of any political significance is epitomized by Willis Cofer's recollection of growing up on the plantation of Eden and Calline Cofer in Wilkes County, Georgia. "Evvy plantation gen'ally had a barbecue and a big dinner for Fourth of July," Willis explained in his WPA interview. "When sev'ral white famblies went in together, dey did have high old times tryin' to see which one of 'em could git deir barbecue done and ready to eat fust." Asked whether he or any of the other slaves on the Cofer plantation understood the origins of the national holiday, Willis responded politely, "No Ma'am, us didn't know nuffin' 'bout what dey wuz celebratin' on Fourth of July, 'cept a big dinner and a good time."[14]

Jim Allen also recalled the holiday as a time of remarkable interracial accord. "July 4th, we would wash up an' have a good time," he said of his summers in Alabama as an enslaved child. "We hallowed dat day wid de white folks." The highlight of the occasion was a barbecue. When served on a large table, which was assembled especially for the occasion, it meant "We was havin' a time now. White folks too."[15]

For slave owners and their supporters, the good-natured gathering of Black and White people every Fourth of July served an additional purpose besides reinforcing the racial status quo. In an era of growing opposition to slavery, it refuted assertions from the North that the South was a place of racial conflict and violence. New Orleans preacher Holland Nimmons McTyeire wrote in a popular proslavery pamphlet, "When the Fourth of July comes or the crop is laid by, why not have a jubilee?" Surely, the barbecuing of beef, mutton, or pork, and the consumption of fresh fruits and vegetables was a fun and enjoyable experience for all in attendance: "One such scene would be to any a refutation of all the preambles, resolutions, reports and speeches made for a whole year in Abolition halls."[16]

Some southern spokesmen mocked the role of enslaved people in Fourth of July festivities to counter northern claims of racial discord. In "Fourth of July among the Slaves," an anonymous writer recalled a "carnival" supposed to have taken place on a plantation belonging to man known as Col. Scott. The Independence Day event began with as many as sixty "well fed, bright-eyed, light-stepping negroes" marching in double file to a sumptuous dinner. During the meal, one of the procession's leaders, "Major-General" Big Nathan, delivered a speech "in genuine African" dialect. "The orator did not know much about politics, but he took a very bold position in favor of his master and the ladies of color, and the excellence of his corn crop." Having dealt several blows to abolitionists' arguments, "he concluded with some original poetry, amid the clatter of dishes and gabble of voices." Several other slaves then spoke of their contentment, insisting they were much better off than the free poor people of the North. "All in all, the occasion was one of rebuke to Abolitionism, and a practical comment upon Southern Slavery, such as a whole book would fail to properly represent."[17]

The evidence offered of halcyon interracial holidays in the antebellum South might have proved persuasive but for the tradition of buying and selling African Americans on the Fourth of July. Indeed, slave auctions held on the nation's anniversary exposed the racism, injustice, and inhumanity that was always at the core of Southern social relations. In historian Anne Bailey's words, slave auctions in general represent "a massive breach in historical memory." There were countless numbers of them in the antebellum era, yet today they are largely forgotten. Undoubtedly, the lapse in historical memory impedes the struggle for equality, for every slave auction revealed "a breach in the very ideals that birthed the United States, in that the auction marked the destruction of the ideals and values encoded in the Declaration of Independence and the American Constitution."[18]

Charles Ball's experience is a case in point. What the escaped slave and author recollected about the Fourth of July in the South was being sold at a public auction. The story began when slave traders marched him and fifty-one other Black people in chains hundreds of miles from Maryland to South Carolina for sale. After completing the long journey, a local jailer promised a crowd of perspective buyers that "he was just about to sell the most valuable lot of slaves that had ever been offered in Columbia." Over the course of the next several hours, consumers purchased many of the captives for as much as $350 per individual. Ball went unsold, so he remained in the town jail until the following morning when he was awakened by music, gunfire, "and all the noise with which I had formerly heard the fourth of July ushered in."[19]

Ball spent Independence Day in his cell. From here he watched as citizens gathered outside, "many of whom were intoxicated, and sang and shouted in honour of free government, and the rights of man." As midday approached, revelers took a seat at a long table where they "continued to eat, and drink, and sing songs in honour of liberty, for more than two hours." When the dinner finished, a local politician stood on his chair at one of the ends of the table and commenced a campaign speech in which he acknowledged both the principle of free government and the idea "that all men were born free and equal." The candidate then humbly asked the group for their votes in the upcoming election.[20]

If Ball and his fellow inmates thought they would avoid sale on this special day, they were mistaken. Early in the morning, the jailer had announced that at five o'clock in the evening "a sale of most valuable slaves would immediately take place." Though prices were higher than the previous day, the captives sold quickly. At sundown, an elderly man offered the "required price" of at least $600 for Ball, and immediately took possession of the prisoner. For the remainder of the evening, Ball sat on a bench outside of a tavern waiting for his new owner, who joined other townsfolk inside drinking toast after toast "in honour of liberty and equality."[21]

Like other fugitive slave authors, Ball published an autobiographical account of his life in bondage to expose the evil of slavery. The effort brought accusations of lying and misrepresentation. In the *Southern Quarterly Journal*, David James McCord, a South Carolina planter and politician, accused Ball "of so many falsehoods and misstatements, as to fix the character of forgery on the whole account." As for the idea that White southerners auctioned Black people on the Fourth of July, McCord considered it a fiction. He presumed Ball invented the story "with a view to contrast his auction with the shouts and songs in honour of free government and the rights of man, yet it is unfortunate in the way of veracity." McCord avowed, "an auction of negroes on a Fourth of July, has never occurred since the Declaration of Independence."[22]

McCord's contention was a bald-faced lie, as the pages of southern newspapers attest. In Savannah, Georgia, Samuel Law alerted prospective buyers to the sale of "the property of Edmund Bacon" in front of the Riceboro courthouse between the hours of ten and two o'clock on "the fourth of July next." The "negro girl named SUE" was available for purchase because she legally belonged to "a minor, deceased."[23] After William Smith's passing in Hartford, Georgia, his estate's administrators advertised the auction of "four likely young negroes" on the following Fourth of July along with "one feather bed and furniture."[24] Leesburg, Virginia's William Franklin offered an entire enslaved family to the highest bidder after their owner defaulted on a deed of trust. Besides the father Allen, the mother Esther, and their two children, other commodities available for sale that "4th day of July" included a horse, cattle, and hogs.[25]

Slave traders in Winchester, Kentucky, offered a bonanza of enslaved people for purchase when three separate auctions took place in front of the local courthouse on the Fourth of July in 1859. In the first, Franklin County Circuit Court Clerk Nathan Frizzell offered "to the highest bidder" a seven-year-old girl named Lizzie. The bidding would begin at $500. With a down payment of $50, the purchase could be made on credit for up to twelve months. In the second, Andrew Erwin alerted buyers that he would only accept cash for the purchase of Charles, Duke, Fancy, and Rachael, all of whom were between the ages of twenty-five and thirty-five. In the remaining auction, J. B. Hawkins did not specify the form of payment he would accept for the land, horse, and buggy—or the eleven Black men, women, and children—he offered for sale on "the 4th day of July next."[26]

A one-of-a-kind Fourth of July slave auction in Columbus, Georgia, highlights the holiday's special place on the antebellum South's proslavery calendar. Before the public sale, Robert Toombs, the US senator from Georgia and administrator for the estate of the recently deceased Henry Pope, advertised the sale of between ninety and one hundred "men, women, boys, etc." on July 4th. All the captives were, he assured, "very likely." All slave auctions were an affront to freedom, yet this one seems particularly revolting when considering the senator's politics.[27]

As much as any other southern politician, Toombs understood the importance of the Fourth of July and other symbols of American freedom in the sectional conflict over slavery. In one instance, to invoke the wrath of his northern adversaries, he confessed his dream of defeating abolitionism and calling "the roll of his slaves at the base of Bunker Hill monument."[28] Despite, or perhaps because of, the remark, Toombs received an invitation to deliver a lecture in Boston. He accepted the invite and after arriving in the Cradle of Liberty delivered an unabashedly racist assault on the Declaration of Independence and its egalitarian ideals. After insisting upon the inferiority of African-descended people, the senator proclaimed that the Declaration of Independence, like the Constitution, was unequivocally proslavery. Besides asserting the creation of a "separate and distinct political community" from Great Britain, Toombs argued that the document did nothing for the cause of equality. "At the time of this declaration slavery was a *fact*," he reminded his listeners. "This declaration was drafted by a slaveholder, adopted by the representatives of slaveholders, and did not emancipate a single African slave." Given Toombs's thinking, it is easy to imagine that his auctioning of nearly one hundred Black people on the Fourth of July was political theater of the most unthinkable kind.[29]

Though nearly forgotten today, Toombs's take on the Declaration of Independence was common in the middle of the nineteenth century. As historian Pauline Maier has pointed out, several decades passed after 1776 before the Declaration became "sacred scripture." Even then, the document's egalitarian assertions often escaped the minds of Americans who saw the Declaration as little more than a pro forma announcement of colonial independence.[30] More recently, British scholar David Armitage has found that this conservative understanding of the Declaration of Independence extended far beyond the borders of the United States. For generations globally, the document's natural rights assertions often failed to find resonance.[31] Nevertheless, growing opposition to slavery in the early nineteenth century forced a reconsideration of the foundational text.

When slavery's opponents argued that the Declaration of Independence's principles applied to all people, slavery's supporters tried to preserve the document's traditional interpretation. During the Missouri Crisis of 1819–1821, New York Congressman James Tallmadge, Jr., introduced legislation to prohibit the spread of slavery into the new state of Missouri.[32] In making his case for the controversial measure, the congressman condemned the hypocrisy of the American people for adopting the Declaration and its egalitarian preamble while allowing slavery.[33] Proslavery legislators responded by arguing that neither the document nor its "abstract principles" had any bearing on the debate over slavery in Missouri—or anywhere else for that matter.[34]

John Randolph was among them. In February 1820, the volatile US representative from Virginia provided one of the most memorable moments of the entire Missouri Crisis. During a rambling three-hour harangue against the Tallmadge Amendment, he ridiculed the "equal rights" doctrine of the Declaration of Independence, calling it a farcical "fanfaronade of metaphysical abstractions."[35] Then, in a dramatic gesture intended to capture the attention of both his colleagues and constituents, he pointed to a framed copy of the document displayed on a wall inside the House of Representative's chamber and demanded its removal.[36] While the fate of the duplicate declaration is unknown, less than a month later Congress ignored Tallmadge's proposal and approved slavery's expansion into Missouri.

Though victorious in their effort to make Missouri a slave state, southern spokesmen remained on the defensive and in subsequent decades escalated their assault on the Declaration of Independence. More than a quarter century after the Missouri Compromise, John C. Calhoun, US senator from South Carolina, predicted that if the union between the North and South dissolved over the issue of slavery, historians would be forced to consider "a proposition which originated in a hypothetical truism, but which, as now expressed and now understood, is the most false and dangerous of all political errors." Calhoun insisted of the Declaration's "proposition" of equality among all men, that there was "not a word of truth in it."[37]

As historians of American holidays have demonstrated, White southerners' disdain for the Declaration of Independence extended to its annual celebration. From the early nineteenth century, writes Matthew Dennis, "The firm association of the Declaration of Independence with the Fourth of July, and the growing interpretation of the text as an instrument of equality and freedom, infused Independence Day with potential power and meaning as a festival of liberation and reform."[38] Consequently, the Fourth of July gradually lost favor among White southerners. For them, it was a source of apprehension and fear as they embarked on a path of secession from a Union that increasingly embraced egalitarian ideals. "Their separatism was driven by a commitment to inequality at a time when," Paul Quigley explains similarly, "the memory of the American Revolution and especially the Declaration of Independence was coming to be defined in terms of the principle of equality."[39]

Evidence of the Fourth of July's demise across the antebellum South abounds in the observations of John Dixon Long. On the eve of the Civil War, the southern-born-and-bred minister lamented how the public commemoration of the United States' anniversary no longer "stimulated sentiments of freedom and liberty" in the slave states. While Independence Day still offered White southerners the opportunity to make bombastic declarations "about the star-spangled banner and the spread-eagle, and our glorious country," they took "little or no interest in the celebration of this anniversary." The reason was obvious: "the occasion recalls to mind too vividly the principles of the immortal Declaration, which, if indiscriminately lauded," could inspire enslaved people to demand their freedom. With its unequivocal assertion of universal equality, the document was now "considered incendiary in its tendency."[40]

After migrating to the North, Long regretted having participated in Fourth of July festivities in the South. He recalled how on one occasion, after a militia company formed in front of a Maryland courthouse, he opened exercises by offering a public prayer. "A young orator followed, with an eulogium on our free country." Long agonized as he listened, for he knew that on the following day, "at the very door of the house where he was then speaking, might have been seen men with as much natural intellect as those who had listened to him, sold to the slave-trader at the highest bid, and handcuffed like criminals, though guilty of no crime." The guilt of having countenanced "so solemn a farce" troubled Long's conscience. For the remainder of his life, he promised not to participate in any Independence Day celebration unless doing so would further the cause of freedom.[41]

Long's testimony reveals how the contrasting interpretations of the Fourth of July reflected the growing sectional conflict over slavery. As the holiday lost favor across the South, it not only retained its significance in the North but acquired new meaning. The change was primarily a result of the organized movement against slavery. "From the very moment of national Independence," writes historian David Waldstreicher, "black and white abolitionists seized upon the Declaration of Independence to show that the American Revolution meant equality for all people, at least as much as it meant American national autonomy."[42] With the founding document serving as "the touchstone, the sacred scripture for" the antislavery and abolitionist movements, slavery's opponents never doubted Independence Day's power as a symbolic weapon in the war against slavery.[43]

Benjamin Lundy showed the emerging significance of the Fourth of July and the Declaration of Independence to slavery's opponents on July 4, 1821. On this day, he published the first edition of the *Genius of Universal Emancipation* with the document's preamble emblazoned across its masthead. The editor explained his reason for issuing his publication on the Fourth of July with the following: "As many of the sentiments contained in that most important state paper, the declaration of independence, coincide with my own ideas," and believing the annual celebration of its issuance an appropriate occasion, "I have

FIGURE 2.1. The caption of this satirical abolitionist engraving reads: "Behold! the degraded son of Africa, reading the Declaration of Independence, handcuffed as he is; and stared at with astonishment by the *Husband* and *Wife*, in front of him, who are also chained; and whose appearance seems to say, 'are these things so.' The *Musicians*, no doubt, could perform better, at least with more ease to themselves, if they had the use of both hands. On the back ground is to be seen, the notorious Judge Linch, with whip in hand, and his foot on the Constitution—bolstered up with bales of Cotton and hogsheads of Tobacco—surrounded by his *Mob Court*, condemning the friends of humanity, and executing them upon the spot, merely for supporting that clause of the Declaration, viz: '*All men are created free and equal*,' and acting in conformity with 192 passages of Holy writ, which are either directly or indirectly, against the system of SLAVERY." "Fourth of July Celebration, or, Southern ideas of Liberty—July 4, '40," by William K. Rhinehart (1840). Courtesy of the American Antiquarian Society.

chosen this day to present the public with the GENIUS OF UNIVERSAL EMANCIPATION."[44]

Over the course of its entire eighteen-year run, Lundy's paper continually conflated the Fourth of July with the Declaration of Independence. On the republic's fiftieth anniversary in 1826, the editor reflected on the historic day that occasioned the assertion of "the bold

and incontrovertible *truths* that 'ALL MEN WERE CREATED EQUAL.'"
For a half century, the American people had reiterated those truths
amid thundering cannon, cheering people, and illuminated cities; yet,
while these citizens were "singing paeans to LIBERTY AND EQUALITY,
and trumpeting their pretended love of JUSTICE to the world," nearly
one and a half million other people were considered "chattel property,
and made the source of the most hellish traffic that ever disgraced and
cursed the most barbarous country upon earth!!!" Though the prospects
of abolishing slavery were grim, Lundy did not despair of the country's
salvation. Among the dark clouds of oppression, he discerned "the solar
rays of universal emancipation."[45]

His protégé, William Lloyd Garrison, was far less optimistic. In 1829,
the brash and bespectacled young journalist earned national notoriety
after delivering an explosive Fourth of July oration inside Boston's Park
Street Church. He asserted that the abuse of alcohol, the proliferation
of violence, and national hubris made the Fourth of July "the worst and
most disastrous day" of the year; nevertheless, slavery was of even greater
concern. Rather than a cause for celebration, "It should make this a day
of fasting and prayer, not of boisterous merriment and idle pageantry,
a day of great lamentation, not of congratulatory joy." It should cause
the spiking of every cannon and the hauling down of every flag. "I am
ashamed of my country," Garrison proclaimed. "I am sick of our un-
meaning declamation in praise of liberty and equality; of our hypocritical cant about the unalienable rights of man." The entire nation was in
danger, for the millions of people held in bondage knew of their natural
right to freedom—and they would, like the republic's founders, stop at
nothing to obtain it.[46]

It was a career-launching address. "What the Boston clergy saw that
afternoon, in the Park Street Church, was the vision of a soul on fire,"
wrote one of Garrison's first biographers, the African American author
Archibald Grimké. "The address was the fiery cry of the young prophet
ere he plunged into the unsubdued wilderness of American slavery."[47]
More recently, historian Henry Mayer judged the speech "the most

forthright and extensive statement of American egalitarian principle written between the Declaration of Independence and the Gettysburg Address."[48]

Garrison's contemporaries were of a different mind. Indeed, just days before the Park Street address—in an obvious attempt to thwart the lecture—authorities ordered Garrison to appear before a local court on July 4th and answer to the charge of failing to muster into the local militia. After borrowing money from a friend and paying several dollars in fines and fees, Garrison made it to the Park Street Church meeting just moments before the scheduled four o'clock start.[49] Subsequent to the speech, local editorialists assailed the orator, criticizing him for everything from his age to his outfit. One editorialist was particularly harsh, calling the oration "one of the most injudicious, intemperate productions ever written."[50]

The reproaches are a reminder that most White northerners abhorred abolitionists and abolitionism. Having enjoyed and embraced the benefits of a society rooted in racism, they saw any effort to opposed slavery as a threat to their privileged position. Their actions in opposition to abolitionism prove two important points about the United States before the Civil War: first, that White supremacy transcended section; and second, that despite the esteemed reputation of abolitionists among scholars and the public today, their contemporaries considered them enemies of the people and treated them accordingly.

Predictably then, abolitionists' efforts to transform Fourth of July celebrations into antislavery affairs often met with great resistance. Time and again, armed, angry, and inebriated mobs of White men, consisting of both native-born citizens and recent European immigrants, terrorized abolitionists on Independence Day. Targeting Black-owned homes, churches, and businesses primarily, they transformed the holiday into a carnival of racial violence.

The tradition had a long history in the antebellum North. The free Philadelphia Black businessman and Revolutionary War veteran James Forten observed during the War of 1812, "It is a well known fact, that black people, upon certain days of public jubilee, dare not to be seen after twelve o'clock in the day, upon the field to enjoy the times; for no sooner do the fumes of that potent devil Liquor, mount into the brain, than the poor black is assailed like the destroying Hyena or the avaricious Wolf!" While all holidays posed a threat to the lives and property of Black people, the Fourth of July was particularly danger-ous. Forten observed sardonically, "Is it not wonderful, that the day set apart for the festival of Liberty, should be abused by the advocates of Freedom, in endeavoring to sully what they profess to adore." Despite Forten's objection, racially motivated Independence Day violence con-tinued and—after the abolitionist movement's emergence in the early 1830s—increased.[51]

The most notorious incident occurred in New York City in 1834 and lasted a week. It began on the Fourth of July during an interracial gath-ering in Chatham Street Chapel. After a reading of the Declaration of Independence by a local physician, the abolitionist icon Lewis Tappan began reciting the Constitution of the American Anti-Slavery Society (AASS), which also declared that all men were created equal. Before he could finish, hundreds of White men burst into the building and cre-ated a disturbance. When another speaker took the stage of the former theater to restore order, the ruffians drowned out his voice by stomping their feet and screaming "Treason! Treason!" Seeing that any engage-ment with the church's invaders "would have served as a pretext for violence," the abolitionists quickly disassembled.[52]

Like other anti-abolitionist mobs, the Chatham Street Chapel ri-oters were motivated by a fear of "amalgamation," a derogatory term for interracial sexual relationships, which they believed were a natural outgrowth of abolitionism.[53] But they also saw an opportunity to re-claim the symbols of freedom from their adversaries. According to one writer, the abolitionists affronted the mob by reading the Declaration of Independence and the AASS's Constitution on the Fourth of July: "*It was considered as a desecration of the day to read the one, after and in con-nection with the other.*" The public display of the AASS's Constitution was also deemed offensive. "On the wall of the building, outside, was suspended the Declaration of the American Anti-Slavery Society, framed, and in the style of a facsimile of the Declaration of American Independence." This, in another writer's mind, was a grave insult to the American people, which justified the mob's actions. "Indeed, if the abolitionists had wished for a row, they could hardly have adopted measures more likely to bring it about."[54]

No blood had been spilled, but that changed three days later when African American worshippers returned to the Chatham Street Chapel to resume the celebration. During another reading of the Declaration of Independence, they were interrupted by a group of European American musicians who demanded the celebrants vacate the premises.[55] Soon, "the whole house was a scene of confusion and violence," as Black and White combatants fought each other with fists and a variety of impromptu weapons, including pieces of broken benches and chairs. Watchmen entered the building and eventually brought the battle to a conclusion, while out in the streets reports surfaced "that the blacks inside were killing the whites."[56] The result was mayhem.

For the next several days, hundreds of rioters unleashed their racist rage across the city. Starting at the Chatham Street Chapel, they proceeded to the famed Bowery Theatre in search of the establishment's English-born operator, Thomas Hamblin, who had recently made remarks deemed un-American. After breaking into the playhouse at dusk on the 9th, the ruffians interrupted a performance of the popular tragedy *Metamora; or, The Last of the Wampanoags*, which dramatized the plight of America's Indigenous people, and then "hissed and pelted poor Hamblin, not regarding the talisman which he relied upon, the American flag, which he waved over his head."[57] The rioters then set their sights on the home of Lewis Tappan, which they promptly looted and destroyed. Over the next forty-eight hours, the horde continued to spiral out of control, ransacking the homes and churches of two of New York's most prominent abolitionist preachers, Samuel Cox and Henry Ludlow.[58]

The White mob reserved its greatest fury for African Americans who lived, worked, and worshipped in and around the city's notorious Five Points district. "The vengeance of the mob appeared to be directed entirely against the blacks," the *New York Commercial Advertiser* recorded; "whenever a colored person appeared, it was a signal of combat, fight and riot."[59] The targets of the rioters' rage generally took flight, but some fought back. Among them was a Black barber known as Marsh. A local report read, "The black intrepidly kept possession of his premises, discharging a pistol three times at his assailants, the last of which unfortunately took effect."[60] By the time local officials finally restored order, more than a dozen Black churches, businesses, and residences lay in ruins. Though no one died in the anti-abolitionist riot, the violence forced as many as 500 African Americans to temporarily abandon their homes.[61]

Because of incidents like this, a growing number of free Black northerners found Independence Day objectionable. Charlotte Forten, the granddaughter of James Forten and an aspiring writer, expressed a common view in a series of diary entries. On July 4th, 1857, she wrote from a suburb outside of Philadelphia, "The celebration of this day! What a mockery it is! My soul sickens of it." A year later she wrote, "Spent the afternoon and eve in *trying* to rest; but in vain, *Patriotic* young America kept up [such] a din in celebrating their glorious *Fourth*, that *rest* was impossible." Forten fumed, "My very soul is sick of such a mockery." She longed to return to New England, where Fourth of July celebrations reckoned with rather than ignored the "hypocrisy" of American slavery.[62]

Considering the Fourth of July little more than a memorial to American hypocrisy, many free Black northerners and increasingly their White allies stopped celebrating the holiday altogether. But rather than disregard the political platform provided by the annual event, they chose alternative days to demonstrate their opposition to slavery and White supremacy. Among the earliest alternatives to the Fourth of July was the Fifth of July. In historian Matthew Dennis's words, the day was "proximate enough to Independence Day to align it with the principles of the Declaration of Independence and to draw attention to their boycott of a day steeped in hypocrisy." It was even more than that. By ignoring the Fourth of July and congregating the following day, protestors demonstrated their attachment to the American nation while refusing to accept its failings.[63]

The first Fifth of July celebration occurred in New York City one day after New York State permanently outlawed slavery. The event was not without controversy. In the days before the law took effect, Black New Yorkers disagreed on when to mark the historic occasion. In *Freedom's Journal*, the first newspaper owned and operated by African Americans in the United States, a writer calling himself CONSISTENCY argued against gathering on the Fourth of July, considering it "a more fit day of mourning, than rejoicing!!"[64] John Russwurm, one of the paper's editors, disagreed. He retorted, "Nothing can be more evident than that the Fourth is the proper day to be observed." Since African Americans had given their lives to birth the republic, there was no reason why they should not celebrate the holiday alongside their European American compatriots.[65]

Also debated was the *way* to mark the occasion. Fearful that a public parade on either the Fourth or Fifth of July would reflect poorly on their communities' values or worse, provoke a violent response from White rioters, Black leaders decided to hold two separate celebrations. *Freedom's Journal* announced in late June, "One party will celebrate the Fourth of July, without any public procession; and the other, the Fifth, with a Grand Procession, Oration and Public Dinner."[66] In the end, the Fifth of July parade, complete with bands, banners, and a grand marshal mounted on horseback, proved a success. Years later, the Black abolitionist medical doctor James McCune Smith recalled, "It was a proud day in the City of New York for our people, that 5th day of July, 1827."[67]

In subsequent years, free Black northerners and their White allies continued to observe the Fifth of July throughout the North, but the First of August eventually surpassed the Fifth of July as an antislavery alternative to the Fourth of July. On August 1, 1834, Great Britain began the gradual abolition of slavery in its West Indian colonies, and then exactly four years later completed the process entirely. Collectively, these events made the First of August a special day for slavery's opponents across the Atlantic world. Despite the obvious global implications of the First of August, there is reason to challenge historian Jeffrey R. Kerr-Ritchie's assertion that these freedom celebrations "did not help shape national political culture" in the United States. To the contrary, when even a small percentage of American citizens disregarded the Fourth of July in favor of an international antislavery holiday, they did so in the spirit of national redemption—not rejection. Rather than forsaking the republic, they endeavored to redeem it.[68]

An early celebration of the First of August in New York City demonstrates. In 1836, Black organizers—Samuel Cornish, Thomas Downing, Henry Sipkins, Theodore Wright, and Thomas Van Rensselaer—swore to use the anniversary of West Indian emancipation to highlight the enslavement of more than two million of their brethren in the United States. They would, along with their "friends the abolitionists," blow the "great trumpet of liberty" while highlighting the evils done "by the *Christian*, church-going, psalm-singing, long-prayer making, lynching, tar and feathering; man-roasting, human-flesh-dealers of America." Having thus exposed the lie of American freedom, "We will *preach* the Declaration of Independence, till it begins to be put into PRACTICE."[69]

Soon the call for First of August celebrations became general among American abolitionists. In 1837, *Freedom's Journal* declared the day one "that should be remembered, observed, and consecrated to gratitude and gladness, by every colored man and his friend."[70] William Lloyd Garrison agreed. "There is no day in the history of human emancipation from bondage so precious as the first of August," he asserted in the summer of 1841. "It deserves to be celebrated more than the fourth of July."[71]

To further their cause, abolitionists endeavored to make the First of August a more respectable holiday than the Fourth of July, which had become synonymous with drunkenness and disorder. Reverend Samuel J. May suggested of the new holiday, "Let us celebrate this day, not by the pomp and circumstance of military parades—not by glittering shows and deafening noises—by the clattering drum—the discordant trumpet—the clangor of arms, or the booming cannon." Slavery's demise in the British colonies was a moral rather than a martial victory; therefore, "the shouts of the people" and the "roar of cannon" were better left to Independence Day.[72] Despite the calls for propriety, May fully intended the First of August to be, in historian Caleb McDaniel's words, "*both* respectable and radical." By carefully commemorating this transcendent international event, the American people would eventually "see its bearing upon the abolition of slavery in our own country."[73]

Abolitionists' desire to peacefully observe the First of August led to the creation of one of its most popular protest traditions—the anti-slavery picnic. In the spring of 1842, Boston pamphleteer John Collins explained the reason for celebrating West Indian Emancipation: "It is absolutely indispensable for the success of our cause, that the benefits of this great and benevolent experiment should be kept constantly before the minds of our people." He recommended "an *Anti-Slavery Pic-Nic*" as an innovative way to observe the occasion. The event would be decorous and orderly, consisting of speeches, songs, and a procession from some agreed-upon place to an outdoor grove. Alcohol was forbidden, while every effort was to be made to include abolitionists "of both sexes" and children in the festivities.[74]

Over the course of the next two decades, abolitionists held hundreds of First of August picnics across the North. The events were so successful that they inspired similar outings on various other summer days, including the Fourth of July. Despite the success of First of August picnics, abolitionists did not limit their celebrations of the anniversary of West Indian emancipation to outdoor gatherings in rural communities. This was done primarily for reasons of accessibility. Out-of-town events, which often required attendees to purchase expensive train tickets and miss a day or more of work, prohibited many abolitionists from participating, especially African Americans who resided in cities.

Boston abolitionists' response to the First of August in 1845 offers an example of both the racial and spatial dynamics that sometimes shaped the celebration of this and other antislavery holidays. When Charles Whipple, a White agent for the Massachusetts Anti-Slavery Society, suggested First of August picnics be held in towns surrounding Boston, local Black leaders responded by offering an urban alternative.[75] A writer using the pseudonym N explained the decision thusly: "Notwithstanding the many inducements to repair to the country, and celebrate the day in the groves, 'God's first temples,' there were those who felt that some demonstration should be made in Boston."[76] Among the organizers of the event was the New England Freedom Association, a group of Black abolitionists dedicated to assisting fugitive slaves. "The colored citizens of Boston and their friends will celebrate the anniversary of West India Emancipation at the Tremont Temple," an advertisement published by one of the group's leaders read, before imploring in the spirit of interracial brotherhood. "We invite the friends of humanity to participate with us on these occasions."[77]

The Boston celebration, which proved a marked success, testifies to the ability of First of August enthusiasts to use the occasion to simultaneously profess their love of country and hatred of slavery.[78] Early in the event, a choir "of colored children" led by Miss Frances Allen offered a rendition of "America (My Country, 'Tis of Thee)" that transformed the popular patriotic anthem into a protest song. The opening lines read:

My country! 'tis of thee
Strong hold of slavery,
Of thee I sing:
Land where my fathers died,
Where men [sic] man's rights deride,
From every mountain side,
Thy deeds shall ring.
My native country! Thee,
Where all men are born free,

> If white their skin;
> I love thy hills and dales,
> Thy mounts and pleasant vales,
> But hate thy negro sales
> As foulest sin.[79]

Far beyond Boston, First of August celebrations took on various forms. In 1842, the students, faculty, and administrators of Ohio's Oberlin College used the occasion to reinforce their commitment to equality.[80] Like abolitionists across the North, the school's racially integrated community considered the day more important than the Fourth of July, "so long as the principles of the declaration of that independence are so utterly disregarded by our slave-holding and pro-slavery citizens." In this case, the idea for the First of August event "originated with, and all the arrangements were made and executed by the colored people, with scarcely a suggestion from others."[81]

The festivities began early in the morning with a prayer meeting in the college's chapel. Following prayers, "many brethren, white and colored" enjoyed a performance of the school's choir and brief orations by the school's most esteemed students and teachers. Chosen especially for the occasion, "the four speakers were representatives of the four classes, the free colored people, the slaves, the slave holders, and the free white people."[82] In the evening, 250 celebrants moved to the Oberlin College Commons Hall for a banquet "where all sat down, without any distinction of caste or sex."[83]

While the First of August at Oberlin suggested the best possibilities of race relations in nineteenth-century America, the holiday's simultaneous celebration in Philadelphia proved the worst. The event started simply enough. At the invitation of the Philadelphia Vigilant Committee, a volunteer organization founded by Robert Purvis and other Black abolitionists to assist fugitive slaves, as many as one thousand African Americans marched down Lombard Street with banners flying high. One of the standards, which marchers intended to symbolize the purpose of the day's events, depicted an emancipated slave, "pointing with one hand to the broken chains at his feet, and with the other to the word 'Liberty,' in gold letters over his head." Behind the Black figure an allegorical scene underscored the great hope inspired by the end of slavery in the British West Indies: a rising sun alongside a sinking ship, "emblematical of the dawn of freedom and the wreck of tyranny."[84]

As the procession got underway, anti-abolitionists spread rumors that the banner displayed something entirely different. Instead of "Liberty," the text purportedly read "*Liberty or Death*." Rather than an icon of an emancipated British slave, the image beneath the slogan was allegedly a representation of the Haitian Revolution, the massive slave revolt that shook French Saint-Domingue at the turn of the nineteenth century. According to the rioters, "the painting exhibited the conflagration of a town in St. Domingo, during the massacre of the whites by their slaves."[85] Another asserted that the image showed "the figure of a black destroying his master's family, as it occurred in St. Dom'o, with the motto, 'Liberty or Death.'"[86]

With that, the lives and property of Black people were in grave danger. The "violators of the peace" began shouting epithets and pelting the marchers with stones, and soon a melee broke out between the two sides, involving the use of sticks, clubs, and bricks. The predominately Irish mob, which quickly grew into the thousands, then set its sights on "the destruction of every church, hall, and public edifice, belonging to the blacks." Among the targets of their rage was the four-story Beneficial Hall, a Black-owned abolitionist institution, which they promptly demolished. While many African Americans took refuge at the local police station, some fought back. In one instance, "some black persons," who had concealed themselves in an upstairs alley apartment, opened fire on the mob below them, wounding at least three of the rioters in the process.[87]

One victim's experience was particularly appalling given his background. Charles Black, an African American veteran of the War of

1812 whose father had fought at the Battle of Bunker Hill, was inside his Lombard Street home when a group of rioters burst through the door and beat him senseless. Only the intervention of several good Samaritans saved the life of this American patriot. Forcefully impressed into military service by the British at the start of the War of 1812, Black "refused to fight against his country, although he had 900 dollars prize money coming to him from the ship." The decision to stay loyal to his homeland was a fateful one, as it landed him in the infamous Dartmoor Prison. As part of a prisoner exchange, Black eventually returned to the United States, where he enlisted in the US Navy and served with distinction at the Battle of Lake Champlain.[88]

Black's beating discloses a great deal about antebellum America. Regardless of section, African Americans were always potential targets of racial hatred and violence. The threat grew significantly on the Fourth of July, the First of August, and any other holiday that held political meaning. In a nation dedicated to freedom but steeped in slavery, it is not surprising that the day set aside for commemorating its birth would become a source of conflict and contestation. Equally unsurprising is that the nation's founding document became a divisive and at times even despised symbol of racial equality.

Today, few Americans remember that as the republic spiraled toward civil war, White southerners' disdain for the Declaration of Independence spread nationwide. During the US Senate debates over slavery's expansion into the Kansas and Nebraska territories in 1854, Indiana's John Pettit called the egalitarian ideals expressed in the text's preamble "a self-evident lie."[89] Two years later, after antislavery stalwarts formed the Republican Party to stop slavery's westward spread, Rufus Choate, a former US senator from Massachusetts, warned of the dangers of this new party, as it had risen on "the glittering and sounding generalities of natural right upon which make the Declaration of Independence."[90] On the eve of the Civil War, Stephen Douglas intentionally tried to transform the founding document into a racist text. The US senator from Illinois informed his colleagues, "I hold that the

Declaration of Independence was only referring to the white man—to the governing race of this country, who were in conflict with Great Britain, and had no reference to the negro race at all, when it declared that all were created equal."[91]

The greatest assault on the Declaration of Independence came in the Supreme Court case of *Dred Scott v. Sandford*, which in 1857 ruled that African Americans, whether free or enslaved, were not and could never be citizens of the United States. In the words of Chief Justice Roger Taney, Black people "had no rights which the white man was bound to respect." As for the nation's founding text, "the enslaved African race were never intended to be included, and formed no part of the people who framed and adopted this declaration."[92]

At a time of ascendant White supremacy, it was left to the great African American thinker, speaker, and writer Frederick Douglass to reclaim the Declaration of Independence from slavery's supporters. As a fugitive slave who found fame as an international advocate of human rights, Douglass was uniquely qualified to articulate the failure of the American republic to reach its potential as stated in its founding document and offer a path to redemption. On the Fifth of July in 1852, he dared an audience in Rochester, New York, to imagine the United States as the world's exemplar of freedom and equality but for slavery. Offering rare insight into the dialectic of race and nation, Douglass's oration is one of the essential speeches in American history. Hence, it is to an analysis of it and its author that this study now turns.

3
THE FIFTH

Frederick Douglass was a sight to behold. Standing more than six feet tall, he towered over the hundreds of men and women who had come to Nantucket, Massachusetts, to hear him speak at a gathering in the island's historic Atheneum Hall in August 1841.[1] His strong and powerful physique, which he acquired from years of hard labor on the tobacco farms of southern Maryland and in the docks and shipyards of East Baltimore, further distinguished him from his audience. So did his distinctive facial features and skin color, which revealed a combination of African and European ancestry.

Unfortunately, there is no record of exactly what Douglass said in this, his first paid public address. According to one observer, "the fugitive slave" was embarrassed when he stepped to the platform and only reluctantly began speaking. But he "gradually rose to the importance of the occasion and the dignity of his theme." Douglass started by condemning the self-professed Christians who across the South held Black people in bondage. Then, in what would become typical of his early orations, "he turned over the terrible Apocalypse of his experiences in slavery."[2]

Douglass discussed his "first speech" in all three editions of his autobiography.[3] "The truth was," he recalled of the anxiety he first felt over addressing the audience, "I felt myself a slave, and the idea of speaking to white people weighed me down."[4] Though trembling and stammering at the start, Douglass quickly regained his composure. Several moments later he experienced a surprising level of comfort, as he confidently addressed the estimated one thousand people in attendance who listened with rapt attention.

The predominately White audience, which included a who's who of the abolitionist movement, was awestruck. Among them was William Lloyd Garrison, who immediately after hearing Douglass speak proclaimed, "that PATRICK HENRY, of revolutionary fame, never made a speech more eloquent in the cause of liberty, than the one we had just listened to from the lips of that hunted fugitive." The editor realized Douglass's potential as a weapon against both slavery and racism. "If Mr. DOUGLASS could be persuaded to consecrate his time and talents to the promotion of the anti-slavery enterprise, a powerful impetus would be given to it" and a devastating blow delivered to racial prejudice.[5]

Garrison's comparison of Patrick Henry and Frederick Douglass was apt. Though the former was a European American slave owner from the Virginia backcountry and the latter an African American slave from Maryland's tidewater, the two men dedicated their lives to public service. Considered among the greatest orators of the eighteenth and nineteenth centuries respectively, they both used their oratorical abilities to inspire others to resist the tyrannical forces that imperiled American freedom. With an extraordinary love of country, the founding father and the fugitive slave risked their own lives to make the United States' republican experiment a success.

While Henry gave his most famous speech, in which he cried out, "Give me liberty, or give me death!" in a Richmond, Virginia, church, on the eve of American independence, Douglass delivered his greatest oration in a Rochester, New York, lecture hall almost a decade before the start of the Civil War. On July 5, 1852, the escaped slave who by then had become an internationally renowned orator and author demanded an answer to a simple question: "What to the Slave is the Fourth of July?"

In what has come to be known as the Fifth of July (or, as some might have it, the Fourth of July) speech, Douglass excoriated the United States for failing to live up to its egalitarian ideals, and in the process offered a memorable, if muted, celebration of American exceptionalism. This is an important idea to consider given the pejorative connotations of the concept today. The belief that the American republic is not only different but superior to other nations has long engendered controversy. It has, for example, fostered foreign and domestic policy that was at times violent, racist, and even genocidal. Accordingly, historians and other scholars have increasingly rejected the idea of American exceptionalism. Despite this, the concept still must be reckoned with, given its powerful history.[6]

Even during the era of slavery, when the republic's shortcomings were so clear, the concept held widespread appeal—even if it did not yet have a name. Among those attracted to the idea of American exceptionalism were some of slavery's staunchest opponents. To them, the republic's renouncement of monarchy and aristocracy in favor of a popular government clearly distinguished it from other nations. So did the widespread enjoyment of the principles espoused in the Declaration of Independence by the republic's White population. They believed that by eliminating slavery and racism, the United States would become a truly exceptional nation—a city on a hill that offered a model of freedom for the rest of the world to follow.

In the antebellum United States, abolitionists' belief in American exceptionalism was conditional. They, to borrow the words of political scientist Lucy Williams, understood American exceptionalism not as an "*accomplished* exceptionalism" that was "uncritical, backward-looking, and self-congratulatory," but rather an "*aspirational* exceptionalism" that was "self-reflective, forward-looking, and ameliorative."[7] It was this aspirational American exceptionalism that Douglass subscribed to and stressed in his Fifth of July oration. Though taking a harsh and highly critical stance, he offered a hopeful vision of America's future. By exposing and condemning the nation's most obvious, enduring, and destructive problems, Douglass endeavored to solve them. Rather than abandoning the struggle to achieve the republic's great destiny, he interrogated the anniversary of national independence to inspire others to join him in the long and difficult fight to secure it.

Douglass's "What to the Slave Is the Fourth of July?" asserted that slavery was a national problem requiring a national solution. By violating

God-given natural rights, the practice degraded slaves and citizens alike, while preventing the republic from fulfilling its egalitarian ideals. To correct course, Douglass invoked and expounded on the United States' revolutionary heritage, arguing that the freedom of all Americans was necessary if the nation was to reach its extraordinary potential. In a masterful appropriation of the Declaration of Independence and the Fourth of July, he claimed both the language and symbols of freedom for himself, enslaved people, and their allies, and in the process revealed their extraordinary power.

───

Frederick Douglass never knew the date of his birth. It was most likely in 1818, the same year the US Congress standardized the national flag. His mother was a dark-skinned field hand, while his father "was a white man" and likely his first owner.[8] Douglass spent the first years of his life on Maryland's Eastern Shore, but before his ninth birthday his owner's death resulted in his being relocated to Baltimore. Life in this burgeoning metropolis was transformative for the young bondman. Here, for the first time, he encountered White people who were opposed to slavery and Black people who were free.

Douglass's acquisition of literacy was equally life-changing. In Baltimore, his owner's wife taught him the alphabet and the rudiments of spelling, but when her husband discovered the indiscretion forbade his wife from offering her apt pupil any further instruction. Convinced that the ability to read and write represented the pathway to freedom, Douglass found creative ways to further his education. From carrying a copy of Noah Webster's spelling book in his pocket, to trading bread and biscuits for impromptu spelling lessons from literate children on the city's waterfront, he became an advanced reader. Among the early treasures in Douglass's personal library was *The Columbian Orator*, "one of the primers through which thousands of American youth improved their reading and practiced syntax and speaking."[9] Among the entries that most appealed to Douglass were those considering the battle between freedom and oppression. "The dialogue and speeches were all redolent of the principles of liberty," he recalled when explaining why he found the volume so compelling, "and poured floods of light on the nature and character of slavery."[10]

Though Douglass conducted himself appropriately in Baltimore, his owners returned him to Maryland's Eastern Shore, where he experienced three back-breaking, mind-numbing, and soul-crushing years of captivity. Only the dream of freedom kept him alive. A turning point came in 1836, when after being caught trying to abscond for the second time, Douglass's owner, who felt he could no longer control the rebellious eighteen-year-old, sent Douglass back to Baltimore. Two years later, Douglass successfully escaped from the hell of slavery by impersonating a free Black sailor and taking two separate trains and a steamboat to New York City.[11]

To pull off the deception, he wore a seaman's outfit and carried a Seamen's Protection Certificate, both of which he borrowed from a friend. With an iconic American eagle emblazoned across its head, the federally issued travel permit was for Douglass—both literally and figuratively—a ticket to freedom. At the turn of the nineteenth century, in response to the growing number of American citizens who were impressed into service on British Navy ships, the US Congress passed an Act for the Relief and Protection of American Seamen. To safeguard individuals sailing "under the protection of the American flag," the law authorized federal customs officials to issue certificates to these sailors proving their nationality.[12] Seaman Protection Papers also proved freedom. They were, in historian Gene Smith's words, "a godsend to black seamen trying desperately to avoid the institution of slavery."[13] Enslaved people in maritime communities understood the power the Seamen's Protection Certificates held. When asked by a conductor on the train from Baltimore for documentation proving his freedom, Douglass responded proudly, "I have a paper with the American Eagle on it, and that will carry me around the world."[14]

Following the successful journey north, Douglass began his new life in New Bedford, Massachusetts, as a free man. He married Anna

Murray, a free Black laundress from Baltimore who had helped him escape and then followed him north, and changed his last name, first to Johnson and then to Douglass, after a character in a Sir Walter Scott poem. Though rarely interrogated by scholars, his full birth name was Frederick Augustus Washington Bailey. Frederick was his mother's preference, while Augustus honored an uncle. Bailey was a family name dating back generations. As for the inspiration behind his second middle name, Washington, Douglass never explained. Biographer David Blight posits, "Perhaps his mother, lonely and sexually abused, with so little to provide for her newborn, sought in a moment of anguished pride to link this child to the father of the country, rather than to a father he could never really know."[15]

The theory makes sense. Today, Washington is the most common surname among African Americans, indicating a long tradition of Black people adopting the surname of the first President of the United States of their own volition.[16] The acclaimed leader and founder of the Tuskegee Institute, Booker T. Washington, offers a well-known example. Known only as Booker prior to the Civil War, the young Virginian informed his first schoolteacher shortly after becoming free that his surname was Washington "as if I had been called by that name all my life."[17] Given this tradition, Harriet Bailey may very well have named her son after the nation's founding father. Whether she did so to increase his claim to an American identity is unknown—as is the reason why Douglass "dispensed with" the name throughout his entire adult life.[18]

In New Bedford, Douglass began attending antislavery lectures and wondered how he might contribute to the movement. Following his Nantucket speech in 1841, he accepted a position with the American Anti-Slavery Society (AASS) and soon became one of the organization's most popular public speakers. Douglass then turned to writing. His autobiography, *Narrative of the Life of Frederick Douglass, an American Slave*, appeared on antislavery bookshelves on May 1, 1845. Selling thirty thousand copies in the next fifteen years, it was, in today's parlance, a blockbuster.[19]

FIGURE 3.1. *Frederick Douglass*, daguerreotype by Samuel J. Miller (circa 1847–1852). Courtesy of the Art Institute of Chicago.

In this small volume, Douglass's conceptualization of slavery in a nationalist framework emerged. By juxtaposing the words *American* and *Slave*, the book's subtitle illuminated the paradox that had imperiled the United States' republican experiment from the beginning. As an "American slave," Douglass contrasted himself with the African-born pioneers of the slave narrative genre who, despite spending years of captivity in the British Empire, identified themselves variously as "an African Prince," "the African," "a Native of Africa," and "the African Preacher."[20] He also distinguished himself from earlier American-born slave narrators who self-identified as "the runaway slave," "formerly a slave," and "a Black Man."[21] From the outset, there was no mistaking Douglass's nationality.

Even so, Douglass continued to assert his Americanness inside the book's covers. In a moving and emotionally raw passage, which invoked both the language and symbols of freedom, he recounted his failed effort to lead himself and several other "noble spirits" out of the house of bondage. The scheme centered on stealing a canoe on the Saturday night before Easter and paddling north on the Chesapeake Bay to Pennsylvania. Douglass and his co-conspirators knew the risks they were taking to become free were far greater than those taken by American revolutionaries—still, they persisted. "In coming to a fixed determination to run away, we did more than Patrick Henry, when he resolved upon liberty or death," Douglass recalled of the group's decision to abscond. "With us it was a doubtful liberty at most, and almost certain death if we failed." By Easter Sunday, the five friends were prepared to die rather than spend another day in captivity. But on the day of their planned escape, an acquaintance revealed the conspiracy to authorities who promptly arrested Douglass and his associates.[22]

Employing a literary agenda that was both abolitionist and nationalist, Douglass's narrative laid the failure of the nation's republican experiment at the door of slavery. This was most apparent in the book's Appendix. In a searing indictment of the "corrupt, slaveholding, women-whipping, cradle-plundering, partial and hypocritical Christianity of this land," Douglass warned his compatriots of the terrible future that awaited them if they failed to change their ways. Turning to the Old Testament, he cited the Hebrew prophet Jeremiah who centuries earlier, in response to the growing sinfulness of the Jewish exiles of ancient Babylon, demanded, "Shall not my soul be avenged on such a nation as this?"[23]

Before Douglass could become, as Blight described him, "an American Jeremiah chastising the flock as he also called them back to their covenants and creeds," circumstances required him to flee the country.[24] Though no fugitive slave in the North was ever entirely safe from slave catchers, Douglass's freedom became especially tenuous after publishing personal information about himself, his owners, and other acquaintances in his autobiography. To avoid being captured, he traveled to the British Isles, where he spent the next eighteen months lecturing to antislavery audiences in London, Dublin, Glasgow, and more than a dozen other cities. Though the themes of his addresses varied, the hypocrisy of American slavery was the most common.

To underscore this hypocrisy for European audiences, Douglass adopted the British-inspired metaphor of a ravenous American eagle. A speech inside a crowded Presbyterian church in Paisley, Scotland, offers an example. The escaped slave explained that he had come to Europe because there was no place in "that boasted land of freedom" across the Atlantic Ocean where an individual like himself could be free. Wherever a fugitive slave traveled, "the American eagle may pursue him on expanded wings." Then, after clutching him in his talons, it could "carry him back in triumph to his blood-thirsty oppressors."[25]

The following year, after British abolitionists purchased Douglass' freedom from his Maryland owner, he prepared to return to the United States a free man. Before embarking, he delivered a farewell speech in London that revealed his increasingly critical style. Published widely on both sides of the Atlantic Ocean, the highly metaphorical address would open Douglass to charges of sedition and subversion. After the hundreds in attendance applauded the orator's arrival to the stage, he reminded them that decades earlier Americans had fought for freedom and asserted the rights of man; "yet at that very time the identical men who drew up that Declaration of Independence, and framed the American democratic constitution, were trafficking in the blood and souls of their fellow men." History proved that the American dream of liberty was a lie and the American people had forfeited their patriotism, "to defend this great falsehood."[26]

For proof of his homeland's hypocrisy, Douglass extended the metaphor of the proslavery American eagle by juxtaposing it with England's antislavery lion. He explained that despite slavery's existence in America, "There is upon our Northern and Western borders a land uncursed by slavery—a territory ruled over by the British power." Borrowing several lines from a popular abolitionist poem, Douglass declared of British Canada:

> The lion at a virgin's feet
> Crouches, and lays his mighty paw
> Upon her lap—an emblem meet
> Of England's queen and England's law.

For decades, fugitive slaves from the United States followed the North Star to a place where "in the mane of the British lion he might find himself secure from the talons and beak of the American eagle."[27]

After ridiculing the republic's national animal, Douglass set his sights on the national flag. Responding to his American critics, who insisted that American slavery was an exclusively domestic concern, he countered that longstanding cultural and economic ties between the United States and Great Britain made the practice a shared problem. As for the fear that bringing the plight of the American slave to the attention of the British people would alarm and affront American slave owners, Douglass declared that that was in fact his intention. Repeating a version of Thomas Campbell's familiar lines, he explained his wish that every Englishman would point to the American flag and say:

> United States! your banner wears
> Two emblems, one of fame:
> Alas! the other that it bears
> Reminds us of your shame.
> The white man's liberty in types
> Stands blazoned on your stars;
> But what's the meaning of your stripes?
> They mean your negroes' scars.

Despite the existence of slavery, Douglass vowed to return to the United States rather than remain in England where the practice was outlawed. "I choose rather to go home; to return to America," he explained. "I glory in the conflict, that I may hereafter exult in the victory."[28]

Upon returning to America, Douglass revealed that his patriotism was complicated and even contradictory. In May 1847, at a gathering of the AASS in New York City's Broadway Tabernacle, he took the stage after a raucous crowd of thousands interrupted a long-winded introduction by William Lloyd Garrison, chanting "'Douglass, Douglass,' from all parts of the house."[29] They had come to hear the fugitive slave sensation, and they were not to be denied. Douglass informed the audience that throughout his visit to "Monarchical England," he never experienced the racial discrimination he commonly faced in the United States. "The instant that I stepped upon the shore and looked into the faces of the crowd around me, I saw in every man a recognition of my manhood, and an absence, a perfect absence, of everything like that disgusting hate with which we are pursued in this country."[30] Regarding race and racism, England was superior to the United States.

This belief led Douglass to deliver one of the most provocative statements of his life. In response to Garrison's congratulation only minutes earlier for having returned from Europe to "his native country," Douglass fired back: "I have no love for America, as such; I have no patriotism. I have no country." In a nation that recognized Black people as property, "I have not, I cannot have, any love for this country, as such, or for its Constitution." Where Douglass agreed with Garrison was a hatred of the American government. "I desire to see it overthrown as speedily as possible and its Constitution shivered in a thousand fragments," rather than allow slavery to continue for another day. Stunned, the audience responded with a combination of "Hisses and cheers."[31]

In the coming days, editorialists across the country denounced Douglass for his remarks.[32] One of the harshest circulated critiques came from the *New York Sun*, "the most widely read newspaper in the world."[33] In reporting the antislavery meeting, the paper protested "the unmitigated abuse heaped upon our country by the coloured man Douglass, who has been so warmly patronized by the English people." In America, the essayist admitted, the freedom of speech allowed public speakers to criticize American institutions. "There is, however, a limit to this very freedom." Just as an invited guest could not enter a gentleman's home and disparage the meal being provided, "we have no right to abuse a country under whose Government we are safely residing and securely protected." Douglass's overseas sojourn, which included the experiencing and promotion of "the doctrine of amalgamation," had apparently convinced the fugitive slave "that the road to preferment and protection in England was in the abuse of this country." Upon returning to America, Douglass's assault on the United States continued. It was time to stop such fanaticism, the writer insisted, for the future of the "Union" was at stake.[34]

Douglass rejected the reproach. In a letter to Willis A. Hodges and Thomas Van Rensselaer, the founders of a short-lived protest paper in New York City, he challenged the *New York Sun* for its "weak, puerile, and characteristic attack upon me." Douglass began sarcastically, calling the editor "truly a patriot" for calling Douglass a colored man rather than a "nigger" or a "monkey." Referring to the analogy presented in the

Sun of a dinner party, he proclaimed that for the Black guests seated at the United States' dinner table, his bill of fare—like the Bill of Rights—paled in comparison to that offered the White guests. "He asks the cook for soup, he gets 'dish water.' For salmon, he gets a serpent; for beef, he gets bull-frogs; for ducks, he gets dogs; for salt, he gets sand; for pepper, he gets powder; and for vinegar he gets gall." This was the type of treatment that African Americans received from the American government. "Its Bill of Rights is to practice towards us a bill of wrongs. Its self-evident truths are self-evident lies. Its majestic liberty, malignant tyranny." The Constitution was nothing more than "a cunningly devised complication of falsehoods, calculated to deceive foreign Nations into a belief that this is a free country." As for the *Sun*'s insistence that Douglass had no right to abuse a country that provided him safety and security, he snapped back: "I am neither safely residing, nor securely protected in this country."[35]

Scholars have been sympathetic to Douglass's apparent anti-Americanism upon his return from Europe. In his study of patriotism's dark side, political scientist Steven Johnston argues that Douglass loved his country "despite his protestations to the contrary."[36] Bernard Boxill suggests that Douglass's comments can only be understood in the context of Douglass's decision to return to his home country after spending several enjoyable years abroad: "This was strange behavior from a man denying any patriotism and any love or attachment to the U.S."[37] Leslie Eckel is equally forgiving, noting that while Douglass denied any attachment to America, "he spent the next sixteen years striving to 'renovate' that very country."[38]

David Blight considers Douglass's renouncement of his American identity a rhetorical device intended to prove an important point. The biographer sees the controversial comments in religious as well as nationalistic terms, concluding that Douglass returned from Europe full of anger, a Black man ready to redeem the republic by exposing its defects. "As the latter-day Jeremiah he spoke as did the ancient prophet, calling the nation to judgment for its mendacity, its wanton violation of its own covenants, and warning of its imminent ruin." Solving the nation's problems required widespread acknowledgment that they existed.[39]

It is worth nothing that while Douglass refused to apologize for the statements made in New York City, he later offered some qualification. In a symbol-laden speech delivered in Syracuse, New York, he acknowledged that America was an extraordinary nation. "Yet the damning fact remains, there is not a rood of earth under the stars and the eagle on your flag, where a man of my complexion can stand free." There was no place that offered sanctuary. "Wherever waves the star-spangled banner there the bondman may be arrested and hurried back to the jaws of Slavery." For many Americans, there was good reason to believe that the United States was the "land of the free" and the "home of the brave." But he reminded the audience, "I never knew what freedom was till I got beyond the limits of the American eagle."[40]

Douglass then addressed the charge of being a "traitor." Recalling the enslavement of his family members in Maryland and Virginia, he inquired, "How can I love a country where the blood of my own blood, the flesh of my own flesh, is now toiling under the lash?" As long as slavery continued, Douglass swore to use his voice to hold America up to the world's scorn. "In doing this, I shall feel myself discharging the duty of a true patriot; for he is a lover of his country who rebukes and does not excuse its sins." Douglass summoned the moral authority of the Scriptures to justify his position, affirming, "It is righteousness that exalteth a nation while sin is a reproach to any people."[41]

In this and other ways, Douglass's views on the United States and its Constitution followed a formula adopted by William Lloyd Garrison. Indeed, just months after escaping from slavery, Douglass became a committed Garrisonian. He wrote of his first encounter with the *Liberator*, "From this time I was brought in contact with the mind of William Lloyd Garrison," and the newspaper "took its place with me next to the bible." Astonished by the *Liberator*'s defiant and uncompromising tone, Douglass recalled, "I not only liked—I *loved* this paper, and its editor." Garrison was an idol whom the fugitive slave from Maryland openly worshipped.[42]

While serving as Garrison's abolitionist apprentice, Douglass adopted many of the beliefs and attitudes of his mentor. Chief among them was that abolition required a moral solution, as slavery already damaged the American political process beyond repair. Closely related to this idea was that the Constitution was a proslavery compact "between the free and slave states" that served the rights and interests of the latter. Early in his abolitionist career, Garrison shared his opinion of the founding document in harsh terms, calling it "the most bloody and heaven-daring arrangement ever made by men for the continuance and protection of a system of the most atrocious villany [*sic*] ever exhibited on earth." By adopting this compact, the Founding Fathers not only brought shame upon the nation but "trampled beneath their feet their own solemn and heaven-attested Declaration, that all men are created equal, and endowed by their Creator with certain inalienable rights—among which are life, liberty, and the pursuit of happiness."[43]

Abolitionist leaders officially embraced Garrison's view of the Constitution a decade later at an antislavery meeting in Boston's famed Faneuil Hall. The interracial and intergender group, which included Garrison, Wendell Phillips, Maria Weston Chapman, Charles Remond, and Samuel May, resolved "That the compact which exists between the North and the South is a 'a covenant with death, and an agreement with hell,'—involving both parties in atrocious criminality; and should be immediately annulled." Portions of the quoted material, which derived from the prophet Isaiah in the Old Testament, were familiar to nineteenth-century Americans. They resonated with those in attendance at the Faneuil Hall meeting, including Frederick Douglass.[44]

Initially, Douglass never questioned Garrison's views on the Constitution or any other major issues. After returning from Great Britain, however, he began distancing himself from his mentor and the entire Garrisonian movement. In December 1847, Douglass established the *North Star*, a weekly abolitionist newspaper, in Rochester, New York, and then moved his family to the city, which served as a major hub for the Underground Railroad. Far removed from the oversight and control of the Boston-based Garrisonians, Douglass experienced a level of intellectual freedom in Rochester that allowed him to challenge some of the key tenets of Garrison's perfectionist philosophy.[45]

In May 1851, Douglass broke from Garrison by renouncing the pro-slavery interpretation of the Constitution and embracing political abolitionism at the Annual Meeting of the AASS in Syracuse. During the first morning session of the three-day conference, New York abolitionist Samuel May set the tone of the event by insisting that it was the patriotic duty of the American people to oppose slavery. Though critics frequently called abolitionists traitors, May proclaimed that "No movement in this country is so patriotic as ours; indeed, any movement which ignores the cause of those in bonds must be unpatriotic, for slavery is jeopardizing the very existence of our country." The crowd cheered, for they welcomed May's avowal that by participating in the struggle against slavery, "We are patriotic in the broadest and best sense of the word."[46]

Douglass amplified May's patriotic theme in the meeting's afternoon session. He claimed that by declaring equality while holding millions of people in bondage, the United States made American slavery an international concern. "By casting out the blacks from the sympathies of this country, from their benevolent regard, and from their institutions for the improvement of mankind, they have presented them to the world, civilized and savage, to take up their cause and plead for them." In the eyes of the world, the republican experiment had failed. Still, all was not lost. For more than any other nation, the United States had a special destiny. "Get American slavery out of the way, and freedom throughout the world will be revived," Douglass demanded before invoking the nation's Puritan ancestors: "get Slavery out of this country, and it will become what it has long preferred to be—the beacon light of liberty to all who have struggled for equal rights throughout the world."[47]

If America was a city on a hill, then the Constitution was a luminous ray emanating from its summit. On the last day of the conference, Douglass explained that when properly interpreted, the Constitution "might be made consistent in its details with the noble purposes avowed in its preamble." Those who shared this belief "should insist upon the application of such rules to that instrument, and demand that it be wielded in behalf of emancipation." Because the Constitution made no explicit reference to slavery, abolitionists previously sought its meaning through an analysis of "the history and practice of the nation under it." This was a mistake. The American government sanctioned and sustained "a system of lawless violence," but slavery "*never was lawful, and never can be made so.*" As a result, it was the duty of every American, "whose conscience permits him so to do, to use his *political* as well as his *moral* power for its overthrow."[48]

Douglass's about-face over the Constitution was one of the most audacious acts in a lifetime full of them. By rejecting one of the central tenets of Garrison's philosophy, he not only forfeited the support of his mentor but the AASS as well. This was a fateful decision that might have ended Douglass's career, but instead it galvanized him and his allies. The reason for this was simple. "Although anathema to the Garrisonians," historian Benjamin Quarles wrote decades ago, "Douglass' new beliefs were held by the majority of abolitionists."[49] The assertion still holds. James Oakes observes in his recent study of emancipation, "Long before the Civil War, antislavery constitutionalism was the conventional wisdom among millions of northerners, not to mention a majority of the northern representatives in Congress."[50]

When Garrison loyalists condemned Douglass for his reversal, he announced his intention to deliver a Fourth of July oration in Corinthian Hall, Rochester's largest and most prestigious public venue, to defend his position.[51] An advertisement, which appeared in *Frederick Douglass' Paper*—the *North Star*'s successor—in June 1851 invited all those who wished to celebrate the "grand Anniversary" to attend the performance. In addition to "spreading the immortal principles of 'the Declaration of Independence," Douglass planned to promote the "great objects for which the American Constitution was ordained and established."[52]

Unfortunately, illness forced Douglass to cancel the event. Years of activism and the added stress of being "an object of special attack" by other abolitionists had taken a toll on his health.[53] For several weeks, Douglass could neither speak nor write. "Bilious fever, sharp, sudden and severe, (brought on no doubt by over exertion and incautious exposure,) prostrated my energies and confined me to my room," he revealed in late July. "As soon as this had subsided, in came my throat difficulty, from which I have suffered periodical attacks during the last five years, and which has made it necessary for me to abstain from much public speaking."[54] The much-anticipated Fourth of July address would have to wait.

As Douglass recovered, he used his newspaper to disseminate his new way of thinking. For months, he published unsolicited correspondence that congratulated him on his "late position on the Anti-Slavery character of the Constitution of the United States."[55] He also reprinted speeches and other commentary by those who shared his view.[56] His efforts had little effect on the Garrisonians; still, he persisted. In the spring of 1852, Douglass attended the AASS's annual meeting, knowing he would be subjected to public scorn. When it was over, Douglass lamented being the target of "bitter reflections and vile insinuations" by some of his closest former friends and associates.[57]

More than a year after declaring his own independence from Garrison and the Garrisonians, Douglass again announced his intention to deliver a Fourth of July oration in Corinthian Hall.[58] This time, he did so at the request of the Rochester Anti-Slavery Sewing Society, an all-female organization that served as the "backbone" of the abolitionist movement in upstate New York.[59] Nearly two centuries later, the speech is still considered one of the greatest in American history. In addition to defining Douglass's antebellum philosophy about slavery and the nation, it demonstrated the power that the annual celebration of the

Declaration of Independence held over the most famous fugitive slave in American history and his allies.

Before examining Douglass's Fifth of July speech, a brief look at his attitude toward the Fourth of July would be helpful. Like other abolitionists, he considered it the most hypocritical day on the national calendar and frequently used the occasion to highlight the morality of their movement. By calling attention to the raucous and rowdy behavior of Independence Day revelers, writes historian Caleb McDaniel, "abolitionists cast themselves as respectable to counteract the caricatures of their enemies."[60] For Douglass, citing the misbehavior of White citizens served the additional purpose of proving the racism that corrupted the republic. He remarked, "If the ringing of bells, waving of banners, irregular discharge of fire-arms, burning powder on the most extravagant scale, confused and tumultuous explosion of crackers, furious driving about the street in carriages, and the uproarious shouts of an apparently purposeless multitude, be an evidence of a love of the great principles of human freedom, as set forth in the American Declaration of Independence," then Rochester's citizens surely loved liberty more than most. "But out of all the thousands that congregated here," few wished to see those principles extended to all people "in this country." Theirs, Douglass lamented, "is a white liberty."[61]

Despite his antipathy for "the anniversary of American hypocrisy," Douglass recognized the powerful political platform that the day provided.[62] Refusing to miss the opportunity to promote his new view of the Constitution for a second year in a row, he advertised in his eponymously named newspaper in mid-June a "CELEBRATION OF THE NATIONAL ANNIVERSARY" at Corinthian Hall. As the Fourth of July fell on the Sabbath, the ad informed readers that the event would take place on the following day, July 5. Interestingly, the selection of the Fifth of July seems to have been purely practical. Neither the notice in Douglass's newspaper nor any of his surviving correspondence references the antislavery tradition of observing the anniversary of American independence on the Fifth of July instead of the previous day. The advertisement further apprised that in addition to Douglass's oration, attendees would be treated to speeches by several other local leaders as well as a reading of the Declaration of Independence. A table full of cheap refreshments, including chicken, eggs, fruit, cake, and cream, ensured that no one would go home hungry.[63]

Below the advertisement, Douglass described the event as a patriotic rally. The goal was to celebrate the ideas of the Declaration of Independence, which were "rapidly being discarded" by the American people. With no end in sight to the practice of "slaveholding, slave-trading, slave-hunting, and slave rule," the time had come to take a strong and permanent stand against slavery. "Come to Rochester then!" Douglass implored. "Bring your wives, sons, daughter and friends, and let us, on the anniversary of the day that gave birth to the immortal *declaration*, come and take earnest counsel together, as to how we may best promote the great principles of Liberty and Justice."[64]

It was a beautiful morning on July 5, 1852, when approximately six hundred people filed into the stately and cavernous Corinthian Hall in downtown Rochester. As the crowd settled into their seats, James Sperry, a leader of the New York State Anti-Slavery Society, called the assembly to order around 10:00 a.m. After the meeting's Chair, Lindley Murray Moore, delivered some opening remarks, Reverend S. Ottman offered a prayer. Following these preliminaries, Reverend Robert R. Raymond, of the First Baptist Church of Syracuse, recited the Declaration of Independence in a manner that was described as both "eloquent and admirable, eliciting much applause throughout." With the crowd's interest peaked, the fugitive slave-turned-international icon rose from his chair and took the podium.[65]

As he looked out over the audience, Douglass began to speak slowly and quietly. Employing a common rhetorical device, which had become a trademark, he humbly confessed an inability to accomplish the task at hand. "The fact is, ladies and gentlemen, the distance between this platform and the slave plantation, from which I escaped, is considerable—and the difficulties to be overcome in getting from the latter to the former, are by no means slight." Therefore, he asked the audience's indulgence. Claiming a lack of experience and education, Douglass warned that he wrote his oration hastily and at the last minute. In fact, he had spent several weeks working on the address.[66] With the audience's expectations tempered by the obeisant introduction, the time to make history had arrived.[67]

David Blight calls the body of Douglass's Fifth of July speech a three-part symphony, but there was nothing harmonious about it.[68] Rather than eliciting the smooth and melodious sounds of flutes, violins, and cellos, the preeminent Black abolitionist in America crushed the classical instruments into oblivion. In an oration celebrating the nation's most sacred secular holiday, Douglass used his legendary baritone voice to produce a dissonant sound that rang painfully in the ears of the predominately White crowd.[69]

For two hours, Douglass reflected on the republic's past, present, and future.[70] In the first of more than one hundred uses of a second-person pronoun, which underscored America's failure to extend freedom to Black people, he announced that the reason for the gathering in Corinthian Hall was to celebrate "the birthday of your National Independence, and of your political freedom."[71] In the previous century, after suffering under the oppressive rule of a foreign government, the American people rose in rebellion. They began by pleading and petitioning in a proper manner. "This, however, did not answer the purpose." So, they declared their independence from Great Britain. Seventy-six years later, the nation remained free, making the anniversary of its birth a moment of great significance.[72]

Invoking a powerful metaphor of bondage and captivity, Douglass stressed the historic importance of America's birth. "The 4th of July is the first great fact in your nation's history—the very ring-bolt in the chain of your yet undeveloped destiny." In case the audience failed to recognize the stark imagery of slavery, he repeated his assertion: "I have said that the Declaration of Independence is the RINGBOLT to the chain of your nation's destiny." The principles endorsed in that document were saving ones that needed to be protected at all costs. "That *bolt* drawn, that *chain* broken, and all is lost."[73]

Douglass then turned to an appraisal of the Founding Fathers. Claiming membership in the nation that years earlier saw his enslavement, he began, "Fellow Citizens, I am not wanting in respect for the fathers of this republic." The men who affixed their signatures to the Declaration of Independence were great men. "They were statesmen, patriots and heroes, and for the good they did, and the principles they contended for, I will unite with you to honor their memory." Among the Founding Fathers' greatest virtues was their love of country, which they considered worth dying for. Through a series of great and selfless acts, "the fathers of this republic, did, most deliberately, under the inspiration of a glorious patriotism, and with a sublime faith in the great principles of justice and freedom, lay deep, the corner-stone of the national super-structure, which has risen and still rises in grandeur around you."[74]

Douglass observed how the sights and sounds of the Fourth of July annually recalled this great accomplishment. Flags and banners flew in the air as fifes and drums joined a cacophony of church bells. People prayed, sang hymns, and listened to sermons, "while the quick martial tramp of a great and multitudinous nation, echoed back by all the hills, valleys and mountains of a vast continent," bespoke an occasion of unmatched importance—"a nation's jubilee." The holiday was much more than an annual celebration of American independence. It was key to the establishment and preservation of a vibrant national culture.[75]

Having completed his brief history lesson, Douglass turned toward the present. As a representative of a reviled race, he wondered what, if anything, African-descended people had to do with American independence. "Are the great principles of political freedom and of natural justice, embodied in that Declaration of Independence, extended to us? and am I, therefore, called upon to bring our humble offering to the national altar, and to confess the benefits and express devout gratitude

for the blessings resulting from your independence to us?" The questions were rhetorical. "I am not included within the pale of this glorious
anniversary," he lamented. "This Fourth July is *yours*, not *mine*. *You* may
rejoice, *I must mourn*."[76]

What started as a warm and sympathetic review of the nation's past
transformed into a devastating critique of its present. By addressing the
issue of "AMERICAN SLAVERY" from the point of view of the enslaved,
Douglass thundered, "I do not hesitate to declare, with all my soul, that
the character and conduct of this nation never looked blacker to me
than on this 4th July!" Whether considering historic declarations or
present professions, "the conduct of the nation seems equally hideous
and revolting." As America was false to the past, present, and future, "I
will, in the name of humanity which is outraged, in the name of liberty
which is fettered, in the name of the constitution and the Bible, which
are disregarded and trampled upon," condemn and denounce slavery—
"the great sin and shame of America!"[77]

For Douglass, the dreams of the Founding Fathers had become a
nightmare. "What, to the American slave, is your 4th of July?" It was
a day that more than any other revealed the hypocrisy of slavery in a
nation that claimed the mantle of freedom. "To him, your celebration
is a sham; your boasted liberty, an unholy license; your national great-
ness, swelling vanity; your sounds of rejoicing are empty and heartless;
your denunciations of tyrants, brass fronted impudence; your shouts
of liberty and equality, hollow mockery; your prayers and hymns, your
sermons and thanksgivings, with all your religious parade, and solem-
nity, are, to him, mere bombast, fraud, deception, impiety, and hypocrisy."
Together, these contrivances concealed the crimes of a savage nation. A
review of the world's most despotic and tyrannical governments proved
that "for revolting barbarity and shameless hypocrisy, America reigns
without rival."[78]

Douglass continued that the clearest contemporary evidence of
the nation's failure was the existence and expansion of the domestic,
or internal, slave trade. In the nearly half-century since the American

government had outlawed the transatlantic slave trade, the traffic of enslaved people across state lines had become a multi-million-dollar industry. The passage of the Fugitive Slave Act of 1850 encouraged the interstate slave trade by empowering slave catchers to cross state lines in pursuit of their prey. "Slavery has been nationalized in its most horrible and revolting form," Douglass explained of the new federal law. "By that act, Mason & Dixon's line has been obliterated; New York has become as Virginia; and the power to hold, hunt, and sell men, women and children, as slaves, remains no longer a mere state institution, but is now an institution of the whole United States." Because of this legislation, slave owners' power extended beyond the South to wherever the "star-spangled banner" waved and American Christians prayed.[79]

The religious reference gave way to an extended reflection on the Christian church's complicity in the national sin of slavery. "It has made itself the bulwark of American slavery," Douglass explained. Its leaders "have taught that man may, properly, be a slave; that the relation of master and slave is ordained of God; that to send back an escaped bondman to his master is clearly the duty of all the followers of the Lord Jesus Christ; and this horrible blasphemy is palmed off upon the world for Christianity." Douglass preferred atheism to America's proslavery church, which championed the oppressors over the oppressed. The situation was different in England. "There, the church, true to its mission of ameliorating, elevating, and improving the condition of mankind," led the movement to end slavery throughout England's empire. In the United States, republican politics and republican religion were equally inconsistent. Given the language in the Declaration of Independence, "The existence of slavery in this country brands your republicanism as a sham, your humanity as a base pretence, and your Christianity as a lie."[80]

With the United States and its church chastised, Douglass turned to his most forceful defense of the Constitution to date. He rejected the idea that slavery was "guaranteed and sanctioned by the Constitution of the United States; that, the right to hold, and to hunt slaves is a part of that Constitution framed by the illustrious Fathers of this Republic." Instead, he considered the charge a slander upon the framers' memory. He credited Gerrit Smith and several other leading abolitionist theorists for vindicating the Constitution from accusations that it supported slavery, and for convincing him to change his own mind about the document's character and intent. "Interpreted, as it *ought* to be interpreted," Douglass proclaimed, the Constitution was "entirely hostile to the existence of slavery."[81]

In bringing the speech to a close, Douglass assured his audience that there was hope for the future, as divine justice would soon rid the United States of its original sin of slavery. Referred to as "millennial nationalism" by David Blight, this religiously inspired idea rendered the American republic "a chosen nation" that would soon realize its great promise.[82] "Notwithstanding the dark picture I have this day presented, of the state of the nation, I do not despair of this country," Douglass explained with an optimism that contrasted with his previous ominousness. "There are forces in operation, which must inevitably, work the downfall of slavery." Besides the Lord's righteousness, "the 'Declaration of Independence,' the great principles it contains, and the genius of American Institutions," ensured slavery's complete and permanent extinction.[83]

It was a masterful speech. For two hours, Douglass had claimed the Fourth of July and the Declaration of Independence for slavery's opponents—and the response was extraordinary. *Frederick Douglass' Paper* reported that after the orator returned to his seat, "there was a universal burst of applause" throughout the auditorium. When William Bloss, one of upstate New York's most respected abolitionist leaders, moved for a vote of gratitude to Douglass, "It was unanimously carried." A request was then made to publish the oration as a pamphlet, "and seven hundred copies of it were subscribed for on the spot."[84]

News of the oration spread quickly. Douglass published the full text of the address in his own newspaper and sold the thirty-nine-page pamphlet version of the speech at his Buffalo Street office in Rochester for ten cents apiece or six dollars per one hundred copies. To assist in the

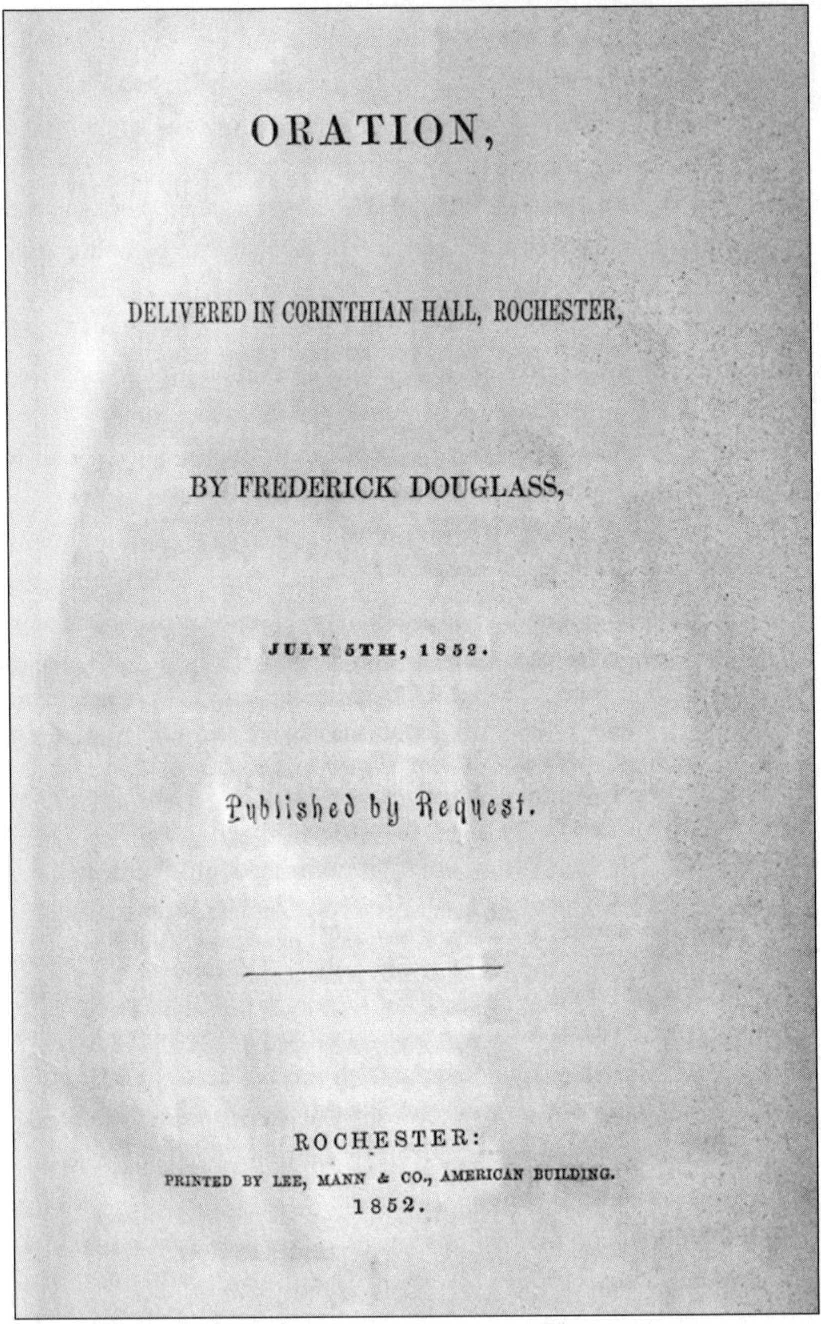

ORATION,

DELIVERED IN CORINTHIAN HALL, ROCHESTER,

BY FREDERICK DOUGLASS,

JULY 5TH, 1852.

Published by Request.

ROCHESTER:

PRINTED BY LEE, MANN & CO., AMERICAN BUILDING.

1852.

FIGURE 3.2. Title page of *ORATION, Delivered in Corinthian Hall, Rochester, by Frederick Douglass, July 5th, 1852* (Rochester: Lee, Mann & Co., 1852). Courtesy of the American Antiquarian Society.

publication and distribution of the pamphlet, more than a dozen individuals contributed the sum of between one and ten dollars each. Gerrit Smith donated twenty-five dollars.[85] Given Douglass's efforts as speaker, promoter, and salesman, it is not surprising that the speech enjoyed a widespread distribution. Following a brief tour of central New York in late July, Douglass proudly reported the sale of "a hundred copies of our 4th July speech."[86]

In subsequent years, the dissemination of Douglass's oration continued apace. In 1855, he included an abridged version of what he entitled, "What to the Slave is the Fourth of July?" in his second published autobiography.[87] At the turn of the twentieth century, African Americans and their allies reprinted the oration in various media and recited its legendary lines during Independence Day observations held at churches, schools, and other public places.[88] Since then, historians and biographers have paid Douglass's oration as much respect as (or in some cases even more than) his contemporaries. A generation ago, William McFeely considered the oration "perhaps the greatest antislavery oration ever given," while more recently David Blight called it "nothing less than the rhetorical masterpiece of American abolitionism."[89]

In his book-length study of the speech, *Frederick Douglass and the Fourth of July*, historian James Colaiaco found the speech's significance lay in the delivery of two separate messages. First, "Instead of renouncing American values and institutions," Douglass condemned America for the hypocrisy of slavery "while at the same time stressing the possibility of redemption." Second, through "a rhetorical 'strategy of appropriation,'" Douglass situated himself "within the beliefs and symbols of the Fourth of July, the most important ritual of the nation's civil religion, to underscore the crime against black Americans." That was not all.[90]

By acclaiming America's birth and offering a plan for the republic's redemption, Douglass demonstrated his faith in, and affinity for, his nation. While other abolitionists mocked the United States' claim to exceptionalism and some sought its ruin through the process of disunion, he offered a path forward. Simply by removing slavery, his oration argued, the American people could achieve the ideals of the Declaration of the Independence and the nation itself.

Though Christianity provided Douglass with a moral certitude that compelled him to seek allies—and fight for oppressed people—across the globe, he understood the problem of slavery in a nationalist framework. Rather than refute the idea that the United States was exceptional, he considered the freedom of all people a touchstone of its national identity. By claiming the Fourth of July for enslaved people, he revealed his faith in America's destiny as a place of freedom and equality. In so doing, he further distinguished himself by becoming one of the United States' greatest critics and crusaders at the same time.

PART II
FIGHTING

4

REBELS

In 1832, more than one hundred Black and White revelers sat down for a Fourth of July dinner on Jacques Bishop's Sumterville, South Carolina, plantation. The guests expected to enjoy an elaborate feast followed by a long evening of relaxing and unwinding. Instead, within minutes of the first course being served, many of them became ill and collapsed to the ground. In the next twenty-four hours, dozens of diners experienced severe stomach pains followed by headaches and vomiting. Several who consumed the celebratory meal, including at least one slave owner, died.[1]

The cause of the sickness was clear. "*Poison was infused into the victuals at our Celebration on the Fourth*," a local writer declared. To bring the perpetrators of the heinous crime to justice, authorities arrested the enslaved cooks who had prepared the meal. Suspicion quickly fell on a man owned by Bishop. In an ad hoc trial that followed, a female food preparer testified to her own innocence, confessing that she, "at the instance of the fellow, made use of a substance, of whose qualities she was ignorant."[2] The jury sentenced the unnamed mastermind to death and officials carried out the execution several days later. What, if any, punishment his female co-conspirator received for participating in the "diabolical tragedy" is unknown.[3]

As was often the case whenever enslaved people killed their captors, southern writers were at a loss for the cause of the mass poisoning; however, at least one northern editorialist ventured to state the obvious. "As horrible as this conduct of the slaves is," the anonymous New Yorker opined, "we cannot but reflect that it was committed by those who were wearing the chains of bondage in a land boasting of its freedom." With enslaved people serving the whims of their owners, deadly events like this were to be expected on the anniversary of the "day on which it was declared that all men were born free and equal."[4]

The cooks who poisoned the Fourth of July dinner left no record of their motivations. As a result, numerous questions remain unanswered. Did they choose the occasion of the nation's most hallowed holiday because of its political significance, or was it simply a matter of convenience? Were they targeting any White slave owners or overseers specifically? Were the Black victims of the poisoning considered collateral damage? Regardless of the answers to these questions, one thing is certain: by attempting to take the lives of their oppressors on Independence Day, these enslaved assassins evoked the nation's revolutionary political tradition—and they were not alone.

Throughout the antebellum era, the language and symbols of American freedom emboldened enslaved people to forcefully resist their subjugation. Though evidence abounds, the historiography of slave resistance is largely silent on the matter for multiple reasons. In an attempt to find foreign influences, for example, recent historians have ignored the extent to which American ideas of liberty and equality reverberated across the antebellum South and fired the hearts and minds of Black captives.[5] Indeed, enslaved people's devotion to the republic's revolutionary founding ideals—which they were willing to fight, kill, and if need be die for—illuminates American nationalism's hold over their imagination for generations.[6]

It also illustrates enslaved peoples' claims to membership in the nation's body politic. Because the United States was born in blood and rebellion, American citizens early approved of the tactics that made the republic's birth possible. The result was a revolutionary political culture and ideology that associated membership in the nation with violence. The idea that individuals who were unwilling to sacrifice their lives for freedom did not deserve citizenship implied that enslaved people were responsible for their own oppression. In historian François Furstenberg's words, "the persistence of millions in chattel slavery suggested that, lacking the virtue to free themselves—having made the choice to submit to fortune rather than to resist or die—slaves *deserved* their obnoxious condition."[7] In other words, they themselves were to blame.

If Americans had an "obligation" to resist their oppressors, then enslaved people repeatedly proved their Americanness by using force and even violence to win their freedom. While revolts, conspiracies, and escapes offer the most obvious evidence of this "virtuous revolutionary resistance," instances of slave suicide, when considered alongside these more recognizable forms of opposition, provide additional proof.[8] Regardless of the type of resistance employed, enslaved people found inspiration in the language and symbols of American freedom. Though denied a place in the United States as persons and citizens, they fought, killed, and even died for the ideas and principles upon which the nation had been built.

In July 1816, as the United States embarked on an "Era of Good Feelings" following its victory over Great Britain in the War of 1812, rebel slaves in Camden, South Carolina, endeavored to make the Fourth of July the most unforgettable Independence Day ever. The group planned to commemorate the national holiday by setting fire to the town, seizing the arsenal, and murdering every White man in the vicinity. As for the White women they encountered along the way, "they intended to have reserved for their own purposes." Or so one local "gentleman" claimed.[9]

Like most American slave revolts, the goal of the uprising was freedom for the rebels and their families. In the days leading up to the national holiday, the conspirators swore themselves to secrecy—and they agreed that the penalty for betraying the plot was death. Despite the threat, "a favorite and confidential slave" disclosed the design to his owner, who quickly informed the authorities. In return for his betrayal, the enslaved informant received his freedom and an annual $50 payment from the state government for the remainder of his life.[10]

Officials moved quickly to bring the accused to justice. Sixteen suspected rebels were arrested, jailed, and tortured. On July 2, the four-member Town Council examined eight of the prisoners, each of whom testified to their knowledge of events. All denied having anything to do with the plot, though several implicated others. The following day, a "drumhead Court" found seven of the defendants guilty of plotting an insurrection. March, Cameron, Isaac, and Spottswood went to the gallows on July 5. Ned met his demise a week later. The two remaining convicts escaped execution. The court sentenced Big Frank to a year imprisonment followed by banishment from the state, while Stephen received a governor's pardon.[11]

With the threat averted, Camden's citizens were left to wonder why the town's enslaved population tried to transform the Fourth of July into a bloodbath. Francis Deliesseline, a Charleston sheriff who was in Camden at the time of the incident, offered a possible explanation. From his perspective, the suspected rebels "had no causes of complaint against their individual masters." As religious and "faithful servants," they were undoubtedly inspired by the "wild and frantic ideas of the rights of man." As for the date of the scheduled uprising, the Fourth of July was selected because "the usual indulgences among us on a day celebrated as a great national jubilee" increased the likelihood of the revolt's success.[12]

While Sheriff Deliesseline displayed a fear of a repetition of the French Revolution's Reign of Terror when he cited Thomas Paine's *Rights of Man*, a writer calling himself "CITIZEN" dreaded a repeat of the Haitian Revolution, the slave revolt that decimated French Saint-Domingue two decades earlier. Five months after the discovery of the Camden plot and as the Christmas holiday approached, CITIZEN expressed his disappointment that local leaders had taken few steps to protect people who daily slept "under the very crater of the volcano, which so recently threatened to burst forth, with such a dreadful explosion." Given the "general license" allowed enslaved people during the holidays, he worried that the streets of Camden would soon "exhibit another

St. Domingo massacre." To prevent such a cataclysm from taking place, CITIZEN proposed the enforcement of existing Slave Codes and an increased police presence "to repress even the hope of insurrection."[13]

The references to the French and Haitian revolutions are remarkable given the Camden rebels planned to rise on an American holiday. While clearly demonstrating the fear of revolutionary violence among slave owners and their supporters, they also testify to the inability of slave owners and their supporters to see the people they held in captivity as compatriots. Notwithstanding the uniqueness of the Camden conspiracy, the reaction of White South Carolinians to the scheme was no anomaly.

Across the antebellum South, slave owners and their supporters refused to recognize slave rebels as American revolutionaries who had imbibed the radical ideals of the republic's founders; instead, they regarded them as racial others who existed beyond the boundaries of the nation despite their obvious and important presence inside of it. Caught in the powerful grip of White supremacy, nothing could convince the South's White population of the Americanness of Black people—not even the largest slave revolt in American history, which, like the conspiracy in Camden fifteen years earlier, was scheduled for the Fourth of July.

The story of Nat Turner's Rebellion is well known. Over the course of two days in August 1831, some seventy bondmen under the command of the charismatic slave preacher stormed across Southampton County, Virginia. Armed with guns, swords, axes, hatchets, and clubs, they murdered as many as sixty White men, women, and children. In response, citizens and militiamen massacred scores of enslaved people—there is no record of the exact number—including many who played no part in the insurrection. After being arrested, Turner spoke with a journalist who quickly published the jailhouse conversation as *The Confessions of Nat Turner*. In this widely disseminated pamphlet, the rebel revealed that he and his followers had planned to launch the revolt several weeks earlier than they did, but an illness delayed the start. "It was intended by us," Turner recalled, "to have begun the work of death on the 4th of July."[14]

The Discovery of Nat Turner.

FIGURE 4.1. Only a brief illness kept Nat Turner from launching his historic uprising on the Fourth of July in 1831. "The Discovery of Nat Turner." Courtesy of the New York Public Library Digital Collections.

Following Turner's revolt, White southerners spent much breath and spilled much ink on the event. Yet they almost universally ignored the originally scheduled date of the insurrection.[15] The reason was obvious: to reinforce the proslavery argument that enslaved people were ignorant of political rituals, symbols, and ideas and thus undeserving of freedom and incapable of citizenship. It was an insidious racial construct that still resonates two centuries later—that African Americans are not American at all.

While slave owners and their supporters denied the significance of the Fourth of July among Black southerners, they readily conceded its importance to White southerners who challenged the section's social and racial order. The bizarre tale of the Clan of the Mystic Confederacy is a case in point.[16] The leader of this criminal gang, John A. Murrell, was a backwoods bandit who stalked the southern frontier for more than a decade. In the summer of 1834, a Jackson, Tennessee, court sentenced the outlaw to ten years of hard labor in the state penitentiary for slave stealing—an increasingly common crime in the era of slave expansion.[17] Given the complicated relationship between slaves and slave stealers, it is not surprising that shortly after Murrell began serving his sentence, rumors spread of a massive slave uprising that the convict had already set in motion.[18]

The source of the rumor was a fictionalized account of Murrell's criminal history written by Virgil Stewart. In this sensationalistic and largely "imagined account," the author depicted the small-time criminal as a cold-blooded killer who recruited slaves across the South to revolt and thus have revenge on their oppressors.[19] The fantasy culminated with Murrell and his interracial army slaughtering slave owners and having their "pockets replenished from the banks, and the desks of rich merchants' houses."[20] The slave revolt was the product of Stewart's overactive literary imagination; nevertheless, many readers took him at his word.

Though Stewart recorded Christmas Eve as the night of the intended uprising, reports circulated across the South that the actual target date was the Fourth of July.[21] Southern citizens trembled at the news because the holiday enabled slaves "to assemble together from the different plantations, and enjoy themselves in uninterrupted feasting and festivity."[22] To thwart the holiday insurrection, authorities and vigilantes alike unleashed a wave of terror against anyone—Black or White—thought to have played a part in the conspiracy.

The reasons for the hysteria are easy to explain. As historian Joshua Rothman points out, the lower Mississippi Valley, the part of the southern frontier most affected by the conspiracy, was experiencing dramatic change. With a rapidly modernizing economic system driven by rampant speculation in cotton, land, and slaves, White anxieties over finances and fortunes often intersected with the fears of an exploding and aggrieved Black population. Life at the "leading edge" of early American capitalism was not only dangerous but at times deadly. A conspiracy among poor European Americans and enslaved American Americans was easily imaginable.[23]

What is more, the 1830s saw northern abolitionists trying to convince their southern countrymen and women of the evils of slavery by publishing millions of pieces of antislavery literature and distributing them nationwide. As the materials made their way through the slave states and territories, White southerners' fears of the people they enslaved intensified. That Murrell, a man with supposed abolitionist sympathies, tried to organize a slave insurrection seemed to these paranoid people not only possible but probable.[24]

What also made White southerners susceptible to the Murrell conspiracy was the very real tradition of Independence Day plots and insurrections—especially the revolt led by Nat Turner. "We had nearly the Southampton scene acted over in this our state," an anonymous Mississippian editorialized. "The negroes (who, by the by, are considerably the largest part of our population,) were, on the night of the 4th July, to have risen in a body, and headed and commanded by white men, to have massacred the whole white population, without regard to ages, sizes, sexes, or conditions." Fortunately, the nightmare had been avoided, and on the Fourth of July in Canton, Mississippi, "thirteen negroes and two white men were hung" for their purported role in the conspiracy.[25]

Even more than slave revolts, what White southerners most feared about Independence Day was enslaved people taking flight. Advertisements offering cash rewards for fugitive slaves who absconded on the nation's anniversary dotted the pages of southern newspapers. In

Orange County, Virginia, George Pannill offered $50 for the apprehension of Rans, a thirty-year-old farmhand who "Ran away from my farm the 4th July" and was most likely headed to the North.[26] Daniel Long of Perry County, Alabama, promised between $25 and $50 for the return of Squire—who also fled on Independence Day—depending on where the arrest took place.[27] John McMurrian offered an astounding $200 for the return of Mose, a "Negro fellow" who escaped from western Georgia "on the 4th of July, inst." The extraordinarily large reward may have resulted from the fact that this was not the first time the twenty-two-year-old had absconded. According to an advertisement placed in the *Southern Argus*, Mose had "a scar or wound near the right shoulder on the back, which was occasioned by a rifle shot."[28]

An enslaved woman's Independence Day escape evinces the blinding influence of racism on White southerners. On Maryland's Eastern Shore, Doll endeavored to reunite with her husband, Daniel Siddens, who resided in an adjacent county, when she fled. Her owner, William Smyth, thought the fugitive would be easy to identify given her appearance. An advertisement noted, she "has a good deal of wool on her head, and generally wears a handkerchief on it—carries her head on one side, has lost all her teeth on one side, and is far gone in pregnancy." The expectant mother's effort to reunite with her spouse seems to have had no impact on Smyth, who promised as much as $50 for her return. Neither did the date of her escape, "the 4th of July last," which went without any additional comment.[29]

Some Fourth of July escapes are particularly notable, for they illuminate just how much was as stake every time White southerners observed the anniversary of national independence. For the notorious Alexandria, Virginia, slave trader Joseph Bruin, there were no holidays from his chosen profession. While conveying an enslaved nineteen-year-old named Henry "on the 4th of July" to a new owner, the prisoner leapt from a moving stagecoach "with his hands fastened with handcuffs." Bruin was sure Henry would "*aim for a free State*," and to ensure the security of his slave-trading services offered $250 "for his return to me, dead or alive, no matter where taken."[30]

While advertisements for fugitive slaves usually ignored the significance of escapes occurring on what was described generically as the "4th July" or the "4th of July," this was not always the case. In one instance, an aggrieved slave owner's use of capital letters illuminated his anger and frustration at having lost possession of a Montgomery, Alabama, bondman named Abram on the holiday. Offering $25 for the return of the dark-skinned twenty-eight-year-old, Zacharius Talliaferro informed readers that the highly skilled carpenter fled "ON THE FOURTH OF JULY." Whether the owner was more upset that Abram escaped, or that he did so on Independence Day, went unrecorded.[31]

In the advertisements described here, no slave owner or official offered an explanation for why these fugitives absconded on the Fourth of July. The implication was that the occurrence of these incidents on the national holiday was coincidental. The refusal to acknowledge the obvious connection is further evidence of the effort of White southerners to strip the escapes of any political meaning and thus deny Black people's place in the nation. Nevertheless, evidence abounds that the Fourth of July, and especially the public remembrance of the Declaration of Independence, inspired enslaved people to abscond.

William Wells Brown's story is an example. While working on a steamship in St. Louis, Missouri, the enslaved teenager heard an impassioned Fourth of July oration by US Senator Thomas Hart Benton, which included a recitation of the Declaration of Independence's preamble. "The boy's young heart leaped with enthusiasm as he listened to the burning eloquence of 'Old Bullion,'" Brown's daughter recalled of her father's reaction that day. "From the moment that William heard the speech of Mr. Benton, he resolved that he would be free." After hearing Benton's address, Brown tried to escape from captivity on more than one occasion. He finally succeeded in 1834 and went on to become one of the nation's most influential abolitionists.[32]

The Declaration of Independence's assertion of equality also inspired William and Ellen Craft to try to free themselves from slavery. In the published account of their unusual escape—which involved the husband, William, posing as the servant of his exceptionally light-skinned wife, Ellen—the couple recalled learning the document's preamble during their enslavement in Macon, Georgia. Having become fully aware of the idea that all men were created equal and endowed with certain un-alienable rights, "we could not understand by what right we were held as 'chattels,'" the two explained in their autobiography. "Therefore, we felt perfectly justified in undertaking the dangerous and exciting task of 'running a thousand miles' in order to obtain those rights which are so vividly set forth in the Declaration."[33]

After successfully escaping from slavery, the couple resided in Boston. Always under the threat of recapture, William "armed himself" and alongside Ellen worked closely with the Boston Vigilance Committee to ensure they stayed free. After avoiding slave catchers for almost two years, the couple emigrated to England, where they remained for nearly two decades. Samuel May, one of the Craft's closest friends and allies, expressed the shame and sorrow that many abolitionists felt about their country, for "a brave young man and a virtuous young woman must fly the American shores, and seek, under the shadow of the British throne, the enjoyment of 'life, liberty, and the pursuit of happiness.'"[34]

Like the Fourth of July and the preamble of the Declaration of Independence, Patrick Henry's "Liberty or Death" speech inspired en-slaved people to forcefully resist captivity. Its history is worth retelling. In March of 1775, in St. John's Church in Richmond, Virginia, Henry deliv-ered an impassioned speech at the Second Virginia Convention, which had gathered to discuss growing colonial opposition to Great Britain. Considering the problems Americans faced as "Nothing less than a ques-tion of freedom or slavery," he urged the delegation to prepare for war. Henry knew that many colonists would not risk their lives for political freedom. "But as for me," he declared, "give me liberty or give me death!"

While the speech's effect on the colonial independence movement is legendary, its impact on enslaved people is almost entirely forgotten.[35]

An insurrection near New Orleans, Louisiana, proves the survival of Henry's famous mantra among rebel slaves more than a half-century after the American Revolution. In February 1846, a White overseer working on the plantation of two local businessmen, James Hewitt and David Heran, ordered the beating of a bondman named Lewis, who, in their estimation, had become unmanageable. Raising an axe in defiance, "The negro replied to this that no white man should ever whip him and live." When the overseer ordered a trusted Black driver to carry out the punishment, the driver refused. Fearing for his life, the overseer sent for help from his neighbors, Sydney Story and another man known only as Batts.[36]

What followed was surely something Patrick Henry had never imagined. As Batts drew a pistol, Lewis charged the slave owner with his axe, daring him to "shoot, shoot, shoot!" The two men engaged in mortal combat until a gunshot sent buckshot deep into Lewis's chest. Despite the grave injury, the rebel continued to fight so furiously that "it required the best efforts of Mr. Story and the overseer to preserve the life of Mr. Batts."[37] Lewis succumbed to his injuries several moments later, but the rebellion continued as the Black driver shouted to dozens of slaves who were watching nearby with shovels and axes at the ready: "Now let us kill them all—Liberty or Death!"[38]

A bloody melee ensued. The three White men received numerous blows from the impromptu weapons being wielded by their Black adversaries but with a sugar cane sword and pistol managed to survive the fray. As the confrontation continued, several White hunters armed with "fowling pieces" arrived on the scene and "checked" the revolt, leaving several of the bondmen badly wounded. To ensure the safety of local civilians, slave owners sent their wives and children by carriage to New Orleans.[39]

The following day, Joseph Cucullu, the sheriff of St. Bernard Parish, summoned a "Jury of Planters" to investigate the incident. The cause of Lewis's death was of particular concern, given his status as property. After reviewing the evidence, the jurors justified the killing, concluding that the bondman died because of his "own improper action."[40] To prevent a similar outbreak for occurring, they ordered the severe flogging of every enslaved man on Hewitt's and Heran's plantation, "which sentence was carried into immediate effect."[41]

As some might dismiss a rebel slaves' invocation of Patrick Henry's revolutionary war cry as apocryphal, it is worth noting that the source of the incident was a local one. Like other patently proslavery southern newspapers, the *New Orleans Delta* had nothing to gain from inventing a story that likened a reviled rebel slave to a revered Founding Father. Indeed, the opposite was the case, which explains why other local media tried to suppress the entire episode. Besides eliminating all references to the rebels' use of Henry's war cry in subsequent published reports, some New Orleans newspapers tried to convince readers that "there was no revolt" at all.[42]

Further evidence of Patrick Henry's words inspiring enslaved people comes from those who after escaping from captivity recorded their experiences for posterity. Prior to earning a reputation as one of the most accomplished Underground Railroad conductors in New York State, Jermain Wesley Loguen spent the first two decades of his life enslaved on the plantation of his White father in Tennessee. A quarter century after escaping across the Ohio River and joining the abolitionist cause, the African Methodist Episcopalian preacher wrote Frederick Douglass, describing the moment he resolved to put his life on the line for freedom. "'Liberty or death!' never came from a more earnest breast than when I uttered it there before my God!" he recalled of his decision to abscond at age twenty-one, "I will be a man—I will wear no chain!"[43]

Israel Campbell never had any intention of fleeing to the North and leaving his family behind in Tennessee. But that changed after learning he was being sold away from his wife and three children with a band of horses. The night before his escape, Campbell armed himself with a double-barrel pistol and "a good old Jackson club," which he kept hidden in a barn. Like Patrick Henry, he recalled in his published autobiography, "I had made up my mind that I was going to try for either liberty or death this time, and intended killing any one who should undertake to stop me." With an indomitable determination to be free, Campbell eventually made his way across the Ohio River and to Canada. His heroic journey from slavery to freedom is rightly regarded as a success; however, despite more than a decade of effort, he never succeeded in reuniting with his family.[44]

The fear of being sold at auction compelled John Henry Hill to abscond. Considered "a dangerous property to keep" because of his love of "Liberty," the skilled carpenter realized he was being separated from his family when his owner brought him to Richmond, Virginia, on "the great annual sale day" of January 1st. Before being placed in handcuffs, Hill resisted his captors "with his fist, knife, and feet," and later made his way to the home of a family friend. For nine months, the twenty-five-year-old husband and father hid in and around Richmond until gaining passage aboard a steamship for Philadelphia with the assistance of an unnamed Underground Railroad agent. On the day of his embarkation, Hill was confident that he would never again wear the chains of slavery, "for I had started from my Den that morning for Liberty or for Death providing myself with a Brace of Pistols."[45]

Rather than a fear of sale, it was being subjected to a sadistic form of torture, which was commonplace across the antebellum South, that convinced Charles Brown to free himself from slavery or die in the process. Known as smoking, the punishment involved being locked inside a smokehouse and brought to the brink of death by a combination of heat, suffocation, and exhaustion. In Brown's case, a concealed pocketknife enabled him to remove the ropes binding his hands and feet. After looking through a crack in the structure's wall and seeing his owner, Garrett Van Metre, preparing "to go off and sell him," Brown decided, "now or never, something must be done for myself—liberty or death." Grabbing an old axe lying on the smokehouse floor, he smashed

the door jamb, dissembled the hinges, and "took to his heels." After reuniting with his half-brother and another acquaintance, Brown eventually crossed the Mason-Dixon Line and settled in the town of Indiana,
Pennsylvania.[46]

The reliability of these accounts of fugitive slaves invoking Patrick
Henry's motto just prior to their escapes is questionable for several reasons. In addition to following a similar formula, each was recorded from
memory long after allegedly taking place. That these recollections appeared in widely disseminated antislavery publications further calls their
veracity into question. Ultimately, the truth of these incidents may never
be proven. What matters is that these enslaved men saw their own self-
liberation as revolutionary acts of resistance that mirrored those of one
of the nation's founders. For them, their attainment of freedom affirmed
a deep personal commitment to a radical political tradition that defined
the American people.

Of course, enslaved women also added to this tradition. Elizabeth
Blakesley is the type of heroine that history has too often ignored. A
young mother who belonged to George Washington Davis, one of
Wilmington, North Carolina's most eminent political and economic
leaders, she repeatedly tried to escape to the North. On one occasion,
the punishment she received for her obstinacy was particularly brutal.
Her "master" lashed her shirtless body until the blood covered her feet—
"he then washed her back in brine, and nailed her by the right ear to
a fence rail, and in her agony, she tore off the outer rim of her ear."
Undeterred, Blakesley continued to plot her escape—even though this
meant separating from her young child.[47]

An opportunity soon arose. After learning that a brig docked in
Wilmington was headed for Boston, Blakesley boarded the vessel the
night before its departure and concealed herself in a narrow passage
beside the ship's cabin. The following day just prior to setting sail, Davis
alerted the captain and together the two men searched the vessel for the
female fugitive. The captain shouted as he advanced, "You had better
come out! I am going to smoke the vessel!" When Blakesley refused to

reveal her hiding spot, the captain burned a combination of sulfur and tobacco, which immediately enveloped the deck of the ship in a cloud of smoke. Where most would have succumbed to the toxic fumes, this woman did not. "I heard him call," she recounted of the incident, "but my mind was liberty or death." Convinced that the stowaway was either dead or disappeared, Davis and the captain abandoned the search. Four weeks later, Blakesley disembarked from the vessel in Boston, where she became a cause célèbre of local abolitionists.[48]

Blakesley's heroism is a reminder that revolutionary slave resistance transcended gender. In their exhaustive study of fugitive slaves in the antebellum South, John Hope Franklin and Loren Schweninger found that the "great majority" of escaped slaves were young males who were either unmarried or had not yet started a family. Fewer females absconded because of their role as mothers and caregivers; nevertheless, "slave women desired freedom as much as slave men and were often as assertive and aggressive on the plantation as male slaves." They were also—as Blakesley's actions attest—just as capable of drawing inspiration from the nation's revolutionary past.[49]

The story of one of the most famous fugitive slaves in history provides additional proof. There is no doubting Harriet Tubman's hold on the public's imagination. Still, the popular image of an elderly and diminutive Black woman in modest Victorian dress belies the revolutionary spirit that moved this authentic American freedom fighter to action. After escaping to the North from a tobacco plantation on Maryland's Eastern Shore in 1849, Tubman returned to the South more than a dozen times and helped scores of enslaved people follow her footsteps to freedom. Fully cognizant of the dangers she faced every time she returned to the South, the inimitable Underground Railroad agent carried a revolver and threatened to use it against anyone—including those she assisted—who threatened the mission's success.[50]

As one of the nation's most notorious outlaws, Tubman kept the details of her life's work private. But in a rare interview with a trusted biographer, she explained her motivation for continually risking her

FIGURE 4.2. Perhaps no individual better embodied the revolutionary nationalism of the abolitionist movement in the middle of the nineteenth century than Harriet Tubman. Photograph by Benjamin Powelson (circa 1868–1869). Courtesy of the Library of Congress.

life and freedom to bring others out of the hell of slavery: "I started with this idea in my head, 'Dere's *two* things I've got a *right* to, and dese are, Death or Liberty—one or tother I mean to have.'" Once free, Tubman vowed to never return to slavery, declaring, "I shall fight for my liberty, and when de time has come for me to go, de Lord will let dem kill me."[51]

When "the Moses of her people" inverted Patrick Henry's refrain, she drew on a long antislavery tradition.[52] Besides comprising the last line of the United States' unofficial national anthem, "Hail, Columbia," the phrase evoked the image of one of the most iconic slave rebels in early popular American culture. In the stage play *Oroonoko: A Tragedy*, which the Irish playwright Thomas Southerne adapted from a fictional tale by the English novelist Aphra Behn, the titular character plots a slave revolt in the Caribbean colony of Suriname. While trying to convince his fellow captives to join the uprising, Oroonoko affirms:

> The Danger will be certain to us all:
> And Death most certain is miscarrying.
> We must expect no Mercy, if we fail:
> Therefore our way must be not to expect:
> We'll put it out of Expectation,
> By Death upon the Place, or Liberty.
> There is no mean, but Death or Liberty.[53]

While Tubman might have been unfamiliar with the fictional Oroonoko, she was almost definitely aware of the very real Gabriel. In 1800, the enslaved Richmond, Virginia, blacksmith recruited hundreds of local bondmen to destroy the city and kill anyone who opposed them. According to one of the rebel leaders, the insurgents were to march to the state capital underneath a silk flag "on which they would have written, 'death or Liberty.'"[54] The betrayal of two enslaved informants thwarted the plot and resulted in the execution of Gabriel and more than two dozen co-conspirators; nevertheless, the intent of the insurrection was clear. "The fact that Gabriel turned the words of Patrick Henry upside down," historian Douglas Egerton concludes in his study of the Revolutionary War era, "suggests that his hope was to do the same with" the slave society that held him in bondage.[55]

For enslaved people who understood the unlikelihood of turning the world upside down, taking one's own life offered a sure escape from captivity. It also established the tenacity of the nation's revolutionary tradition. A case in upstate New York demonstrates the point. The incident occurred after an escaped steamship cook named Davis gained passage aboard a packet boat to Canada. While en route, a White "scoundrel" hoping to collect a posted $50 reward seized the Black fugitive and forcefully disembarked him at Buffalo. As two slave catchers prepared to return Davis to Kentucky, he made a fateful decision. Crying out "Give me liberty or death! or death!!" he removed a razor from his pocket and "drew it across his throat." Convinced the fugitive was dead or dying, the slave catchers abandoned their mission and returned to the South. They were, however, mistaken. Davis managed to survive the grievous wound and after a long recovery made his way to Canada.[56]

Historians have long disagreed on the motivation for slave suicide. In an important work on the subject, Diane Miller Sommerville rejects an influential body of scholarship, which contends that for enslaved people self-destruction was "a noble act of rebellion and resistance, a defiant challenge to a master's authority." She argues instead that most slave suicides were non-ideological. Rather than an intentional act of defiance, "Self-murder was an escape from personal misery, emotional fatigue, and torment. That, not a swipe at the institution, was the immediate goal."[57] While this interpretation makes sense, the accounts of enslaved suicide victims invoking Patrick Henry proves the political calculations that often underlie the decision to take one's own life.[58]

Abolitionists were the first to discern the important implications of slave suicide, though to be clear, as historian Richard Bell points out, their interpretation of this phenomenon changed over time. While initially viewing enslaved self-annihilators as noble warriors in a life-and-death struggle against their oppressors, abolitionists later depicted these same men and women as weak, helpless, and pathetic sufferers who were in desperate need of saving. By mid-century, as sectionalism's threat to the nation became existential, abolitionists saw slave suicide as a form of resistance that "could echo the patriotic struggles of the Founding Fathers."[59]

The latter interpretation is evident in a plethora of articles published in northern newspapers entitled "Liberty or Death" or a close variation. In them, abolitionists compared enslaved self-destroyers to the Revolutionary-era citizen-soldiers who also sacrificed their lives for freedom. While the examples are numerous, some stand out for their sympathetic and even supportive tone. The *Liberator* reported that when passengers sailing on a brig from Mobile, Alabama, to Providence, Rhode Island, discovered a "*fugitive slave*" on board, Captain Samuel Remington ordered to the crew to "bout ship" and return home. As the vessel reversed course, the commander demanded the prisoner explain his presence, but the stowaway remained silent. Enraged, Remington seized a rope for the purpose "of compelling answers to his inquiry." Refusing to be either whipped or re-enslaved, the "trembling captive" grabbed a firm hold of the ship's rigging and leapt overboard. Slowly lowering himself from the vessel, "he dropped into the ocean, and the passengers, rushing to the side, saw the blue wave close over him forever."[60]

The Black abolitionist Martin Delany described a similar incident in his short-lived weekly, the *Pittsburgh Mystery*. A White couple in southern Georgia promised in their last will and testament to free an enslaved mechanic named George in return for his years of faithful service. After their passing, however, "the unjust heirs broke the will, seized his person, and thrust him into the dark caverns of slavery again!" When George found himself on a steamboat headed for "a new residence," he became despondent. One night, as the ship glided down the Ocmulgee River, a loud noise awoke the crew and passengers who quickly discovered the mechanic was missing along with the boat's grindstone. A search of the river the following morning revealed George's body "with the *grindstone tied to his neck!*" Though abolitionists ordinarily condemned suicide, Delany admitted he admired George for "preferring as a *man, Death* before slavery!"[61]

Emblazoning Patrick Henry's "Liberty or Death" atop these harrowing accounts inscribed suicide with powerful political meaning. Indeed, by imparting the language of American freedom to enslaved self-destroyers, abolitionists put these sufferers in the pantheon of the nation's revolutionary founders and thus demanded their recognitions as compatriots. If the Founding Fathers deserved the nation's respect and admiration for risking their lives to throw off the yoke of their oppressor, then so too did the enslaved people who took their own lives for the same reason.

Articles entitled "Liberty or Death" that described slave suicides compelled readers to consider the political context of the deadly act. After an enslaved farmhand drowned himself in a Maryland creek rather than submit to a posse seeking his capture, one writer argued that the incident proved enslaved people possessed the same spirit that drove "Patrick Henry to say 'give me liberty or give me death.'"[62] Reports of a slave intentionally drowning himself in Alabama's Coosa River led the *Washington (D.C.) National Era* to censure the American public for its hypocrisy. Across the country, Americans celebrated Patrick Henry for his famous declaration. "But here is a poor despised, sorrow-stricken man, who acts out the sentiment which the orator merely proclaimed," and these same citizens did not give the tragedy "a second thought."[63] The suicide of a fugitive slave off the Virginia coast and a subsequent court battle over his market value occasioned another critique of the glaring double standard. The *National Anti-Slavery Standard* was incensed. While a White Virginian had once become a national hero for declaring, "Give me Liberty or give me Death!," the reaction to the self-destruction of a Black Virginian, "whose acts attests how well he believed in the truth of these words," was a valuation of his corpse.[64]

A particularly gruesome suicide in Cincinnati, Ohio, which evoked Patrick Henry's famous lines, proved the lengths enslaved people would go to be free. The incident occurred after a Dayton, Ohio, judge ordered Thomas Mitchell, a fugitive from Kentucky, to be returned to his owner. The night before being transported south, while being held in a room on the fourth floor of Cincinnati's Main Street Hotel, Mitchell made a fateful decision. He opened a window "and resolving on liberty or death, threw himself from it (an elevation of more than forty feet,) upon the pavement below." Though surviving the fall, Mitchell suffered a concussion along with several broken bones and dislocated joints. When a doctor arrived on the scene and began to treat the various injuries, this Black Patrick Henry "violently forced every bone again out of place, declaring at the same time, he would rather die than be a slave." He expired the next day.[65]

In an angry article called "Give me Liberty or give me Death," a writer calling himself X. Z. excoriated those who remained silent after learning of Mitchell's suicide. He noted that if an enslaved White man had committed the same act, "he would have been commended as the possessor of a noble soul that scorned to be a slave, and the recollection of his melancholy fate, would have been cherished by his fellow citizens." In this case, the reaction was silence. Lest anyone misunderstand what motivated this "humble being" to take such extreme measures to avoid being returned to slavery, X. Z. fumed, "The same feeling which prompted Patrick Henry to utter, upon the floor of Congress, the thrilling sentiment, which has immortalized his name, 'give me liberty or give me *death*,'—the same feeling which animated the signers of the Declaration of Independence, to pledge life, fortune and sacred honor of liberty, determined poor Thomas to be free or die."[66]

The *New York Daily Tribune* suggested that it was not only the words of Patrick Henry but also Thomas Jefferson that emboldened a fugitive slave in Baton Rouge, Louisiana, to hang himself to death rather than submit to his captors. "Give me Liberty or give me Death," the piece began, has throughout the republic been passed down from generation to generation since first falling from Henry's patriotic lips. "Yet when a rude and almost savage African attempts to put in practice this principle of the great Virginian, and rather than longer submit to the galling chains and blood-clotted cowskin of Slavery deliberately and boldly meets death," slave owners dismissed the deed as the act of an "obstinate nigger." In fact, something much bigger had occurred. Having fled from captivity near the Fourth of July, the fugitive was almost certainly inspired by Jefferson's assertion that all men were "created equal" and thus "set out in 'the pursuit of happiness.'"[67]

As abolitionists well understood, enslaved people who resisted their captivity by revolting, absconding, or taking their own lives repeatedly put the radical egalitarian ideology of the nation's revolutionary generation into practice. While slavery alone incited slave resistance of all kinds, rebel, fugitive, and suicidal slaves drew additional inspiration from the language and symbols of American freedom. Acutely aware of the United States' radical history and heritage, these Black men and women sought nothing less than the equality promised to all Americans by their national ancestors.

Though the republic's founders did not share the blessings of liberty with African Americans, the revolutionary nationalism they fought and died for resonated with enslaved people in the antebellum South. By scheduling insurrections for the Fourth of July or crying out "Liberty or Death" as they faced off with their oppressors, captive men and women revealed the fierce and often bloody struggle over what it meant to be an American in the decades before the Civil War. In so doing, they helped fuel a growing sectional conflict that centered not only on slavery but on the nature and meaning of freedom.

Whenever slave resisters claimed both their freedom and their Americanness, they offered their allies fresh ammunition in the war against slavery. For decades, abolitionists scoured a variety of southern sources, including newspapers, pamphlets, and periodicals in search of examples of slave resistance. When they found what they were looking for, they responded with a profusion of books, pamphlets, articles,

and illustrations that attested to both the humanity and heroism of enslaved people. In some cases, when defiant Black captives responded to
the language and symbols of American freedom, abolitionists flew to
their defense by offering a powerful narrative of national sacrifice and
martyrdom that legitimized slavery's revolutionary overthrow. A nearly
forgotten fugitive slave rebellion, which occurred over the Fourth of July
weekend in 1845 and is the subject of the next chapter, demonstrates.

5
DISCIPLES

On the Fourth of July in 1845, residents of Rockville, Maryland, a small farming village several miles north of Washington, DC, gathered underneath the shade of a large oak tree to celebrate the anniversary of American independence. It was a memorable day filled with prayer, songs, and speeches, as young and old, rich and poor, urban and rural, remembered the sacrifices of their national ancestors and rededicated themselves to the cause of freedom. The diversity of the throng excited one spectator, who observed members of every class and condition of society, "The farmer, the mechanic, the merchant, the doctor, the lawyer and the reverend and venerable clergy, all, with their wives, sons and daughters." The oratory was equally exhilarating, as it lacked "everything of a party character, and breathing a spirit purely national and American." The Montgomery Volunteers led a large procession through the town center "with their Eagles blazing in the sun, laying their devotions upon the altar of patriotism."[1]

The euphoria was short-lived. Days later, Rockville became the focus of national attention when the same Montgomery Volunteers clashed with dozens of fugitive slaves who had escaped from plantations in and around Port Tobacco in Charles County, Maryland, some fifty miles to the south. After passing directly through the nation's capital, the armed bondmen continued their march toward the Pennsylvania border until they encountered the local militiamen and other concerned citizens. Following a brief but bloody battle near Rockville, most of the fugitive slave rebels were arrested and jailed. Some were returned to their owners. Others were put up for sale to the Deep South.[2]

Still, the collective effort at freedom was not in vain. In the coming weeks and months, abolitionists rose to the defense of these Black freedom fighters, and on the pages of a variety of antislavery newspapers exposed the glaring gap between the rhetoric of the Declaration of Independence, which Americans celebrated every Independence Day, and the reality of slavery. Launching a literary assault on the South's peculiar institution, these antislavery crusaders demanded their fellow citizens cease making a mockery of freedom by annually commemorating the abstract concept, and instead—like the fugitive slaves who took flight over the Fourth of July weekend—embrace the concrete idea.[3]

Slavery's supporters countered in proslavery publications with a radically different interpretation of events. Ignoring any connection to the Fourth of July and the natural rights philosophy of the Declaration of Independence, they accused White northerners, free Black southerners, and foreigners of inciting slave insurrections and escapes in Rockville as well as other southern cities and towns. Intended to defend and protect the South's peculiar institution, these defensive and paranoid assertions revealed a growing anxiety among slavery's defenders. Especially along the northern–southern border, where fugitive slaves traversed in substantial numbers, slave owners and their advocates were angry and frustrated with their inability to control those held in bondage.

As to the reason the Rockville rebels took flight and fought for their freedom when they did, a definitive answer does not exist. Unfortunately, no record of their motivation survives. That they, like countless other enslaved Americans before and after them, intentionally marked the annual celebration of American Independence by escaping their captors is possible and even probable—but can only be speculated. All that can be said for certain is that their abolitionist allies believed that the rebellion's initiation over the Fourth of July weekend was no coincidence. Rejecting its characterization by proslavery speakers and writers as a random act of resistance, they interpreted it as an act of civil disobedience that belonged to the national tradition of revolutionary resistance to tyranny that began on July 4, 1776.

An analysis of the "fugitive slave rebellion" at Rockville and the public response reveals how collective efforts at "self-liberation" could engage enslaved people in political action.[4] Today, historians readily acknowledge the prominent and often preeminent role that free and in many cases formerly enslaved African Americans played in the northern abolitionist movement.[5] They also recognize the role that the fear of slave resistance played in shaping the attitudes and ideas of White southerners.[6] Yet they still underestimate the ability of enslaved people, especially those residing near the seat of the federal government, to affect the political process. When slavery's opponents mobilized support for their movement by showing how the language and symbols of American freedom inspired the Rockville rebels, and slavery's supporters deepened their proslavery phalanx by denying such inspiration, the political power of enslaved people revealed itself. The result was an intensification of the sectional conflict over slavery that brought the nation ever closer to civil war.

During the 1840s, enslaved people comprised two-thirds of the population of Charles County, Maryland, a large agricultural district south of Washington, DC, which extended along the eastern edge of the Potomac River toward the mouth of the Chesapeake Bay. While many labored in the fields and farms of their owners, others worked as servants, sailors, and stevedores for the traders and merchants who coursed the waterways between the nation's capital and the Atlantic Ocean more than one hundred miles to the southeast. Regardless of their occupation, bondpeople in southern Maryland never received compensation for their labor and in other ways daily suffered the injustices of slavery. Consequently, many of them tried to escape. Fleeing by themselves or in small groups, these absconders rarely attracted public attention outside of the local communities from which they had fled. But in 1845, when scores of them together took flight over the Fourth of July weekend and tried to fight their way to freedom, the entire country took notice.[7]

Little information on the public observances of the anniversary of American independence in Charles County in 1845 survives. In the county seat, the *Port Tobacco Times* recorded a local gathering to hear an oration "in commemoration of the day" by James Fergusson, a recent Yale University graduate and aspiring politician. The crowd also heard a reading of the Declaration of Independence by a well-respected lawyer named Richard Alvey. Following these addresses, revelers retired to the Farmers and Planters' Hotel for a party hosted by the establishment's owner.[8]

Undoubtedly, the festivities went beyond those described in the town paper. If Fourth of July celebrations across the nation were any indication, Port Tobacco's citizens assembled in private and public spaces from the early morning to late night. While some imbibed their favorite drink and others did not, all delighted in a cacophony of sounds, including the shouting of huzzahs, the ringing of church bells, the firing of national salutes, and the explosion of fireworks and cannon.

As for the town's enslaved residents, there are no records indicating how they experienced the holiday or whether they heard the public reading of the Declaration of Independence in the town square and hence resolved to be free. What is recorded is that the next day as many as seventy-five of them, under the leadership of a "powerful and muscular negro" named William Wheeler, agreed to abscond.[9] Arming themselves with scythes, knives, bludgeons, clubs, "and some guns," they proceeded north under the dark of night—directly toward the nation's capital.[10]

Almost nothing is known of the identities of these fugitives besides their names and gender. All were men. Several of them belonged to some of the most prominent families in southern Maryland. Wheeler was the property of Benjamin Contee, a state assembly member descended from a revolutionary war hero and U.S. congressman of the same name. Henry and John belonged to John Grant Chapman, a recent gubernatorial candidate and newly elected member of the U.S. House of Representatives. Tom, Joe, Phil, Jim, Hamilton, John, Dick, Cato, and Manuel Beall all shared the same owner, John R. Fergusson, a respected Port Tobacco doctor.[11] At least one of the fugitives was a free man. Thirty-year-old Mark Caesar was a literate carpenter who recently became free upon the death of his owner.[12]

After walking almost two days and about forty miles northward through Charles and Prince George's County, the fugitives arrived at the southern shore of the Eastern Branch of the Anacostia River, the boundary between Maryland and Washington, DC. They first arrived on the Maryland side of the Navy Yard Bridge shortly after midnight, but a bridge-keeper thwarted their crossing by raising the wooden draw. The group then advanced a quarter of a mile to the north, where after reaching the southern wharf of the Eastern Branch Bridge they split into two separate groups. A smaller band of as many as three dozen men proceeded along the edge of the Eastern Branch further into Prince George's County. Whether they originally intended to enter the federal district—or later regretted the decision not to—is a mystery. Nevertheless, the larger contingent of about forty men crossed the bridge without any resistance. Once they stepped inside the district's borders, they progressed toward 7th Street and continued north with their "knives, pitchforks, scythes, old pistols, or bludgeons," in full display. Passing within a mile of the US Capitol, which dominated the landscape with its imposing white neoclassical dome, they were "fully prepared to take life if necessary to the attainment of freedom."[13]

The decision to proceed through Washington, DC, is important to consider given the sectional contest over both slavery and the interstate slave trade in the capital. In the aftermath of the American Revolution, federal lawmakers took several years to determine the location of the seat of the new government. The delay owed largely to northern and southern politicians insisting that the national capital reside in their part of the country. The sectional stalemate broke in the summer of 1790 when congressmen, as part of a compromise that secured southern votes for Alexander Hamilton's proposed economic plan, agreed to locate the federal district on the Potomac River fifteen miles upstream from President George Washington's Mount Vernon home.[14]

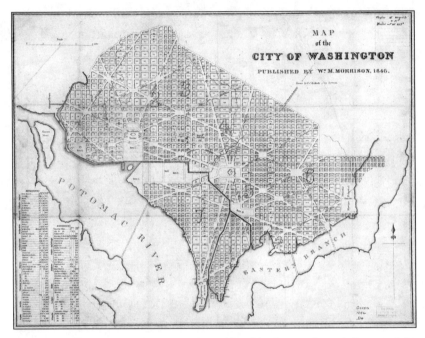

FIGURE 5.1. This contemporary map shows where the fugitive slave rebels entered the District of Columbia, across the easternmost of the two bridges spanning the Eastern Branch of the Potomac River. "MAP of the CITY OF WASHINGTON" (Washington: William M. Morrison, 1846). Courtesy of the Library of Congress.

Despite its southern location and the existence of slavery, the District of Columbia's status as a proslavery territory was insecure.[15] Article I, Section 8, of the US Constitution gives Congress the power "To exercise exclusive Legislation in all Cases whatsoever" over the government seat;[16] therefore, almost as soon as Washington officially began functioning as the national capital, slavery's opponents lobbied federal officials to outlaw the institution in the district. Terrified at the precedent such a measure would set regarding the federal government's power to legislate against slavery, slave owners and their allies became defiant. They vowed to resist any effort to impinge upon the rights of White citizens to own Black people both in the capital and beyond. The situation escalated dramatically in the 1830s when abolitionists flooded Congress with dozens of petitions signed by thousands of people demanding the abolition of slavery and the domestic slave trade in Washington. After the House of Representatives adopted a "gag rule" in 1836, which forbade all discussion of antislavery petitions and proposals, the measure became a matter of even greater national concern.[17]

Indeed, as scholars attest, the controversy over slavery and the internal slave trade in the nation's capital had by the 1840s become one of the most divisive political issues in the United States. "There was no other place quite like the District of Columbia," historian James Oakes concludes in his study of antislavery politics in the antebellum era. "Yet the issues raised by the abolition of slavery in Washington, D.C., were broad and general. At stake was the legitimacy of slavery itself, the right versus the wrong of 'property in man.'"[18] While abolitionists considered slavery's survival in Washington a national disgrace, they focused their energy on outlawing the internal slave trade in the city. Abolishing the inhumane traffic in the nation's capital was, in their calculation, a more realistic goal than abolishing the institution entirely; nevertheless, it was a daunting challenge. "Before the Civil War," writes local historian Mary Beth Corrigan, "the District of Columbia had the most active slave depot in the nation." Undeterred, abolitionists persisted, and through speeches, newspapers, posters, and pamphlets propelled the capital city into "the vortex of the national debate over slavery."[19]

The American Anti-Slavery Society's broadside SLAVE MARKET OF AMERICA offers an example. Through its nine illustrated vignettes, and quotations from the Bible, the Declaration of Independence, the US Constitution, and several state constitutions, it highlights the hypocrisy of slavery in America. Of these pictures, an image entitled "THE LAND OF THE FREE," epitomizes abolitionists ability' to use the nation's capital as a symbolic weapon in their war against slavery. It shows the Founding Fathers reading the Declaration of Independence, juxtaposed with the famous scene first described by Jesse Torrey under the title "THE HOME OF THE OPPRESSED," showing the chained bondman signing "Hail Columbia" in front of the Capitol.[20]

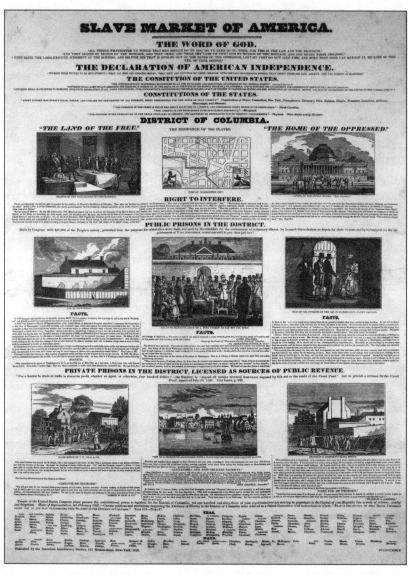

FIGURE 5.2. William S. Dorr, *SLAVE MARKET OF AMERICA* (New York: American Anti-Slavery Society, 1836). Courtesy of the Library of Congress.

The bondman's demonstration proved that enslaved people understood the paradox of slavery in the seat of the American government long before the fugitive slave rebellion at Rockville. Consequently, it is easy to imagine that decades later the armed and escaped slaves from southern Maryland who crossed the Eastern Branch Bridge and proceeded through the federal district were aware of the prior incident involving the shackled vocalist. It is also conceivable that like their famous forerunners, they also recognized the political symbolism of their march out of bondage through the national capital of a republic birthed in freedom. Without any proof of their thinking, however, this is impossible to determine.

What is provable is that in July 1845 the sight of dozens of armed Black men marching six abreast in a column formation behind a sword-wielding "Captain" spread fear throughout Washington.[21] Residents in the District's southeastern section fled toward the heavily fortified Navy Yard, where Marine Corps Commandant Archibald Henderson welcomed them inside the compound's walls and established a "triple guard" around the enclosure.[22] He moreover armed the members of a local fire company, "who volunteered their services to give chase to the colored fugitives."[23] The response of local citizens was equally impressive, proving historian Sally Hadden's argument that "all white Southerners recognized their collective responsibility for maintaining dominance over the black slaves among them."[24] By late Monday night on July 7 as many as two hundred residents from Washington and surrounding communities had joined the marines and firemen in hunting the fugitives down.

A summary of the chaotic scene comes from a northern newspaper correspondent in Washington, who was troubled by the overwhelming and unnecessary display of force. As word spread "of an insurrection among the negroes," it seemed that "every body was in expectation of a momentary descent across the eastern branch, of a posse of a thousand indignant slaves, armed to the teeth, and carrying death and destruction in their march." Even on Capitol Hill, every man "capable of bearing arms turned out to repel the dreaded African invasion." Through day and night, women and children "clustered upon the stoops and thresholds of their several dwellings, forgetful of every thing but the impending danger," while armed men on horseback raced along the city's streets looking for any signs of the enemy. By the following morning, however, the "black cloud" had disappeared. Rather than an insurrection, "It appears that a gang of slaves, variously reported at ten, twenty and thirty had made an attempt to run away in the pursuit of liberty."[25]

The collaborative effort of citizens and soldiers to capture the fugitives proved successful. The first arrests occurred on the night of the seventh when authorities apprehended four of the bondmen inside the district limits. Soon thereafter, a former local sheriff named Thomas Baldwin rounded up eighteen more in nearby Bladensburg, "he having previously had an intimation of their escape."[26] These captives belonged to the smaller group of fugitives that decided against crossing the Eastern Branch Bridge and thus never entered the capital.

Events played out differently near Rockville. At dawn on Tuesday, July 8, the larger contingent of about forty fugitives pushed past a turnpike gate and continued north on Frederick Road beyond the town. About twenty White men from Washington followed closely behind them, carrying "double-barreled guns, revolving pistols, &c., on horseback and in buggies."[27] Several hours later mounted members of the Montgomery Volunteers commanded by Captain John Braddock and a civilian posse led by Rockville Sheriff Daniel Candler joined the pursuit. Moving north on Frederick Road from Rockville they surprised the fugitives, who immediately took shelter in the woods nearby. Six of the volunteers gave chase while the remainder stayed on the turnpike, thinking "the negroes would again enter the road" and surrender.[28]

Instead, the fugitives turned rebels and emerged from the woods ready to fight. The result was what one Rockville writer called a "Grand Negro

Battle." It began on Benjamin Gaither's farm when Braddock's men surrounded the rebels and demanded an immediate surrender—but they refused. Wheeler ordered his companions to "resist to the last," and they responded by closing ranks and opening fire on their pursuers. When the rebels' guns malfunctioned, they charged forward with stones and bludgeons until a hail of gunfire forced them to retreat into a swamp. As several of them fell to the ground wounded, twenty-three others surrendered.[29] "The rest," including Wheeler, "made off."[30] By the end of the day, officials captured eight of these individuals, bringing the total number of fugitives secured in the Rockville jail to thirty-one. Of the two hundred White men believed to have been involved in the manhunt and subsequent arrests, only one received injuries worthy of attention.[31]

The fate of all the Rockville rebels is difficult to determine. A local newspaper published the names of the thirty-one captives confined in the local jail, along with the names of their owners. Sheriff Candler attached a brief note to the list, requesting the owners come forward and collect their property by paying the appropriate charges, "otherwise they will be discharged as the law directs."[32] The owners did as instructed and, according to witnesses, the captives "were all marched with ox chains, handcuffs, &c., and driven through Washington yesterday, on their way to their homes." Ten among them bore physical proof of having resisted their enslavement:[33]

Ferdinand, a slave of Wm. Brawner, slight shot in the left neck; James, slave of Edwin Jones, wounded in the back from a rifle shot; Samuel, slave of Dr. Hodges, slightly wounded in the back and face, David, a slave of John Hamet, slightly wounded in the back and face, David, a slave of John Hamet, shot through the right arm with a musket ball—badly wounded; James, slave of Barnes' estate—wounded in the side, face and neck; Mark, do, in the back of the neck with a pistol ball; Jas. Gray, belonging to Charles Pye, wounded in the side face, Lewis Key, do, to Col. Miller, in the side face; Henry, to General Chapman, slightly shot.[34]

A subsequent manhunt throughout central and western Maryland resulted in the apprehension of seven other rebels, including Wheeler. When finally confronted by White vigilantes in Howard County, "he was armed with a long sword, but suffering for want of food, he made no resistance."[35] All told, U.S. Marines, militiamen, and ordinary citizens helped arrest and return more than fifty fugitive slave rebels to their owners. At least two of the bondmen appear to have died as the result of their wounds, though accounts vary.[36]

The number of prisoners is important, because it substantiates the fact that some of the rebels avoided recapture. Northern newspapers offer additional proof. In late July, nine fugitive slaves passed through upstate New York and entered Canada. "They were," according to one widely disseminated report from Oswego, "a portion of those seventy-seven it is said in all, who escaped from their pursuers, in the recent movement in Maryland."[37] While some doubted the veracity of the account, an announcement published a week later independently confirmed it. The brief statement read, "Nine of the slaves who ran away from Maryland, have arrived in Canada."[38]

Regardless of how many of the Rockville rebels reached Canada and became free, the aftershocks of their efforts reverberated far beyond the farms and plantations from where they began. By assaulting slavery in and around the nation's capital while the smoke and aroma of the fireworks celebrating the Fourth of July still floated in the air, these enslaved people proved the United States' failure to fulfill the promise of freedom and equality proclaimed in the Declaration of Independence. At the same time, they offered powerful images of slave sacrifice and suffering in the name of these American ideals, which abolitionists then deployed as part of a national argument to end slavery.

Of course, the Rockville rebellion was not the first time that slave resisters in or around Washington inspired abolitionist agitation. In 1815, a Black woman named Anna learned of her impending sale to a trader and hurled herself out of the garret window of a three-story Tavern on F Street to the pavement below. Though she survived the fall, the young wife and mother broke both of her arms and shattered her lower spine. While lying in a bed recuperating from her injuries, Anna shared her story with Jesse Torrey, who published parts of the conversation in the *Portraiture of Domestic Slavery* and a revised text entitled *American Slave Trade*.[39]

To illuminate the irony of Anna's actions in the "Metropolis of Liberty," Torrey included an engraving of the failed suicide attempt that despite the artist's intentions stretches incredulity.[40] "Technically," writes a knowledgeable observer, "nearly everything in the illustration/ engraving is wrong."[41] Anna's body is far too large to have climbed out of the garret window, and it levitates in midair instead of falling towards the cobblestones below. What is more, the static and generic scenery belies the event having taken place in Washington at all. Despite its flaws, the image proved the lengths enslaved people would go to escape captivity in the nation's capital, which in large part explains its resonance among abolitionists for decades.

By repeating Anna's story, abolitionists made her one of the movement's early female icons—and the District of Columbia a site of national infamy.[42] Benjamin Lundy reflected on the significance of Torrey's interview with Anna and other trafficked people thusly: "The sketches given by him of the scenes which he beheld at the city of Washington, his description of the cruelties and misery as he there witnessed them, produced by the internal slave trade," were enough "to make every American citizen hang his head in shame for the country of his birth."[43] The remark proved prescient.

Three decades later, as news of the violent suppression of the Rockville rebels spread, abolitionists adopted what had by them become one of the trusted tactics in the fight against slavery—what historian Caleb McDaniel calls the mobilization of "patriotic shame."[44] In William Lloyd Garrison's first comments on the episode, the editor offered the violence meted out in Maryland as another example "of the oppressive and bloody deeds which are daily perpetrated in the South." Garrison wondered how anyone could read of the heroic effort

" . . . But I did not want to go, and I jump'd out of the window."

FIGURE 5.3. "But I did not want to go, and I jump'd out of the window," from Jesse Torrey, *American Slave Trade: or, An Account of the Manner in which the Slave Dealers take Free People from some of the United States of America, and carry them away, and sell them as Slaves in other of the States; and of the horrible Cruelties practiced in the carrying on of this most infamous Traffic* (London: J. M. Cobbett, 1822). Courtesy of the New York Public Library.

of these enslaved people to become free following the Fourth of July, and the manner in which they were captured and marched through Washington in chains, "without groaning in spirit, and being ashamed of the American name?"[45]

An anonymous New Englander sharing Garrison's view argued that the mistreatment of the Rockville rebels revealed how the young republic had forsaken its foundational ideals by shamefully serving slave owners' interests. An anonymous editorialist in the *Hartford Daily Courant* explained that these resisters were human beings "born with *inalienable rights to life, liberty and the pursuit of happiness.*" Consequently, they were justified in running away from their owners. Though legally considered chattel, these individuals were in fact free men. Having lived "under the very shadow of the lofty porches of Freedom's own temple, the capitol at Washington," it was to be expected that "they longed to taste that liberty, which they every day heard was the inalienable right of every man." The use of federal soldiers to shoot, capture, and kill these people was particularly troubling, for the victims "were men, of inalienable rights, their right to escape from their masters perfect and unquestionable."[46]

In an indignant article called "Liberty or Death!" a *New York Tribune* editorialist expressed similar frustration with the American government's shameful proslavery position. The article reminded readers how only days earlier, citizens across the republic had celebrated national independence "with cannon, bonfires, pistols, squibs, crackers, and every conceivable manifestation of Democratic exultation and fervor." Orators praised the union of states "as 'the land of the *Free* and the home of the Brave'—a favored portion of God's footstool, from which Old-World tyranny and oppression had been utterly banished by the men of '76 and their worthy descendants." Pastors and ministers offered up thanks for the freedom of the people, while millions listened to a reading of the Declaration of Independence, "as its fundamental, all-essential assumption was propounded." Americans had good reason to be proud that Fourth of July.[47]

Yet something was amiss. For among those who had heard the bomb blasts and the flowery orations were the Rockville rebels. "They listened and were convinced—the National sentiment coincided with theirs, exactly," but their situations ran counter to the nation's noble sentiments. Their friends and family were "mere chattels, liable to be bought, sold, swapped, flogged, branded, kicked, cuffed, and outraged at the caprice of those deniers and contemners of the truths asserted by Jefferson and his compeers in the Congress of '76." As enslaved people, the rebels could not fight for their unalienable rights as the founding fathers did, "so gloriously (it is said every 4th of July;)" because they lacked all the advantages of their oppressors. Their only hope was to escape to the North, where the ideas of the Declaration of Independence still resonated. Failure was anticipated, because they needed to travel more than one hundred miles through a slave state and territory. Though the laws of the United States protected slave owners and their slave-catching allies, there was a tribunal that they could not escape, "and where the oppressor is confronted with his victim."[48]

An evangelical Bostonian also appealed to a higher authority when defending the Rockville rebels. He recalled that the Founding Fathers dedicated themselves to "liberty or death" when confronted with British taxes that enslaved them to the British Empire, "and for this they have been immortalized in song and story, and on the grave page of history." But the revolutionary right they asserted was not the result of education, ancestry, or color; it was a gift of God, "and it is as truly the gift of God to the negro who swelters on the 'plantation,' as it was to George Washington or Patrick Henry." The recent "battle" near the nation's capital "was as strictly justifiable, by the law of human rights, as was the battle of Bunker Hill or Yorktown." In this case, the "gallant defenders of their rights" did not intend to harm anyone. "They only wished to go quietly away from a crushing bondage, and in *attempting* to go they wronged no man,—wronged no man." Like the founding fathers, they refused to submit to their enslavers, and by offering their blood for free-dom only "obeyed the undying instincts of humanity."[49]

Given the revolutionary motivations of the Rockville rebels, the writer warned of the danger facing the entire republic should slavery continue to exist. "Our fourth of July celebrations are not unknown to them," he explained. "Our glad huzzas are wafted to their ears, and what if, hearing the sound and catching the spirit of our national rejoicings, they should determine to be as free as we, and should rise to execute their will?" The American people would condemn them, despite their having once rejected "a tyranny not a millionth part as grievous as the slave complains of." The future was clear. Aware of their natural rights, enslaved Americans would adopt the same doctrines held dear by the nation's founders, and to protect their own lives and that of their fami-lies take freedom in their own hands. "That day if it comes, will be the day of doom to oppressors, for on earth there is nothing so terrible to contend with as the spirit of liberty, restrained, disappointed, wronged, and goaded to madness. And in such a conflict Heaven takes the part of the weak and the injured."[50]

In his defense of the Rockville rebels, James Russell Lowell joined the abolitionist tactics of patriotic shaming and appealing to a higher power. The Massachusetts poet's antislavery attitudes were still relatively new when he learned of the "disciples of the Declaration of Independence," who, while escaping from bondage near the nation's capital, were sub-jected to "an act of unparalleled inhumanity," which the national media failed to address adequately. "It seems strange that a burst of indignation, from one end of our free country to the other, did not follow so atro-cious a deed," Lowell lamented. "At least, it seemed a proper occasion for sympathy on the part of our daily papers, which, a year or two ago, endorsed Lord Morpeth's sentiment, that 'Who would be free, them-selves must strike the blow.'"[51]

Lowell abhorred violence, but the bravery of these Black rebels, who endeavored to "convert themselves from chattel into men," moved him to compose an impassioned antislavery poem. Highlighting the hypocrisy of American patriotism, the rhyming couplets condemned those who worshiped the freedom fighters buried beneath the earth's surface while ignoring those who still walked upon it.

> Shame on the costly mockery of piling stone on stone
> To those who won our liberty, the heroes dead and gone,
> While we look coldly on, and see law-shielded ruffians slay
> The men who fain would win their own, the heroes of to-day!

Lowell then challenged readers to remember their faith in a higher authority since their government had abandoned its egalitarian mission so entirely.

> Man is more than Constitutions: better rot beneath the sod,
> Than be true to Church and State, while we are doubly false to God;
> We owe allegiance to the State; but deeper, truer, more,
> To the sympathies that God hath set within our spirit's core:
> Our country claims our fealty; we grant it so, but then
> Before Man made us citizens, great Nature made us men.[52]

The poem struck a chord, appearing widely in abolitionist and antislavery publications for the next two decades.[53]

Extensive coverage of the Rockville rebellion in local and national newspapers demonstrates the political power of enslaved people, especially as it relates to the rise of American abolitionism. Fugitive slaves were the abolition movement's "most effective emissaries," writes historian Manisha Sinha. In the case of the Rockville rebels, they were also rank-and-file soldiers on the front lines of the growing sectional battle over the essence of American freedom. Consequently, their story adds to the burgeoning historiography on the nineteenth-century Black struggle to both end slavery and secure equal rights.[54]

Still, because of the entrenched power of White supremacy, slavery's defenders refused to credit the Rockville rebels for inspiring abolitionists and instead argued that the reverse had taken place. A report from Maryland informed that Charles County slave owners were "overrunning with fire and brimstone for the Northern Abolitionists" whom they believed bore responsibility for the rebellion. Having nearly lost their valuable enslaved property, they were thankful "for the bravery, activity, and patriotism of the citizen soldiery of Rockville."[55]

In the proslavery publications that blamed abolitionists for the Rockville rebellion, the fact that the incident started on Independence Day weekend went unmentioned. A Baltimore writer attributed the incident "to the intermeddling of Northern abolitionists, who, by infusing discontent and disaffection amongst the slaves, have produced the necessity for more rigid laws, and a more exact surveillance."[56] An editorialist in the Georgetown section of the nation's capital confessed the conspiracy was "daringly conceived," but because of the slaves' inherent submissiveness, "we strongly suspect that some of our demure northern philanthropists had a hand in bringing about this business."[57] An incensed Louisianan divulged whom he held responsible for the Rockville rebellion when he demanded, "Hang the abolitionists and whip the negroes until they are sick of it."[58]

Northern newspapers at times amplified the anti-abolitionism of their southern counterparts. A New York editor insisted that the incident was the result of "the recent agitation of the slavery question, both north and south, and various movements of the abolitionists in the free States." Given abolitionists' efforts, incidents like that which had taken place at Rockville would undoubtedly increase along the North–South border. He wondered, "What is there to prevent the organization of large bands of negroes in all the States adjacent to free States, and a universal system of insurrection and rebellion, all produced by the agitation of the rabid politicians and frantic fanatics who are marshalled under the banner of abolitionism?"[59]

There were, in fact, reasons for slave owners and their supporters to be concerned. In 1841, Charles Torrey, a radical White abolitionist from Massachusetts, had relocated to the district and with the assistance of a small interracial band of men and women began leading enslaved people out of the city and toward freedom. Over the course of the next two decades, as historian Stanley Harrold has demonstrated, the Underground Railroad line operated by this interracial cadre helped an estimated four hundred enslaved people escape. In return for forcefully challenging slavery, Torrey in December 1844 landed behind the bars of the Maryland Penitentiary in Baltimore, where he died of tuberculosis a year and a half later.[60]

Among Torrey's key accomplices was Thomas Smallwood, a free Black Washingtonian and former Maryland bondman, whose thoughts on Independence Day offer additional clues as to the holiday's meaning among enslaved and formerly enslaved people. In June 1843, Smallwood moved to Canada to avoid arrest. Arriving in Toronto on July 4 purely by happenstance, he wondered how he would have spent the day in the United States surrounded by so many White citizens who failed to recognize the failure of America's national ideals. "There I would have been compelled painfully to witness as I had done for many years their hypocritical demonstrations in honour of a day, which they say, brought to them freedom," he wrote in his autobiography. "But I sorrowfully knew that it was in honour of a day which brought to me, and my race among them, the most degrading, tyrannical and soul-withering bondage that ever disgraced the world or a nation." Considering Smallwood's contempt for the Fourth of July, and the fact that he on at least one occasion returned to Washington to resume his Underground Railroad activity, it is tempting to speculate that he or his associates contributed to the Rockville rebellion. That a multiracial band of abolitionists tried to conduct seventy-seven slaves from Washington aboard the schooner *Pearl* in 1848, in the largest attempted slave escape in US history, is further cause for speculation. Regardless, the Rockville rebels appear to have acted on their own.[61]

That did not stop their owners and other proslavery Marylanders from holding a series of public meetings in the wake of the rebellion, where they blamed foreigners, White northerners, and free Black southerners for the affair. According to an ad hoc committee organized at a "very large" gathering in front of the Port Tobacco courthouse, these congregations were the direct result of "having watched with deep concern the tendency of the late movement of foreign governments and the reckless efforts of fanaticism in the northern portion of the United States to subvert the institutions of the state." Given recent events, it was clear that abolitionists intended to "invade the peace of our people by the sacrifice of our property at the risk of our lives and the destruction of our constitutional rights." Besides that, a rising population of free Black men and women represented a "growing evil" that required immediate redress.[62]

The proslavery assemblies, in which any references to the rebellion having occurred on the Fourth of July weekend were conspicuously absent, resulted in the adoption of a series of resolutions that newspapers printed statewide to encourage a political consensus among White residents. Though variations existed, the intent of the resolves was always the same—"to adopt such rules and regulations as will effectually counteract the causes which instigate their slaves to elope, and the means by which many of them do escape." The proposals encouraged an increase of law enforcement resources and the further restriction of the rights of enslaved people. The most radical encouraged policy makers to secure legislation that would permanently banish free Black people from the state.[63]

To justify this extreme measure, a Prince George's County editorialist calling himself "CITIZEN" invoked a racist trope that had become part and parcel of the White supremacist argument against racial equality. The philippic proclaimed, "the time has arrived at last when I hope every white man in Prince George's will feel the necessity of ridding ourselves of the presence of that lazy, degraded, vicious and worthless class of citizens—*free negroes*—who infest our neighborhoods and disturb our peace." Rather than the daily injustice of slavery, it was these criminals, vagrants, and rabble rousers who rendered "our slaves dissatisfied and unhappy." Referring to Caesar, the only free Black man counted among the Rockville rebels, and Caesar's enslaved accomplices, CITIZEN warned "that we sleep upon the very mouth of a volcano—its first rumblings have been heard and felt." Similar eruptions were inevitable, "and unless we are on our guard we may be overwhelmed ere we appreciate the danger."[64]

In the end, state and local administrators made few of the recommended changes. While the presence of slave patrols increased in some areas, proposed legislation to remove free Black people from the state failed. There were several reasons; however, the fear of the loss of labor was paramount. "Whatever white Marylanders might say or think about the danger and mischief of the free black population," writes historian Barbara Fields in her study of mid-nineteenth-century Maryland, "the economy of the state could not dispense with them."[65]

Responding to the failed reform effort, former Maryland assembly member Walter Millar recommended the increased oppression of enslaved people. After all, he submitted, unchecked abolitionism made "it necessary for the master to draw tighter the ligatures of slavery, and finally to sever the cord which binds them together, and consigns the slave to a more ungenial clime and a less compassionate taskmaster." Whether any slave owners heeded Millar's advice is unknown, but the process repeatedly played itself out across the South. "When slaveholders cracked down in the aftermath of revolts and revolt scares," writes Walter Johnson, "they treated slave revolts as if they could be ended by more vigilance—more mastery—on the part of white people, as if, that is to say, those revolts were aspects of their own agency." Almost incapable of acknowledging the potential of the people they held in captivity, "They responded to, without ever fully imagining, the politics of black revolt."[66]

Further evidence of the political impact of the Rockville fugitive slave rebellion came in late August 1845, when the Charles County

Court charged William Wheeler and Mark Caesar, the rebellions' two alleged "ringleaders," with the capital crime of inciting a slave insurrection. In two separate trials, a veritable who's who of Maryland's most powerful public officials volunteered their services. Former state assemblyman Clement Dorsey and former state senator Alexander Contee Magruder presided as judges, while George Brent, a Harvard-educated state's attorney, and Thomas F. Bowie, a current member of the Maryland House of Delegates, served as prosecutors. It is not clear how John Causin became counsel for the two defendants, but the former U.S. congressman performed his duties admirably despite the White public's disdain for his Black clients. As one Baltimore writer later put it, "never (in the opinion of the writer) has he deserved better of his friends and country than when, as counselor for the accused on the late occasion, he stood forward solitary and alone the eloquent advocate and the fearless man."[67]

The trials occurred in September 1845. Wheeler's, which went first, lasted only two days. Based on the testimony of several witnesses, "a fair and impartial jury" reached "a verdict of *guilty*" after only a brief absence from the courtroom. The court then sentenced the defendant to death by hanging.[68] Caesar's trial came next. It lasted a week, though a lengthy adjournment similarly left only two days for testimony. In this case, after hours of deliberation, the twelve-man jury was unable to reach a consensus and thus found the defendant not guilty. There were two reasons for Caesar's acquittal. First was a dispute over the "technical construction" of an 1809 law defining the word *insurrection*. Causin argued "that the meeting of negroes, with fire arms in their hands, to run away, was not an insurrectionary movement, within the meaning of the statute." Therefore, the defendant could not be convicted of such a crime. Second was the question of Caesar's freedom, which the court ultimately admitted after reviewing the will of his recently deceased owner.[69]

Under the presumption that the common law protection of double jeopardy did not apply to African Americans, the Charles County

Court immediately impaneled a new jury and two weeks later retried Caesar "as a free negro aiding and abetting slaves in making their escape from their masters." This time, the jury found Caesar guilty of ten separate counts of the charge, each of which carried a sentence of four years, "making the whole term of his imprisonment forty years." Having failed in his effort to free others from slavery, Caesar spent five years in Baltimore's penitentiary before dying of consumption in 1850.[70]

Wheeler experienced a far different fate. While awaiting his execution in the Port Tobacco jail, "a memorial very numerously and respectably signed" arrived on the desk of Governor Thomas Pratt. The petition called on the state's chief executive to reduce "the punishment in this case" to life imprisonment. In his annual message to the General Assembly in December 1845, Pratt confessed that he also wanted to modify the prisoner's sentence from death to life imprisonment; however, existing laws prohibited him from taking such action in cases involving slaves. Pratt asked the assembly to take the necessary steps to allow the state penitentiary to receive the convicted bondman into its custody and confine him for the rest of his life. Three months later the legislature did just that, passing a law that ordered the prison's administrators "to receive and keep negro William Wheeler, now under sentence of death into the Penitentiary, in the event of the commutation of his sentence by the Governor."[71]

While there are several possible explanations for the governors' and other prominent slave owners' desire to commute a rebellious fugitive slave's death sentence, one—which had nothing to do with any concern over Wheeler's well-being—stands out. In the first half of the nineteenth century, as the sectional gulf between the northern and southern states widened, White southerners expanded their efforts to ensure the future of their most profitable and peculiar institution. Eager to convince outsiders of slavery's positive good, they tried to suppress and even eliminate examples of extreme violence against enslaved people. In the words of abolitionist Angelina Grimké Weld, who recalled of slave owners in her native South Carolina, "Everything cruel and revolting is carefully concealed from strangers, especially those from the north." Given the widespread coverage of the Rockville fugitive slave rebellion in the northern press, it is not surprising that Maryland's proslavery political leaders preferred to see Wheeler's body safely secured behind the bars of a private prison cell rather than dangling lifelessly from the public gallows.[72]

That being said, Wheeler had no intention of spending the rest of his life behind bars or hanging from a noose. Just days after the General Assembly passed the law allowing Wheeler's incarceration in the Baltimore jail, which caused Governor Pratt to officially commute the prisoner's death sentence, the *Port Tobacco Times* announced: "On Saturday night last, negro BILL WHEELER, convicted of insurrection during the term of last August Court and sentenced to be hung, but whose sentence, by a special act of the Legislature, was remitted to imprisonment in the Penitentiary during his natural life, broke from the jail of the sheriff of this county and made his escape." The Charles County Sheriff offered a $100 reward for Wheeler's capture, but it appears the prize went uncollected. The absence of Wheeler's name in subsequent editions of the paper and other local contemporary sources suggests that this disciple of the Declaration achieved liberty over death.[73]

When William Wheeler and the other Rockville rebels fled from enslavement over the Fourth of July weekend and fought for their freedom days later, they did more than challenge their captivity. Their dramatic actions, which demonstrated the nation's failure to secure the rights enunciated in the Declaration of Independence for all people, ignited an intense cross-sectional conversation on slavery. While most citizens preferred to postpone the controversial issue until a later date, the Rockville rebels made such a delay impossible. Setting the national agenda—even if only temporarily and partially—they showed how the politics of slave resistance shaped the public discourse on slavery and freedom.[74]

Following the fugitive slave rebellion at Rockville, abolitionists continued to come to the defense of enslaved people who in response to the language and symbols of American freedom resisted captivity. The result was a radicalization of their movement, which helped put the nation on the path to civil war. With no end to slavery in sight, the free men and women of various races, ethnicities, and classes who for decades had tried to secure slavery' abolishment by peaceful means decided to change tactics. Embracing the revolutionary nationalism of the republic's founders, they joined their enslaved compatriots in seeking slavery's destruction by force and even violence.

6

RADICALS

James Blunt's first encounter with fugitive slaves was unforgettable. While visiting Cincinnati on business, the antislavery physician followed with two local abolitionists, the wealthy White merchant Levi Coffin and the free Black painter Thomas Dorum, to a secret location just beyond the city limits. Upon entering the undisclosed Underground Railroad depot around midnight, Blunt came face-to-face with fourteen escaped slaves who had arrived from Kentucky only moments earlier. Everything about these brave Black men and women impressed Blunt, but nothing more so than the cache of firearms they openly brandished. Recalling Patrick Henry's immortal oration, the doctor encouraged the fugitives to do everything in their power to remain free. "Let your watchword be liberty or death," he imparted. "Die in your tracks boys, rather than be taken back to slavery."[1]

Coffin revolted at the suggestion. A Quaker pacifist, he rejected violence in any form and thus implored the group to "throw away" their firearms "and look to a higher power for protection." Despite Coffin's reputation as the President of the Underground Railroad, his recommendation went unheeded. Blunt continued to encourage the fugitives to fight for their liberation "and gave them all the money he had with him to help them on their way." Armed and ready for battle, the fugitives left the depot and continued their perilous journey toward freedom.[2]

Blunt's advocacy of violence to oppose slavery proved prophetic. Inspired by the incident in Cincinnati, he later moved westward and for years fought in the bloody frontier battles over slave expansion that came to be known as Bleeding Kansas. He then ascended to the rank of major general in the Union Army during the Civil War, earning a reputation as one of the military's most ardent abolitionist officers.[3] When Coffin learned of Blunt's military success during the war, he still refused to condone violence for any reason; however, he wrote proudly of the forces serving under Blunt's command: "They have one General who will fight for liberty or die, and if slaves come inside his lines, they will never be given up to their masters."[4]

Throughout the antebellum era, the brave and heroic acts of enslaved people encouraged and convinced their abolitionist allies to accept violence as a viable means of slave opposition. As Levi Coffin's above comments attests, most abolitionists never abandoned the strategy of nonviolence. But some, like James Blunt, did. For these radicals, resistance to tyranny in the form of slavery was a revolutionary right that was deeply rooted in the nation's history and tradition. Taking the founding generation at its word, they considered it their responsibility—even their obligation—as Americans to honor and emulate the sacrifices of their national ancestors by waging war against the enemies of freedom.

While James Blunt represents the archetypal abolitionist as an educated and affluent White man, the advocates of revolutionary nationalism in the pursuit of slavery's destruction represented a cross-section of the antebellum North. As the historiography of American antislavery makes clear, African Americans, including many formerly enslaved people, were always in the vanguard of radical abolitionism—but they were not alone. By the middle of the nineteenth century, and especially after the US Congress's passage of the Fugitive Slave Act, White men and women of various economic, social, and ethnic backgrounds joined their free Black compatriots in calling for slavery's destruction by force and even violence.[5]

———

In December 1833, sixty-three delegates meeting at Philadelphia's Adelphi Hall launched the American Anti-Slavery Society (AASS), the first national organization dedicated to the total and immediate abolition of slavery. At the convention's conclusion, the group issued a

Declaration of Sentiments, which acknowledged the symbolism behind Philadelphia's selection as the site of the historic gathering. The statement, written by William Lloyd Garrison, began with a reference to 1776: "More than fifty-seven years have elapsed since a band of patriots" laid the cornerstone of the "Temple of Freedom" on the bedrock of the idea "that all men are created equal; that they are endowed by their Creator with certain inalienable rights; that among these are life, LIBERTY, and the pursuit of happiness." When millions of patriots responded to the call to resist their oppressors, the result was American freedom.[6]

The AASS's Declaration of Sentiments provided "the dramaturgical framework in which the fledgling organization linked itself to the American revolutionary tradition," writes Henry Mayer, Garrison's preeminent biographer.[7] It also demonstrated that while the society's organizers revered the nation's founders, they rejected the violence those revolutionaries employed to win independence. Referring to those eighteenth-century freedom fighters, the declaration clarified, "*Their* principles led them to wage war against their oppressors, and to spill human blood like water, in order to be free. *Ours* forbid the doing of evil that good may come, and lead us to reject, and to entreat the oppressed to reject, the use of all carnal weapons for deliverance from bondage." Rather than force and arms, the AASS vowed to destroy slavery with the "power of love."[8]

For the next two decades, nonviolence, or non-resistance as it was then called, remained the preeminent ethos of the organized effort to end slavery in the United States. To accomplish this, abolitionists across the country seized upon the idea of "moral suasion"—that is, the apolitical effort to persuade slave owners and their supporters of the evils of slavery, and thus convince them to cease the practice peacefully and voluntarily. While the abolitionist commitment to this conservative strategy was widespread, it was not universal.

Inspired by the language and symbols of freedom, a small number of African Americans early embraced the revolutionary violence of their national forebears. The group included David Walker, a free North Carolinian who spent much of his youth seeing the horrors of slavery firsthand. When he migrated from the South in his late twenties, he swore, "As true as God reigns, I will be avenged for the sorrow which my people have suffered."[9] Upon settling in Boston, Walker owned and operated a used clothing store while authoring a series of articles that appeared in the United States' first Black-owned newspaper, *Freedom's Journal.*[10]

In 1829, Walker gained national attention when he published *Walker's Appeal, in Four Articles; Together with a Preamble, to the Coloured Citizens of the World, but in Particular, and Very Expressly, to Those of the United States of America.* In this radical pamphlet, which is widely considered the most incendiary antislavery publication in the antebellum era, he assailed White Americans for making their Black countrymen and women "the most degraded, wretched, and abject set of beings that ever lived since the world began." Given slavery's entrenchment in the South, Walker urged the people being held captive across the region to strike for freedom. If they were unwilling to do so, he thought that they deserved to remain in bondage forever.[11]

Walker's call for racial revolution has endeared him to scholars of Black nationalism.[12] Throughout his *Appeal,* the author acknowledged a shared history and experience that united Africans and their descendants across time and space. In one compelling passage, he reveled in the accomplishments of his racial brethren, including the building of Egypt's ancient pyramids and the defeat of the Roman army by the great North African general Hannibal—who Walker insisted was Black. Based on his reading of history, Walker believed that if slavery continued, White Americans would face violent retribution from the ancestors of these great Africans. For those who doubted the capacity of enslaved people to secure freedom forcefully, he pointed to the Black republic of Haiti.[13]

Despite Walker's fascination with Black diasporic history, there is reason to believe that, as biographer Peter Hinks suggests, "Walker's stature as an architect of black nationalism is overstated."[14] The *Appeal* demonstrates that Walker felt a deep attachment to the United States, repeatedly claiming it for himself and all African Americans. On at least five separate occasions in his pamphlet, he reminded Black readers that the United States was their nation as much as anyone else's. Indeed, because of hundreds of years of enslavement, Walker concluded, "America is more our country, than it is the whites—we have enriched it with our *blood and tears*."[15]

Walker did not publish the *Appeal* to damage the United States or its reputation. Instead, anticipating Frederick Douglass's Fifth of July Speech a quarter of a century later, he did it to ensure its survival. With slavery ascendant, he feared that the republic's days were numbered, and the lives of its citizens were in grave danger. "O Americans! Americans!!" Walker pleaded. "I call God—I call angels—I call men, to witness, that your DESTRUCTION *is at hand*, and will be speedily consummated unless you REPENT." Should slavery continue, the end would be a violent one. African Americans would have freedom—or they would have revenge.[16]

Walker's devotion to violent slave resistance owed in large part to his veneration of the nation's history. "He frankly admired revolutionary America," writes Hinks, for it unleashed "constructive and righteous individual energies" that "would lead inevitably to universal emancipation."[17] Walker revealed his affinity for the republic's founding ideals by inserting the text of the Declaration of Independence at the close of his pamphlet. Repeating the document's preamble and its affirmation of both the right and duty of Americans to overthrow their oppressors, he asked White Americans who continued to hold Black people in bondage, "Do you understand your own language?"[18]

Two centuries after the *Appeal*'s publication, Walker's reputation as a global Black revolutionary remains secure. But his American nationalism is nearly forgotten. "Although Walker mocked the pretensions of 'American' liberty,'" Stephen Kantrowitz explains in his study of the African American struggle for civil rights, "he and his comrades nevertheless claimed the American Revolution as their birthright."[19] Had he not passed away shortly after publishing his tract, Walker might have guided the abolitionist movement down a different and more radical path than it eventually followed.

Nevertheless, his legacy lived on in the minds of other Black abolitionists like James Forten, a Revolutionary War veteran and accomplished Philadelphia entrepreneur. A year after Walker's death, upon learning of the flogging of a free man of color in North Carolina, Forten wrote a letter to William Lloyd Garrison that, according to biographer Julie Winch, bore the "unmistakable echoes" of Walker's *Appeal*.[20] Referring to the United States as "this boasted land of liberty" and "the worst place for colored persons in the known world," Forten wondered if revolutionary violence was the only solution to the problem of slavery. He predicted that soon the "words 'Fight for liberty, or die in the attempt,' will be sounded in every African ear throughout the world." When that happened, "he will throw off his fetters, and flock to the banner which will be then floating in the air with the following words inscribed upon it—'Liberty or Death.'"[21]

Henry Highland Garnet also continued Walker's legacy. Born enslaved on Maryland's Eastern Shore in 1815, Garnet escaped to New York with his family before his tenth birthday. Three decades later, after becoming an accomplished preacher and educator, he delivered an historic speech before the National Negro Convention at Buffalo, New York. Addressed "TO THE SLAVES OF THE UNITED STATES," the talk revisited many of the themes of Walker's *Appeal* with one exception. Where Walker tried to save the republic from a vengeful slave uprising, Garnet thought it was too late.[22]

Citing the republic's revolutionary origins, Garnet called for slave insurrection. He explained that in the previous century, when colonists declared their independence from England in a "glorious document," they cried out with one voice, "LIBERTY OR DEATH." Those words fired their souls like a bolt of electricity and nerved their arms "to fight in the holy cause of freedom." Since winning independence, some Americans had questioned the use of force, but Garnet assured his imagined audience of enslaved people, "We are among those who do not." History proved that liberty required bloodshed; thus, "If you must bleed, let it all come at once—rather, *die freemen, than live to be slaves.*"[23]

Garnet concluded by stating that enslaved people were far more predisposed to revolution than the nation's founders. From an early age, he reminded his Black brethren, "you have been accustomed to nothing else but hardships." Unlike the "heroes of the American Revolution," who never experienced true suffering and were thus enervated, slavery had "prepared you for any emergency." Having become accustomed to pain and suffering, Garnet bellowed, "In the name of the merciful God, and by all that life is worth, let it no longer be a debatable question, whether it is better to choose *Liberty or Death.*" Then, after invoking the names of some of the most notorious Black rebels in history, he called on enslaved Americans to strike for their freedom. "Let your motto be resistance! *resistance!* RESISTANCE!"[24]

The audience was stunned. Some who were initially moved to tears had by the end of the oration dried their eyes, clenched their fists, and leapt from their seats "under the words and action of the speaker." Because of the excitement in the room, one observer thought "it would have been dangerous to a slave-holder to have been in sight." Garnet's words were so stimulating "that one of the first clergymen of the city, an anti-abolitionist, was heard on going out, to declare, that were he to act from the impulse of the moment, he should shoulder his musket and march South."[25]

Despite the audience's approval, the convention's delegates rejected a motion to officially adopt the Address or support its publication.[26] Among them was Frederick Douglass, who, because he was at the time still committed to moral suasion, argued "that there was too much physical force" in it. If Garnet's words reached enslaved people, the result would be a slave insurrection, which Douglass "wished in no way to have any agency in bringing about."[27] The delegates' refusal to adopt the motion testifies to the hesitancy of Black abolitionists to endorse

FIGURE 6.1. Henry Highland Garnet (circa 1881). Courtesy of the National Portrait Gallery, Smithsonian Institution.

revolutionary slave violence. Despite that, the narrow vote (19–18) over the motion shows a shift in their thinking. In the words of historian Howard Bell, "this convention came within a trifle of advocating an insurrection of slaves."[28]

The near endorsement of violent slave resistance was unsurprising given the commitment of the Colored Convention movement to Furstenberg's idea of "virtuous revolutionary resistance."[29] Across the antebellum era, delegates at local and national meetings proudly cited the martial contribution of Black men to national independence as proof of qualification for citizenship. In Albany, New York, three years before Garnet's address, convention-goers reminded their "Fellow-Citizens" that in the American Revolution and the War of 1812, when the clarion call of Freedom rang out across the country, "the dark-browned man stood side by side with the fairer fellow citizens, with firm determination and indomitable spirit." In these conflicts, Black men fought for the principles enshrined in the Declaration of Independence and as a result, "Their blood is mingled with the soil of every battlefield, made glorious by revolutionary reminiscence; and their bones have enriched the most productive lands of the country." Because of these battlefield sacrifices, one thing was certain of African-descended people in the United States: "*We are Americans.*"[30]

While support of violent slave resistance often distinguished Black abolitionists from their White counterparts, veneration of the nation's revolutionary heritage sometimes made the two groups indistinguishable. William Lloyd Garrison's career is a case in point. The historiography of American abolitionism rightly recognizes this reformer's lifelong commitment to nonviolence. Yet it understates his long-held sympathy for enslaved people who fought for freedom. The sentiment, as historian Kellie Carter Jackson points out, derived partially from Garrison's fear of alienating his primary audience, which was predominately Black and radical.[31] Something else was at work as well. Decades after America's revolutionary generation sealed the republic's independence with their blood, the idea that freedom required violence permeated American political culture.[32] Infusing Garrison's thinking on many issues, it often led him, and other White abolitionists, to take a paradoxical position on violent slave resistance.

When some accused abolitionists of inciting Nat Turner's rebellion in Southampton, Virginia, in 1831, Garrison blamed slavery along with the United States' revolutionary tradition. "The slaves need no incentives at our hands," he elucidated in the *Liberator*. "They will find them in their stripes—in their emaciated bodies—in their ceaseless toil—in their ignorant minds—in every field, in every valley, on every hill-top and mountain, wherever you and your fathers have fought for liberty." They would also find reason to revolt in the speeches, writings, and celebrations of "Ye patriotic hypocrites." While there was never any justification for violence, Garrison thought Turner and his rebel army deserved no more censure than "our fathers in slaughtering the British."[33]

Several years later, Garrison expanded on his enigmatic view of violent slave resistance in a Fourth of July speech steeped in the language and symbols of American freedom. While imploring his "enslaved countrymen" not to imitate the violence of the nation's founders in the pursuit of freedom, he compared Nat Turner's insurrection to the American Revolution and thus undermined his pacifism. Garrison likened "the black patriot" to Washington, Lafayette, and Hancock for similarly embracing the Revolutionary War-era motto: "Resistance to tyrants is obedience to God." Then, after asserting that Turner wanted nothing more than the "revolutionaries of 1776," demanded of his audience, "are the people ready to say, no chains ought to be broken by the hand of violence, and no blood spilt in defence of inalienable human rights, in any quarter of the globe?" In claiming the right to fight for freedom, "the American people necessarily concede it to all mankind." If they chose to tyrannize any part of the human race, "they voluntarily seal their own death-warrant, and confess that they deserve to perish."[34]

Growing sympathy for the idea of revolutionary nationalism made it difficult for Garrison and other nonresistant abolitionists to repudiate slave violence entirely. Following Turner's insurrection, White abolitionists with long-held pacifist views decried the double standard of assailing rebel slaves for doing the same thing that the nation's founders had done a half-century earlier. At a Maine peace society meeting, Reverend Rufus Phineas Stebbins, the son of a Revolutionary War soldier, wondered why citizens praised the Founding Fathers for purchasing "our freedom by blood and violence," while Turner and his army "were treated as rebels and murderous assassins, and were ruthlessly hung, or shot like wolves," for attempting to purchase their own freedom.[35]

Rather than Turner's execution, it was the murder of Elijah Lovejoy by an anti-abolitionist mob in Alton, Ohio, that prompted Henry Clarke Wright to assert the "RIGHT OF SELF-DEFENCE" based on national precedent. After editorialists blasted Lovejoy for violently resisting his attackers, the renowned pacifist denounced as "Hypocrites!" all those who eulogized the nation's founders for fighting in self-defense while vilifying Lovejoy for doing the same thing. As to the charge that Lovejoy's actions would incite slave rebellion, Wright asserted that the language and symbols of American freedom were more likely to produce such an event. "Our 4th of July orations, our celebration of Independence, our ringing of bells and firing cannons, and shoutings in honor of the Revolution, our proclamations and messages of Governors and Presidents, extolling the blessings of liberty, and those who bled for liberty, all say to the slave, '*you have a right to butcher your masters to gain your freedom.*'"[36]

The revolutionary language of Black and White abolitionists testifies to an underlying tension that always existed within American abolitionism yet has rarely attracted historians' attention. Despite a genuine commitment to nonviolence, abolitionists of all types—Black and White, male and female, rich and poor—frequently defended, justified, and in some cases even encouraged violent slave resistance. The republic's revolutionary history drove this paradoxical position. Indeed, for slavery's opponents, the national precedent of using force to obtain freedom was impossible to ignore.

Even so, the abolitionist movement remained nonviolent—that is, until the passage of the Fugitive Slave Act. Included in the Compromise of 1850, which the US Congress adopted after the Mexican-American War to resolve the growing sectional conflict over slave expansion, the measure was the culmination of years of intense lobbying by southern politicians for increased federal protections for slavery. Despite a Constitutional provision requiring the arrest and rendition of escaped slaves, and a 1793 federal law reinforcing this provision, slave owners often struggled to regain possession of their absconded property. Especially after the emergence of the abolitionist movement and the Underground Railroad, the ability to recover escaped slaves became increasingly difficult.

The Fugitive Slave Act was one of the most important and controversial pieces of legislation ever passed by the American government. "It was meant to be a remedy and salve," writes historian Andrew Delbanco, "but it turned out to be an incendiary event that lit the fuse that led to Civil War."[37] The dispute over the law stemmed from its intent to do more than reinforce the Constitution's fugitive slave clause. In addition to ending jury trials for suspected fugitives, the edict put the cases in the hands of federal commissioners who would receive ten dollars for sentencing an accused fugitive to slavery but only five dollars if they declared the fugitive free. The law also imposed harsh penalties, including six-months' imprisonment and a $1,000 fine, on anyone who aided fugitive slaves or in any other way obstructed the law's enforcement. For abolitionists who long suspected slave owners exerted undue influence over the federal government, the law offered irrefutable proof of the Slave Power.

Even before the implementation of the new legislation, free Black leaders openly espoused violence in principle. At Cazenovia, New York, members of a "Fugitive Slave Law Convention" informed their enslaved brethren that while some abolitionists remained committed to nonresistance, they did not. As "fugitives from Slavery," they vowed to help those escaping from captivity by any means. Even in the case of a slave insurrection, "the great majority of the colored men of the North" would "be found by your side, with deep-stored and long-accumulated revenge in their hearts, and with death-dealing weapons in their hands." The nation's history justified the use of violence to achieve freedom. "If the American revolutionists had excuse for shedding but one drop of blood, then have the American slaves excuse for making blood to flow 'even unto the horse-bridles.'"[38]

Once the Fugitive Slave Act took effect, Black abolitionists across the North appropriated the language and symbols of American freedom in calling for violent opposition to the statute. At a meeting at Samuel Snowden's A.M.E. Church in Boston, Black speakers entreated audience members "to do and dare all, in imitation of Patrick Henry's immortal sentiment, *Liberty or Death!*"[39] In Philadelphia's Brick Wesley Church, "colored citizens" proclaimed their opposition to the Fugitive Slave Act based on the self-evident truths of the Declaration of Independence. As part of ten agreed-upon resolutions, attendees endorsed "to the full, the sentiment of the Revolutionary period of Virginia, and, should the awful alternative be presented to us, will act fully up to it—'Give me Liberty, or give me Death.'"[40] Two thousand "colored people" and a "sprinkling of white abolitionists" crowded into New York City's Zion Temple, where they encouraged fugitive slaves to adopt the principles of Patrick Henry, George Washington, and Madison Washington—the leader of the revolt aboard the slave ship *Creole*—and "resist unto death."[41] At a meeting in Providence, Rhode Island, formerly enslaved attendees resolved to remain free by adopting the "inestimable motto—Liberty or Death." Because some of them likely descended from the members of the 1st Rhode Island Regiment, one of the Continental Army's racially integrated combat units during the American Revolution, the *National Anti-Slavery Standard* cautioned anyone against trying to re-enslave them: "Revolutionary blood courses through their veins, and let the kidnapper beware how he stirs it."[42]

Black embracement of Patrick Henry's war cry extended as far west as Cincinnati, Ohio. In a letter sent to Frederick Douglass from the Queen

City, William P. Newman accused President Millard Fillmore and his "political followers" of doing the devil's work by agreeing to "that bill of abominations." As an escaped slave from Virginia, Newman swore that he would kill any man, including the president, who tried to return him or his brethren to bondage. "I am proud to say, that Patrick Henry's motto is mine—'Give me Liberty or give me Death.'" Newman censured anyone who opposed resisting the new law yet idolized "the spirits of '76 for their noble defence of their inalienable rights." By forcefully resisting the Fugitive Slave Act, he hoped to add his name to the list of revolutionary patriots the American people extolled every Fourth of July.[43]

As federal enforcement of the Fugitive Slave Act became widespread, White abolitionists joined their Black brethren by taking up Patrick Henry's mantra. In Marshfield, Massachusetts, "citizens" who refused to "repudiate the principles of the Declaration of Independence" promised to oppose the law's enforcement because of the self-evident idea "that all men are free and equal, and have an inalienable right to liberty." They encouraged fugitive slaves to adopt Patrick Henry's "glorious sentiment" and "use all the means that God will justify" to gain and protect their freedom. Should any fugitives die while fighting for freedom, their sacrifice would not be in vain. Their last words, "Give me liberty, or give me death!" would inspire others like them to claim their birthright.[44]

Even immigrant abolitionists embraced the revolutionary nationalism inspired by the Fugitive Slave Act. At a rally inside Boston's Tremont Temple, while discussing the ways for abolitionists to thwart slave catchers working throughout the city, a Scottish-born weaver named M'Clure rose to his feet. Having seized the audience's attention, he "denounced as a coward any man who would allow his arm to hang loosely by his side while a fugitive was being carried off." Though claiming to be a man of peace, the Scotsman shouted to the crowd, "Liberty or death—resistance to tyrants is obedience to God."[45]

Among those listening to M'Clure's outcry was Theodore Parker. A White Unitarian minister and Transcendentalist reformer, he kept a loaded pistol and "a drawn sword" in his house to safeguard the Black members of his congregation from arrest under the Fugitive Slave Act. This may have been peculiar behavior for a preacher, but it was expected from someone who descended from a long line of American patriots. Parker remarked of his ancestors, "My grandfather drew the first sword in the Revolution; my fathers fired the first shot; the blood which flowed there was kindred to this which courses in my veins to-day." In honor of his forebears, he hung two of his grandfather's guns on the wall of his home—one used in the Battle of Lexington and the other believed to be "the first gun taken in the Revolution." With "these symbols" offering inspiration, Parker vowed to protect and defend fugitive slaves "to the last."[46] He implored others to join him by resisting the new federal law, "peaceably if they can, forcibly if they must." By doing so, "We can make it like the Stamp Act of the last century, which Britain could not enforce against disobedient Americans."[47]

Parker's militancy was more than just talk. In the words of biographer Paul Teed, the abolitionist drew from a deep well of American memory "to establish an enclave of antislavery unity" in Boston that flourished for more than a decade. As a founder and leader of the 250-member Boston Vigilance Committee, "he presided over an organization that brought radical abolitionists, antislavery politicians, as well as the city's Black leaders together in mobilizing resistance to the hated Fugitive Slave Act."[48] The effects of Parker and his committee were profound. Besides protecting and defending the lives of countless Black people, they revitalized revolutionary American nationalism and in turn fueled an explosion of violent abolitionism in the decade before the Civil War.

Throughout the 1850s, a series of violent clashes among fugitive slaves, abolitionists, and slave catchers rocked the nation. In most of these high-profile cases, which historian Gordon Barker terms "fugitive slave dramas," combatants suffered little more than bloodied noses and bruised egos.[49] In at least two instances, however, radical abolitionists killed men who were trying to enforce the Fugitive Slave Act. The first, a bloody battle in September 1851 near the North–South border in Christiana, Pennsylvania, resulted in the liberation of four fugitive slaves and the

FIGURE 6.2. Theodore Parker (circa 1855).
Courtesy of the Boston Public Library.

death of their infamous owner, Edward Gorsuch. The second, which occurred three later, centered on the arrest of an enslaved Virginian named Anthony Burns in Boston. After federal agents apprehended the suspected fugitive, abolitionists stormed a federal courthouse, and in a riotous confrontation with authorities, stabbed US Marshal James Batchelder to death. In the end, the effort to thwart Burn's rendition failed, as federal troops returned the captive to Virginia and slavery.[50]

Abolitionists' reactions to the incidents in Christiana and Boston confirm their commitment to the republic's revolutionary tradition. Inside Columbus, Ohio's African Methodist Episcopalian Church, Black committee members celebrated the fugitive slaves who won their freedom at Christiana just days earlier. Having fled from a place "where they were unjustly claimed as property," these fugitives not only embraced the egalitarian ethos of the Declaration of Independence but adopted Patrick Henry's 'Give me *Liberty*, or give me *Death*,' as their motto." Following the example "of the Fathers of '76," they secured their freedom the only way they could—through force of arms; "therefore, we cannot only sympathize with, but must extol and commend our Pennsylvanian brethren, for resisting unto death rather than be returned to the Southern 'prison house of bondage.'"[51]

At an interracial gathering near the site of the "late Christiana tragedy," tempers flared when participants considered declaring the Fugitive Slave Act "*null and void*." In a "thrilling speech" supporting the measure, Samuel Aaron, a White "preacher, temperance lecturer, educator and ardent abolitionist," shocked many in attendance when imagining himself as a fugitive slave, he swore that if a slave hunter ever attempted to return him or his family to slavery, "I would blow out his brains, and so would you." After reviewing the recent events in Christiana, Aaron admitted his sympathy lie with the escaped slaves rather than Gorsuch because "Those colored men were only following the example of Washington and the American heroes of '76." If the federal government were to punish the Christiana rebels for treason, Aaron argued that it should also tear up the Declaration of Independence, "tumble and grind to powder every revolutionary monument," and forget that the name Washington ever existed.[52]

Not everyone in attendance approved of Aaron's position. Several White audience members dissented, insisting that it was God's law to love one's enemies and "do good to those who hurt you." It was a polite and respectful rebuttal rooted in Christian theology, yet it compelled Robert Purvis, one of the movement's most respected Black leaders, who "had not designed to speak," to comment. In a dramatic and intentional display of interracial solidarity, the AASS cofounder rose from his seat and "in the name of the colored people" thanked Aaron for his remarks. At Christiana, Purvis rejoiced, "the first battle of liberty had been fought!" More were sure to follow.[53]

As news of Christiana spread nationwide, Frederick Douglass's mailbox filled with letters applauding the revolutionary spirit of the Christiana rebels. In this unsolicited correspondence, which the editor promptly published in his self-titled weekly, abolitionists of all stripes showed their devotion to the United States' revolutionary tradition as well as the nation itself. In the process, they encouraged Douglass and his readers to do the same.

White working-class men, who comprised many of Douglass's subscribers, made their opinions public. Elijah McKinney Glen, a middle-aged farmer and Underground Railroad operative, applauded the "conduct of the negroes" in Christiana because the blood they spilled was an investment in freedom. He declared, "I hold that the right of Revolution belongs to every man, *to black, as well as white*, that these men had as perfect a right to fight for their liberty as our revolutionary fathers did for theirs." Glen urged Douglass to discover the names of any of the freedom fighters who may have fallen in the battle, "and give them to the world, that they may descend to posterity with the names of Warren, and the brave patriots who fell on Bunker Hill."[54]

Albro S. Brown, a New York wagonmaker, was outraged. Whenever fugitive slaves like those who had taken a stand at Christiana displayed "the patriotism and bravery that inspired the souls of our Revolutionary Fathers, in their struggle for freedom, and like them," dispatched their oppressors, cries of "blood, treason, and murder" echoed nationwide. Yet slave owners and officials had no right to hunt down men who adopted and acted "out the sentiments of Patrick Henry," who proclaimed, "give me liberty, or give me death." For acting in self-defense and leaving the slave hunter Gorsuch dead, the Christiana rebels would likely swing from the gallows. This, Brown closed, was what constituted "the patriotism, the philanthropy and justice of our nation, at the middle of the nineteenth century."[55]

Out of a fear of reprisals, the authors of the letters sent to Douglass sometimes used pseudonyms to protect their identities. Hannibal, a pen name for the ancient African general, encouraged enslaved people to emulate the violent actions of the Christiana rebels and free themselves from captivity. "It appears to me, that it is high time they should come to an understanding and realization that the self-evident truths of the declaration of Independence of 1776, 'That all men are created equal,' having 'certain unalienable rights, among which are life, LIBERTY, and the pursuit of happiness'—are as applicable to themselves as to others." Like the Founding Fathers, the motto of enslaved Americans should be, "liberty or death."[56]

"SANS NOM" offered more than encouragement. He proposed the creation of a "Fugitives' Arms Fund" to supply guns and knives to escaped slaves. Armed with these weapons, they "would soon make Gorsuch cases so plentiful as to cause the profession of men-hunter to" vanish. Fully aware that the establishment of such a fund would offend those who did not adopt Patrick Henry's motto as their own, SANS NOM recalled that according to the Declaration of Independence, "*All men* have '*certain inalienable rights,*'" including liberty. Accordingly, every man was entitled to fight for their freedom; "therefore, let him be provided with efficient arms."[57]

Though the individuals who wrote to Douglass in support of the Christiana rebels did not know it at the time, the editor had put his own life and liberty in jeopardy by helping several of the rebel leaders avoid arrest. The three men arrived in Rochester by train two days after the incident, and Douglass sheltered them in his home until securing them safe passage out of the country. Before embarking on a steamship to Toronto, Canada, one of the fugitives, William Parker, gifted Douglass the revolver used to kill Gorsuch. It was an extraordinary moment according to Underground Railroad historian Fergus Bordewich: "The gun was a symbol, both men knew, that the war against slavery had taken a new and deadly turn, and that more, perhaps much more, violence lay ahead."[58]

Julia Griffiths, Douglass's "faithful friend," also helped the Christiana rebels get to Canada.[59] Subsequently, she became one of the first writers in the United States to draw a direct parallel between the Battle of Christiana and the American Revolution. In Douglass's paper, she rejected the argument that the abolitionists and fugitives who fought the slave catchers at Christiana were "traitors" as some had suggested. Instead, she considered them "heroes" for fighting their tyrannical oppressors "and having for their watchword, 'Liberty or Death.'"[60]

Following the first anniversary of the Battle of Christiana, Griffiths amplified abolitionists' growing commitment to revolutionary nationalism in *Autographs for Freedom*, an anthology of poems, letters, essays, and short stories from the movement's most respected voices. The compilation included a piece by George W. Perkins that asked, "Can slaves rightfully resist and fight?" Looking back to the previous century, the Connecticut preacher reasoned, "*If* it was right in 1776 to resist, fight, and kill, to secure liberty,—it is right to do the same in 1852." Perkins swore that he did not endorse violent slave resistance, yet he believed that if three million colonists were justified in waging a bloody war to vindicate their rights in the eighteenth century, then so were "three millions of slaves" in the nineteenth century—"and any black Washington who shall lead his countrymen to victory and liberty, even through carnage, will merit our veneration."[61]

Before abolitionists could fully understand the significance of Christiana, their attention turned to Boston where Anthony Burns's arrest and rendition resulted in a bloody riot that took the life of a federal marshal trying to enforce the Fugitive Slave Act. In the aftermath of this fatal affair, radical abolitionists made no apologies for the violence used in the attempt to preserve Burns's freedom. To the contrary, drawing from the nation's revolutionary tradition, they defended the lethal actions taken in Boston on Burns's behalf—and they vowed to prevent other fugitive slave renditions from taking place.

For some, the use of violence was a question of natural law. A group of "colored men" in Philadelphia declared that following Burns's re-enslavement they no longer owed any allegiance to the American government's proslavery edicts. "We hereby declare ourselves absolved from all obligations to obey its slaveholding behests, and fall back upon our natural rights—that we adopt and advise all oppressed to adopt the motto, 'Liberty or Death,' nor will we allow any fellow beings to be enslaved if we can prevent it." Resistance to slave hunters was "obedience to God"; thus, they pledged "to resist all such laws by such means as we shall deem right and expedient."[62]

For others, like William J. Watkins, the use of violence was a matter of masculinity.[63] The Black educator and newspaper editor appreciated abolitionists' adoption of Patrick Henry's mantra as their own but worried that those "manly words" would not be fully executed. "If we wish our enemies to respect us," he explained, "we must develop our manhood." Foreshadowing the immortal lines of Claude McKay's early twentieth century anti-lynching poem, "If We Must Die," Watkins wished that with God-given natural rights, African Americans would "not ingloriously retreat from the land in which our fathers' bones lie buried, but will, if need be, die, though we die struggling to be free."[64]

An anonymous contributor to Frederick Douglass's newspaper, who lacked Watkins's literary style, agreed. He argued, "*A good revolver, a steady hand, and a determination to shoot down any man attempting to kidnap*" was the only remedy for the Fugitive Slave Act. To stop the act's enforcement, "every colored man" needed to be willing to die rather than live another day without freedom for himself or his brethren. Like the close of the previous century, the time for cowardice had passed. "Oh! That we had a little more of the manly indifference to death, which characterized the Heroes of the American Revolution."[65]

As far as Charlotte Forten was concerned, the parallels between Burns's rendition and the American Revolution derived from the Boston backdrop more than any gendered assertions of masculinity. The Black teenager conveyed the dismay free African Americans felt as they followed Burns's arrest and re-enslavement. "Our worst fears are realized," she began in her journal. "The decision was against poor Burns, and he has been sent back to a bondage worse, a thousand times worse than death." Just days earlier, his rescue proved impossible because of the presence of soldiers who with fixed bayonets and loaded cannons did the Slave Power's bidding. It was a disgraceful scene, especially since it occurred "on the very soil where the revolution of 1776 began; in sight of the battlefield, where thousands of brave men fought and died in opposing British tyranny, which was nothing compared with the American oppression of today." Though abolitionists had failed in their effort to free Burns by force of arms, Forten concluded, "all honor should be given to those who bravely made the attempt."[66]

Like Forten, the location of Burns's rendition infused Frederick Douglass's response to the incident. "A Kidnapper has been shot dead, while attempting to execute the fugitive Slave Bill in Boston," an editorial began. "The streets of Boston in sight of Bunker Hill Monument, have been stained with the warm blood of a man in the act of perpetrating the most atrocious robbery which one man can possibly commit upon another." The killing of the federal marshal was justified, Douglass argued, because that man "took upon himself the revolting business of a kidnapper." That most Americans disagreed was an affront to the nation's ideals.[67]

Indeed, Douglass considered the public condemnation of Burns's rescuers for resorting to violence an insult to the nation and its founders. "It was glorious for Patrick Henry to say, '*Give me liberty or give me death!*' It was glorious for Americans to drench the soil, and crimson the seal with blood, *to escape the payment of a threepenny tax upon tea.*" But it was a crime to shoot a slave hunter to save a Black man from a bondage, which in Jefferson's words, "is worse than ages of that which our fathers rose in rebellion to oppose." Until the American people were willing to forfeit their own right to self-defense and cease "to glory in the deeds of Hancock, Adams, and Warren—and cease to look with pride and patriotic admiration upon the somber pile at Bunker Hill," Douglass deemed it hypocritical to "brand as *murderers*" those who killed the "blood-hound" who sought to return Burns to slavery.[68]

On this point, William Lloyd Garrison was in full agreement with his former protégé. In Boston's Melodeon Temple, he asserted that fighting for freedom was the birthright of every American. If Burns

FIGURE 6.3. Charlotte Forten Grimké (circa 1870).
Courtesy of the New York Public Library.

were to drive a knife into the heart of anyone who claimed him as his property, "he would be doing just such an act as our revolutionary fathers committed." The Declaration of Independence not only outlawed tyranny but pronounced a death sentence against all tyrants. Americans honored the memories of the Founding Fathers for taking up arms and killing their oppressors; therefore, "If the millions whom this nation consigns to chains shall imitate their example, shall they not be equally justified?" As for the killing of a US marshal, Garrison was remorseless. He insisted that Burns and the abolitionists who came to his defense were just as patriotic "as were those who threw tea into Boston harbor, or fought for freedom on Bunker Hill."[69]

Despite having forcefully defended those who violently resisted the Fugitive Slave Act, Garrison was not finished. A month later, while standing underneath an inverted American flag at a Fourth of July meeting in Framingham, Massachusetts, he bewailed the Slave Power's grip over the republic. Where the antislavery sentiments of George Washington, Thomas Jefferson, and Patrick Henry once brought commendation and admiration, they now brought criticism and abuse. The disrespect toward the nation's revolutionary history and tradition reached the US Senate, where politicians derided the Declaration of Independence "as a tissue of lies and absurdities!!!" To prove his hatred of the nation's proslavery stance, Garrison produced a copy of the Fugitive Slave Act and the judge's ruling, which he promptly set on fire. Then, holding a copy of the US Constitution, "he branded it as the source and parent of all the other atrocities,—'a covenant with death, and an agreement with hell,'—and consumed it to ashes on the spot."[70]

The speech is remarkable for more than its fiery conclusion. Rather than inspiring and uplifting, Garrison was dark and depressing. "There was a sorrowful tone in the editor's oratory that most people had never heard before," writes biographer Henry Mayer. "He spoke gloomily of the evil in the world, of a Europe beset by reaction and an America compromised by slavery and deceived by the empty form of a republic."[71] Even so, Garrison had not lost faith in the nation entirely. Though finished with the Constitution, he still revered the Declaration of Independence, considering its creation "the greatest political event in the annals of time."[72]

As abolitionists' reactions to the deadly incidents at Christiana and Boston reveal, the Fugitive Slave Act forced a reconsideration of the tactics needed to end slavery. Where the movement long advocated nonresistance, it now embraced force and even violence. In justifying the shift in philosophy to themselves and others, abolitionists repeatedly pointed to the principles and precedent of the American Revolution. As citizens of a nation born in rebellion, they considered it not only their right but their duty to resist tyranny in all its forms, including the Fugitive Slave Act.

FIGURE 6.4. William Lloyd Garrison (circa 1870). Courtesy of the Library of Congress.

At the twenty-fifth meeting of the Massachusetts Anti-Slavery Society in Boston, the chief auxiliary of the AASS, abolitionists revealed just how widespread support for revolutionary violence had become among them. On the first night of the assembly, Henry Clarke Wright proposed a series of resolutions asserting the revolutionary right of enslaved people to fight for their freedom. "I believe that resistance to tyrants is obedience to God," the erstwhile pacifist explained, "and the man who believes in fighting at all, is a traitor to his principles if he does not assert the right of the American slave to armed resistance." Should anyone listening to Wright's words misunderstand, he added as a point of clarification that moving forward, "non-resistance is not the doctrine of the Abolitionists generally, nor of the disunionists generally."[73]

Some thought Wright went too far. James Buffum, a wealthy Massachusetts financier and philanthropist, dissented by reading the AASS's Declaration of Sentiments, which two decades earlier recorded the group's opposition to "the use of violence, of arms and bloodshed" in the struggle against slavery.[74] The Unitarian preacher and Transcendentalist poet David Atwood Wasson also opposed the resolution. Rather than abandon his commitment to nonviolence, he preferred enslaved people and their allies continue to let the political process play out, regardless of how long it took. He explained, "If emancipation can be attained without blood by waiting, I am willing to wait twenty-five years, if necessary, and the negroes ought to be willing to wait" as well.[75]

Wright's supporters pushed back, citing the nation's revolutionary tradition as evidence of the righteousness of violent slave resistance. "We are taking the American people on their own ground, and judging of them by their own standard," William Lloyd Garrison declared. "We have a right to demand that a nation shall act in consistency with that which it avows to be its rule of faith and practice." While some might wait a quarter-century to avoid a slave insurrection, the human soul continually cried out, "Give me liberty, or give me death." An American bondman was duty bound to pursue freedom, "and he must seek it in a manner accordant with his own ideas of right, deciding that point for himself." Abbey Kelley Foster stressed that the blood of enslaved people already flowed across the South. In that part of the country, "all the evils of war, violations of life, liberty, property, and every other right, are *now going on*, and *increasing*." With such blatant violations of national principles and ideals, all that remained to be decided was whether the blood of slave owners would spill as well. "Certainly every friend of liberty here would rejoice to hear to-night that the slaves of Louisiana or of Tennessee had risen against their masters." Wendell Phillips insisted that "If a negro kills his master to-night," his name deserved mentioning alongside those of Joseph Warren and John Hancock. Patriotic Americans acknowledged "that every slave has a right to seize his liberty on the spot."[76]

When given the chance to defend the resolutions, Wright drew upon the idea of "virtuous revolutionary resistance," which had once inspired only the most radical abolitionists.[77] He avowed, "The slaves of George Washington had as good a right to cut their master's throat as he had to throw his cannon ball and bombshells from Dorchester Heights upon the British in Boston harbor." Though generations had passed, the principles of the American Revolution persisted; therefore, it was both "the right and duty" of enslaved people "to kill their masters as really as it was of our fathers to kill their oppressor at Bunker Hill and Yorktown." As for the citizens who already enjoyed freedom, they should "encourage and assist the slaves to resist, by arms, those who enslave them."[78]

After two days of spirited debate, Wright won the day. Delegates unanimously adopted his resolutions, two of which proved the movement's radicalization. The first proclaimed that whenever enslaved people tried to win their freedom, "whether by flight or insurrection, our sympathies are, and ever must be, with him, and against his oppressor; and we pledge ourselves that we will do all in our power which we, as individuals, deem right and most fitting to aid the enslaved in their struggle for liberty." The second revealed that the justification for the revised position lie in the nation's revolutionary heritage. It asserted, "those who hold the right of armed resistance to oppression, and glorify their Revolutionary sires for their bloody conflict with British tyrants, are recreant to their own principles if they do not recognize this right on the part of the slaves against their tyrant masters, and assist them to achieve their complete enfranchisement."[79]

It was an extraordinary moment. While nonresistance and moral suasion had dominated the abolitionist movement since the 1830s, slavery's growth and expansion called these tactics into question. The federal government's implementation of the Fugitive Slave Act proved a turning point, as it convinced abolitionists that the time for peace had passed. In response to this and other patently proslavery measures in the 1850s, they encouraged and on occasion even enacted forceful and violent resistance to slavery. Still, the institution endured.

In a nation planted in the soil of freedom and watered with revolution, a destructive war over slavery seemed inevitable. Among those who subscribed to this view was John Brown, an abolitionist known for leading Free State forces into battle against their Slave State adversaries in Bloody Kansas. Long inspired by the language and symbols of American freedom, Brown believed it was his patriotic duty to fight, and if necessary, die for the cause of freedom. Frustrated by the failure of the United States to secure the principles of the Declaration of Independence for all people, he and a small band of followers set out in the fall of 1859 to destroy slavery and save the republic by launching a second and more complete American Revolution.

7

REVOLUTIONARIES

John Brown was for most of his life a pacifist. He had seen the War of 1812 on the northern frontier in his youth, and the experience made him averse to "military affairs." As a young adult, he avoided serving in the armed forces by various methods. Refusing to dress, drill, or train for combat, he paid fines and generally "got along like a Quaker" until middle age disqualified him from military service altogether. His commitment to nonviolence endured for three decades until slavery's survival set him on a different path.[1]

By the late 1840s, Brown had begun developing a revolutionary plan to destroy slavery, which he shared with a small group of Black friends and associates. While working as a wool merchant in Springfield, Massachusetts, he invited Thomas Thomas, a friend and coworker, to join his "enterprise for the liberation of the slaves," which the former bondman promptly accepted.[2] The following year, after consulting with Henry Highland Garnet and Martin Delany, Brown welcomed Frederick Douglass into his Springfield, Massachusetts, home. Pointing to the Appalachian Mountains on a map of the United States, Brown informed Douglass of his intention to station dozens of armed men along the base of the mountains, where they would "run off the slaves in large numbers." When Douglass expressed concerns over the plan, Brown responded that "Slavery was a state of war, and the slave had a right to anything necessary to his freedom."[3]

Brown further demonstrated his martial turn months later during a trip to Europe. He had crossed the Atlantic Ocean to find a market for his company's wool, but there was an ulterior motive as well. Years later, an associate of Brown's recalled of a conversation he had with Brown about the European excursion, "He then told me that he had kept the contest against slavery in mind while traveling on the continent, and had made an especial study of the European armies and battle-fields." Brown toured places where Napoleon had fought and examined first-hand the maneuvers of Austrian and French troops, both of which left a strong impression.[4]

Upon returning to America, Brown's focus turned from plotting's slavery's destruction to the more practical matter of protecting his Black friends and neighbors from arrest under the Fugitive Slave Act. In Springfield, where resistance to the new legislation had already begun, Black residents embraced Brown's proposal to create a paramilitary force christened the "Springfield Branch of the United States League of Gileadites."[5] Named after the biblical Israelites, who though greatly outnumbered at Mount Gilead managed to vanquish their Midianite oppressors, the group vowed to resist slave catchers with force of arms and kill any "traitors" who betrayed the cause.[6]

The Gileadites espoused an American identity premised on the idea of racial and gender equality. An "AGREEMENT" and nine Resolutions written by Brown and signed by forty-four Black men and women in Springfield in January 1851 revealed the group's commitment to forming an interracial band of militants, "whether male or female," who endeavored to secure the "inalienable rights" of all people. "As citizens of the United States of America," they vowed, "*we will ever be true to the flag of our beloved country, always acting under it.*" The patriotic declaration was extraordinary, especially when considering its author would become the first person executed for treason in the history of the United States.[7]

Like other clandestine organizations that emerged across the North in response to the Fugitive Slave Act, little evidence of the Gileadites' actions survives. What is known is that the group carried out their mission, even after Brown left Massachusetts for the Kansas Territory. In one instance, a group of as many as fifteen Gileadites, "all armed to the teeth and swearing vengeance upon the heads of any who should attempt to take them," forced several slave catchers to abandon their mission and seek refuge elsewhere. From that point forward, "No fugitive slave was ever afterward disturbed at Springfield."[8]

The militancy of John Brown and the Gileadites is easy to explain. As proud patriots of the United States, they considered it their duty as citizens to oppose slavery and its evils, including the Fugitive Slave Act. To rid the republic of slavery, they adopted the ideas and tactics of its founders. By continuing the legacy of these iconic revolutionaries, they endeavored to further the project of building a nation in which all people were free and equal.

Where historians once argued that John Brown was a madman who manipulated others into joining his extreme effort to oppose slavery, the evidence proves otherwise. Instead of an outlier, his radicalization was part and parcel of the mid-century transformation of the abolitionist movement in response to the federal government's proslavery policies. The actions of Brown and his allies, which culminated in a violent assault on the federal arsenal at Harpers Ferry, Virginia (now West Virginia), in October 1859, reveal the powerful influence of the language and symbols of American freedom on slavery's fiercest opponents on the eve of the Civil War. Inspired by a love of country and a hatred of tyranny and oppression, Brown and his allies took up the mantle of revolutionary nationalism and launched a violent insurrection to both destroy slavery and redeem the republic.

————

John Brown understood the power of symbols. This in part explains his motivation for traveling with Thomas Thomas to the studio of the Black portraitist Augustus Washington in Hartford, Connecticut, in the mid-1840s.[9] During the visit, Brown sat for three glass-plated photographs, or daguerreotypes as they were called, of which two survive.[10] The first reveals a fit and clean-shaven man with short brown hair in the prime of his life. Crossed arms and a half-smile just below two opaque grey eyes suggest a calm and quiet confidence. The second offers a far more serious subject staring directly into the camera. With his right hand raised slightly above his shoulder, Brown takes an oath of fidelity to the red, white, and blue flag that his left hand holds firmly at his waist. Though the primitive coloring process makes it difficult to determine, the standard is not the American flag. As no copies of the third daguerreotype survive, a description by one of Brown's earliest biographers suffices. The image shows Brown standing with a hand on the shoulder of "a colored man, presumably Thomas," who holds "a small banneret, lettered 'S.P.W.'" an abbreviation for "Subterranean Pass Way," the name of Brown's secret plan to spirit enslaved people to freedom along the Appalachian Mountains. The flag is the same one displayed by Brown in the second photograph.[11]

The decision to include the S.P.W. flag in the two daguerreotypes—rather than the Stars and Stripes—is worth brief consideration. While the choice of standards might indicate Brown's disillusionment with, or even contempt of, the United States, the evidence proves otherwise. Indeed, the actions he took to oppose slavery in the last years of his life proved his devotion to the American nation and its ideals as articulated in the Declaration of Independence.

A decade after sitting down in Washington's studio, Brown's career as an American revolutionary advanced quickly. In response to the Kansas and Nebraska Act, which allowed slavery in the two new territories based on the idea of popular sovereignty, he relocated to the disputed area. Organizing five of his sons and their associates into a "Liberty Guard," the group spent three years fighting proslavery settlers over the issue of slave expansion.[12] Of the many conflicts Brown's band endured, none proved their mettle more than the Pottawatomie Massacre. The incident was a direct response to two events that took place within a twenty-four-hour period and more than one thousand miles apart: first, the sacking of the antislavery community in Lawrence, Kansas, by hundreds of proslavery ruffians; and second, the brutal assault on the abolitionist US Senator Charles Sumner of Massachusetts in the US Senate by South Carolina congressman Preston Brooks. To avenge these

FIGURE 7.1. *John Brown*, daguerreotype by Augustus Washington (circa 1846–1847). Courtesy of the National Portrait Gallery, Smithsonian Institution.

humiliating abolitionist defeats, Brown and his guardsmen murdered five proslavery men near Pottawatomie Creek with broadswords.[13]

While some abolitionists were appalled with the Liberty Guard's violent actions, others thought they recalled the sacrifices of the nation's founders. An anonymous "friend," who traveled to Kansas to determine "the true condition of the territory," spent a few hours with the guardsmen after the killings and came away impressed. "Until now, I never could realize the forbearance, patience, and courage of the heroes of the American revolution," he affirmed. "The free-state people of Kansas will equal those of that revolution, both men and women." Eager to spend their lives for freedom, "Their motto is, 'Liberty or death.'"[14]

James Redpath also met Brown in Kansas shortly after the slayings. When many were beginning to question Brown's sanity, the British émigré journalist did not. He encouraged those seeking an explanation for Brown's violent actions to look no further than the nation's revolutionary tradition. "He admired Nat Turner, the negro patriot, equally with George Washington, the white American deliverer," Redpath wrote of Brown. "He could not see that it was heroic to fight against a petty tax on tea, and war seven years long for a political principle; yet wrong to restore, by force of arms, to an outraged race, the rights with which their Maker had endowed them, but of which the South, for two centuries, had robbed them." After his brief visit with Brown, Redpath was sure he had met "the predestined leader of the second and the holier American Revolution."[15]

Following the Pottawatomie Massacre, Brown went on the lam. To avoid arrest, he fled Kansas and returned to the North where he promoted his plan to destroy slavery, which now included an armed assault on the federal arsenal at Harpers Ferry in western Virginia. At a private gathering in Medford, Massachusetts, Brown explained his revolutionary ideology to some of New England's most prominent people, including Massachusetts Governor John Andrews, Ralph Waldo Emerson, and Henry David Thoreau, in chilling terms: "I consider the Golden Rule and the Declaration of Independence one and inseparable," Brown announced, "and it is better that a whole generation of men, women, and children should be swept away than that this crime of slavery should exist one day longer." He offered a similar statement while visiting with Judge Thomas Russell in Boston, avowing, "It would be better that a whole generation should perish from the earth than that one truth in the Sermon on the Mount or the Declaration of Independence should be forgotten among men."[16]

Franklin Sanborn agreed. The grandson of a Revolutionary War soldier, the Harvard-educated schoolteacher first met Brown in January 1857 and instantly became an admirer. In a letter to fellow abolitionist Thomas Wentworth Higginson, Sanborn defended Brown's sanity and supported his plan "to overthrow slavery in a large part of the country." Convinced of the failure of the "Union" of northern and southern states, Sanborn suspected that a second and more complete American Revolution was afoot. "Treason will not be treason much longer, but patriotism."[17]

Sanborn's thoughts are revealing. By interpreting Brown's thoughts and actions in the context of heroic patriotic sacrifice, they confirm the findings of biographer Evan Carton, who sees Brown as a national martyr. "If American patriotism is defined as unqualified commitment to the nation's founding religious and political ideas—a commitment both to live by them and to die for them," Carton concludes, "then Brown may count as one of America's first patriots, though he was not born until 1800 and was hanged for treason in 1859."[18]

Of course, patriotism did not ensure support. When Brown failed to receive significant financial assistance from New England's Brahmins, he appealed to their sense of both regional and national pride. In a document entitled "Old Brown's Farewell. To the Plymouth Rocks, Bunker Hill Monuments, Charter Oaks, and Uncle Tom's Cabin," which detailed his failure to secure arms and other materiel for his devoted group of Kansas "minutemen," Brown vented his frustration. He explained that in addition to exhausting his own personal resources, he had endured cold, hunger, illness, and imprisonment "in order to sustain a cause which every citizen of this 'glorious Republic' is under equal moral obligation to do, and for the neglect of which he will be held accountable by God." Given the resources and power of New England's population—many of whom descended from the region's first colonists and later patriots—Brown found his inability to secure "even the necessary supplies of the common soldier" reprehensible.[19]

Seemingly forsaken by his compatriots, Brown went to British Canada, where he expected to find a more receptive audience among Her Majesty's rising population of fugitive slaves. In 1850, approximately 75,000 African Americans resided in the imperial outpost, and as many as half of them had fled from enslavement in the southern United States. More than just shelters and sanctuaries for passengers on the Underground Railroad, the settlements along the Canadian border where these Black people resided, flourished. Indeed, despite the racism that afflicted the British territory, Black churches, schools, farms, and businesses thrived in towns like St. Catharines and Chatham.[20]

Like most Americans opposed to slavery, Brown held Canada in high regard. As part of the British Empire, the province outlawed slavery in 1834. It also, since even before that time, welcomed fugitive slaves from the United States and refused to extradite them south of the border. Even so, Brown never expressed a preference for Canada, or any other foreign nation for that matter, over his homeland. Even when helping fugitive slaves escape to Canada, Brown's primary objective was always to spread freedom throughout the United States. "His purpose was not to populate a Queen's colony," Redpath recorded, "but to save a Republic."[21]

By April 1858, Brown and at least a dozen close associates had arrived in Canada seeking recruits for their interracial revolutionary army. At St. Catharines, on the opposite side of the Niagara River from Buffalo, New York, Brown met with leaders of the city's Black community. The group included Harriet Tubman, the formerly enslaved Underground Railroad conductor, who had moved to the city with her family following the passage of the Fugitive Slave Act.[22] From St. Catharines, Brown and his band ventured more than one hundred miles west to Chatham, Canada's most famous Underground Railroad terminus. While staying at the homes of several prominent Black people, Brown, with Martin Delany's assistance, called for a clandestine convention to initiate his plan to destroy slavery.[23]

The convention occurred on Saturday, May 8, and Monday, May 10. While most of the meetings took place in Chatham's First Baptist Church on King Street, others transpired at a local schoolhouse or nearby fire station. On the first day, the twelve White men and thirty-four Black men in attendance began by electing the church's minister, William Charles Monroe, the convention's President, and one of Brown's close associates, John Henri Kagi, its secretary. Attention then turned to the ratification of a "Provisional Constitution and Ordinances for the people of the United States," which Brown had drafted several months earlier while staying at Frederick Douglass's Rochester home. After a brief but spirited debate, convention delegates unanimously adopted the document and swore an oath to uphold it.[24]

Establishing a plan for an American government that would ostensibly replace the one centered in Washington, DC, the Provisional Constitution was a truly revolutionary text.[25] Consisting of a Preamble and forty-eight Articles, it follows the outline and structure of the US Constitution. It also copies some of its predecessor's elemental precepts, such as the idea of three separate and equal branches of government: legislative, executive, and judicial. The new charter also called for a president and vice president. That is where the similarities end. Among the many peculiarities of the new constitution were the encouragement of all persons "of sound mind" to openly carry arms and a prohibition on profanity, indecent exposure, and intoxication. "Unlawful intercourse of the sexes" was also declared unconstitutional.[26]

The most striking difference between Brown's constitution and the one penned in Philadelphia the previous century was the outlawing of both slavery and White supremacy. The Provisional Constitution asserted in its preamble that slavery in the United States was a "barbarous, unprovoked, and unjustifiable war of one portion of its citizens upon another portion." It existed and endured "in utter disregard and violation of those eternal and self-evident truths set forth in our Declaration of Independence." In an obvious allusion to the Dred Scott decision, the preamble concluded, "Therefore We, *citizens of the United States, and the Oppressed People, who, by a recent decision of the Supreme Court are declared to have no rights which the White Man is bound to respect; ordain and establish ourselves, the following* PROVISIONAL CONSTITUTION *and* ORDINANCES, *the better to protect our Persons, Property, Lives, and Liberties; and to govern our actions.*"[27]

When word of Brown's Provisional Constitution reached the United States, even some of his strongest supporters were critical. Franklin Sanborn thought it "desperate in character, wholly inadequate in its provision of means, and of most uncertain result." Still, he respected Brown's effort to "restore our slave-cursed republic to the principles of the Declaration of Independence."[28] Frederick Douglass was equally critical, considering the constitution impractical and "something of a bore." His refusal to attend the proceedings at Chatham despite several invitations to do so offers additional evidence of his disapproval.[29] Decades later, biographer Oswald Garrison Villard, William Lloyd Garrison's grandson, spoke for many of Brown's friends and allies when writing that it was best "not to attempt to analyze the Chatham Constitution, but to admire its wording and its composition, and lay it aside as a temporary aberration of a mind that in its other manifestations defies successful classification as unhinged or altogether unbalanced."[30]

Only in the twenty-first century have scholars reconsidered the Chatham constitution, reimagining it primarily as a symbol. In *Patriotic Treason: John Brown and the Soul of America*, Evan Carton celebrates the constitution for combining "a practical and symbolic dimension." Attacking "both the institutional and attitudinal expression of prejudice and inequality," it was a "blueprint for a second American Revolution and a new American nation that would fulfill the betrayed promise of the old."[31] David Reynolds, the author of *John Brown, Abolitionist,* reaches a similar conclusion regarding the government suggested in the Provisional Constitution. "Taken symbolically," he contends, "the government had great significance." It imagined a society in which all people were equal; at the same time, it was entirely national in sentiment. Brown "saw it as a natural fulfillment of the ideal of equality announced in the Declaration of Independence. It was what the American government really *was*, underneath the racism and corruption that currently spoiled it."[32]

These reinterpretations of Brown's Provisional Constitution rely in large part on a newfound appreciation of Article 46. It began, "The foregoing Articles shall not be construed so as in any way to encourage the overthrow of any State Government of the United States: and look to no dissolution of the Union, but simply to Amendment and Repeal." The final sentence was equally explicit: "our flag shall be the same that our Fathers fought under in the Revolution."[33]

Of the forty-eight articles in Brown's proposed charter, Article 46 was the only one the convention delegates considered rejecting. On the event's first day, George J. Reynolds, an escaped slave and accomplished Underground Railroad operative, offered a motion to strike the Article from the document.[34] He left no record of his motivation for doing so; nevertheless, it is easy to imagine why. In a revolutionary new constitution that outlawed both slavery and White supremacy, a vow to preserve a racist government and its flag made little sense.

Despite the rationale, Reynolds's motion failed. Immediately after hearing the proposal to "strike out" Article 46, Martin Delany, William Charles Munroe, and Thomas Kinnard, "all colored," strenuously objected. John Brown, his son Owen, and several other White delegates also opposed the measure. In the end, every delegate at the Chatham Convention except Reynolds voted to keep the pledge to the United States and its flag in the new constitution.[35]

While the convention debate over Article 46 is familiar to scholars, a little-known, behind-the-scenes exchange is even more revealing. According to James Monroe Jones, a respected Black gunsmith, engraver, and justice of the peace, convention delegates spent evenings inside his Chatham gun shop discussing pressing issues. On one occasion, the question arose concerning the use of a flag when carrying out Brown's revolutionary plan. Some of the Black delegates, recalling years spent in captivity, declared they would never fight "under the hated 'Stars and Stripes,' for they carried their emblem on their backs." In response, "Brown said the old flag was good enough for him; under it, freedom had been won from the tyrants of the old world, for white men; now he intended to make it do duty for black men. He declared emphatically that he would not give up the Stars and Stripes." According to Jones, "That settled the question."[36]

Back at the convention, Brown offered additional evidence of his love of country. When some delegates suggested he delay his uprising until the United States became involved in a foreign conflict—which would increase the uprising's chances of success—Brown took offense. Rising from his seat, he retorted: "Mr. Chairman, I am no traitor; I would be the last one to take advantage of my country in the face of a foreign foe." Jones thought the response proved Brown's patriotism: "In his conversation during his stay here, he appeared intensely American. He never for a moment thought of fighting the United States, as such, but simply the defenders of slavery in the States." Brown's only interest was cutting the "ulcer" of slavery "from the body politic."[37]

Having successfully secured support for his Provisional Constitution, Brown returned to Kansas to set his plan into motion; however, fate intervened yet again. In December 1858, an enslaved Missourian named Jim Daniels, whose family was being sold to a slave owner in Texas, "begged" the now fully bearded and gray-haired Brown for assistance. Days later, Brown and twenty of his followers flew across the Kansas–Missouri border under the dark of night. Speeding across farms along the Little Osage River, they freed a total of eleven enslaved people, including Daniels, and killed a local slave owner "who fought against the liberation." Following the raid, Brown and his confederates conducted the fugitives hundreds of miles through Kansas, Nebraska, Iowa, Illinois, and Michigan, until eventually crossing into Canada.[38]

Before reentering Canada, Brown shared his thoughts on the history of American slavery with a Kansas correspondent of the *New York Tribune*, William Addison Phillips. The Scottish-born writer recalled of the conversation, "He said the founders of the Republic were all opposed to slavery, and that the whole spirit and genius of the American Constitution antagonized it, and contemplated its early overthrow." Despite this, slavery endured and expanded, while the government fell under the influence of slave profiteers. "Then began an era of political compromises, and men full of professions of love of country were willing, for peace, to sacrifice everything for which the Republic was founded." Because of this, Brown assured, "we have reached a point where nothing but war can settle the question." Fortunately, slavery's proponents had failed to conquer Kansas, because if they did, "it would have been the death-knell of republicanism in America." The Slave Power would never relinquish its control over the government, and if forced to do so the result would be civil war "until American republicanism and freedom are overthrown." Brown refused to allow the forces of slavery to triumph. He avowed, "I drew my sword in Kansas when they attacked us, and I will never sheathe it until this war is over."[39]

With Bloody Kansas behind him, Brown again traversed the North in a final effort to secure financial support for his project. This time, the trip proved successful. From a disparate array of abolitionists, he secured thousands of dollars, which allowed him to stockpile weapons, including hundreds of rifles and revolvers. Brown also completed the purchase of one thousand six-foot-long iron-tipped pikes, which he intended to distribute to enslaved people after the Harpers Ferry raid.[40]

Naturally, Brown planned his revolution for the Fourth of July—though the idea was not his alone. During one of the conversations he had with Harriet Tubman in the previous year, the "Moses of her People" offered to support Brown's effort to destroy slavery.[41] As to the day designated to commence the great work, she "suggested the 4th of July as a good time to 'raise the mill.'" The idea took. In a letter written in early June 1859, Sanborn recorded, "Brown means to be on the ground as soon as he can, perhaps so as to begin by the 4th of July."[42]

A series of delays kept Brown from initiating his insurrectionary movement on Independence Day; nevertheless, the event still held great symbolic meaning for him and his followers. On July 3, an eccentric Free State fighter named John Cook who had come to Harpers Ferry to scout the location for Brown, reflected on the holiday's significance. As he looked over the picturesque mountains, which breathed "a mournful song of liberty," Cook confessed that he could think of nothing else besides what he owed his God and his country. "To-morrow is the Fourth!" he lamented. "The glorious day which saw our Freedom's birth, but left sad hearts beneath the slave lash and clanking chain." As the cup of slavery was bitter, Cook knew that he and his companions had a duty to "*drain it to the very dregs.*"[43]

When Brown finally arrived in western Maryland, he joined Cook and a small group of followers at a farmstead several miles east of Harpers Ferry. Among his first undertakings was to formally articulate his reasons for assaulting the nation's largest arsenal. Composing what biographer Tony Horwitz calls a "political manifesto," Brown reiterated his commitment to the nation and its egalitarian ideals.[44] Dated "——4th, 1859," in an obvious reference to the Fourth of July, the hand-written document is titled, "A DECLARATION OF LIBERTY BY THE REPRESENTATIVES OF THE SLAVE POPULATION OF THE UNITED STATES OF AMERICA."[45]

Offering a major revision of the Declaration of Independence, Brown's handwritten manuscript is an historic text. It begins by copying much of its predecessor's preamble word-for-word. Then, after asserting the right of oppressed and rebellious people to "declare the causes which incite them to this just & worthy action," it announces: "We hold these truths to be Self Evident; That All Men are Created Equal; That they are endowed by their Creator with certain unalienable rights. That among these are Life, Liberty; & the persuit [*sic*] of happiness." The 1776 declaration infuses the remainder of the 1859 text. An example is the inclusion of a list of abuses suffered at the hands of a tyrannical government. Among the "enormous atrocities" committed by the United States were the Fugitive Slave Act, the Dred Scott decision, and the domestic slave trade.[46]

Everything else about Brown's declaration was unique, including the use of the first person. Written primarily in the voice of enslaved people, the text abounds in the use of plural pronouns such as *we, us,* and *our,* which modern readers might find offensive. "By today's standards, John Brown's efforts to write for black people might be attributed to the presumptions of white privilege," writes biographer Louis DeCaro, Jr., before countering, "To the contrary, the overwhelming number of black critics, including the most strident disputants of the white community, have credited Brown for backing up his words with militant action, almost to the degree of turning white privilege on its head." In the end, the literary device employed by this White man was a testament to his extraordinary sympathy for, and solidarity with, Black people.[47]

Above all else, Brown's declaration was an indictment of the United States. With slavery being "the embodiment of all that is Evil, and ruinous to a Nation," the republic was a failure. While its leaders held the people in contempt, its laws betrayed "the words spirit, & intention, of the Constitution of the United States, & the Declaration of Independence." Denying the universality of natural rights, they stained the character and honor "of any Nation" that claimed the mantle of civilization.[48]

For Brown, the days of the republic were numbered. Long enamored with the idea of "virtuous revolutionary resistance," he recognized that the "oppressed Citizens of the Slave States" had no choice but to fight for their freedom.[49] Indeed, the declaration affirmed, "It is their Right, it is their Duty to resist & change such Government, & provide safeguards for their future Liberty." Influenced and inspired by the "Sacred Instrument" of 1776, enslaved people demanded the freedom and natural rights "of faithful Citizens of the United States." Anything less was unacceptable. "We will Obtain these rights," the document warned in the spirit of Patrick Henry, "or Die in the struggle to obtain them."[50]

The conclusion of Brown's declaration stressed enslaved people's right to rise against their oppressors. "As free, & Independent Citizens" of the nation, they had "a perfect right, a sufficient & just cause, to defend themselves against the tyrany [sic] of their oppressors." They were also entitled to seek the assistance of the friends of freedom, foreign or domestic, "& to do all other acts & things which free independent Citizens may of right do." Brown welcomed a revolution over slavery, for he knew who would emerge victorious in such a contest. Borrowing one of the most memorable lines of Thomas Jefferson's *Notes on the State of Virginia*, he acknowledged: "I tremble for my Country, when I reflect; that God is Just; And that his Justice; will not sleep forever."[51] By demonstrating a close reading of, and respect for, the primary author of the Declaration of Independence, the quotation revealed Brown not only as an admirer of Jefferson but a revolutionary heir.

Three months after drafting the "Declaration of Liberty," the time for Brown and eighteen of his most devoted disciples to finish the revolutionary work of the Founding Fathers had finally arrived. On Sunday night, October 16, 1859, the heavily armed abolitionists stormed into the small hamlet of Harpers Ferry, which was located at the confluence of the Shenandoah and Potomac Rivers on the Virginia side of the Virginia-Maryland border, and quickly seized the federal armory and arsenal. They also took possession of a fire engine house that doubled as a guard station. The interracial band then began liberating enslaved people and capturing slave owners throughout the area. From here on, there was no turning back.

Around midnight, Brown's men accomplished one of their most symbolic objectives. Before the raid, John Cook had met Colonel Lewis Washington, a great-grandnephew of George Washington, who lived just outside of Harpers Ferry. During the meeting, Cook learned that Lewis owned items that once belonged to his famous ancestor, including a dress sword given to the first president by the Prussian King Frederick the Great. At Cook's suggestion, Brown's men confiscated the symbolic relics during the raid's early hours. Osborne Anderson, one of the five African American raiders, first took possession of the commemorative sword, but for the remainder of the raid Brown carried the weapon at his side.[52]

In addition to weapons, Brown's raiders also appropriated the Founding Fathers' words. Shortly after invading Lewis Washington's home, Cook and three other raiders arrived on the doorstep of a local slave owner named Terence Byrne. Entering the residence with guns drawn, Cook demanded the liberation of all enslaved people on the property. At the same time, he delivered an extemporaneous "higher law speech" before an audience of terrified family members. With his mind focused on keeping his family safe, Byrne ignored most of the abolitionist's invective; nevertheless, he later recalled Cook's assertion that the use of force to free enslaved people was justified because, according to the Declaration of Independence, "all men were created equal."[53]

Amidst the chaos and confusion of the raid's first hours, Brown made a fateful mistake. Several of his men forced a train passing through the town to halt, but at dawn allowed it to proceed toward its destination. At its next stop, the train's conductor telegraphed a Baltimore & Ohio Railroad official that "armed abolitionists" numbering "about one hundred and fifty strong" had taken Harpers Ferry. Three-and-a-half hours later, the report reached the White House in Washington and the governor's mansions in Maryland and Virginia. Immediately, hundreds of state and federal troops boarded trains and rushed to Harpers Ferry to retake the town.[54]

In the meantime, armed citizens and local militiamen engaged Brown's men in mortal combat, which led him to twice offer a flag of truce. In both cases, the offer to negotiate was refused; thus, the fight raged into Monday evening. When one hundred US Marines under the command of Colonel Robert E. Lee arrived and assumed authority of the local forces, Brown and four of his men, along with eight hostages and a similar number of escaped slaves, retreated into the fire station. Early Tuesday morning, the marines smashed through the building's front door and after a brief scuffle took the bruised and bloodied abolitionists who survived the melee, including Brown, into custody. In total, four civilians and ten abolitionists died in the Harpers Ferry raid.[55]

In the aftermath of the Harpers Ferry raid, the entire nation pondered its significance. Why would a White man offer his life for the freedom of Black people? Did all abolitionists endeavor to incite slave insurrections? Was there any way to prevent a similar event from taking place in the future? The answers to these questions were unknown.

Brown's fate, by contrast, was sealed. In November, a Virginia jury sentenced him to death for the crimes of treason, murder, and inciting a slave insurrection. Before making his way to the gallows, Brown handed a small slip of paper to his jailor, which revealed his expectations of a national cataclysm brought on by the sin of slavery. The hand-written statement read, "I, John Brown, am now quite certain that the crimes of this guilty land: will never be purged away; but with Blood."[56] It was a prescient "violent final message" that illuminated its author's enduring belief in the revolutionary destruction of American slavery.[57]

Hours after officials lowered Brown's lifeless body from the scaffold, abolitionists poured into Boston's Tremont Temple in an extraordinary display of solidarity with the deceased.[58] The two-thousand-person capacity auditorium filled more than a half-hour before the beginning of the memorial's scheduled start, forcing an estimated three thousand supporters to remain outside. Organizers decorated the temple's interior walls with abolitionist "emblems and mottos," including a placard reading, "*Give me Liberty, or give me Death!*" Most prominent of all the ornamentation was a large painted banner of the Virginia State Seal. Emblazoned with the official state motto, "sic semper tyrannis" ("*Thus Always to Tyrants*"), the circular vignette centered on an image of Virtus, the Roman god of courage and bravery, standing with his foot on the neck of a prostrate and defeated Tyrant. Underscoring the hypocrisy of the execution of a modern revolutionary in a state that gave the nation Patrick Henry, Thomas Jefferson, and George Washington, the standard showed "that John Brown was directly upheld, in his attempt to set free the slaves of Virginia, by the present instructions, as well as by the early example, of Virginia herself."[59]

Following opening remarks and a number of speeches by some of Boston's best and brightest, William Lloyd Garrison took the podium and sent the audience into a frenzy. He avowed that Brown was, like the Founding Fathers, justified in using revolutionary violence to end oppression—in fact, even more so. "If men are justified in striking a blow for freedom, when the question is one of a threepenny tax on tea, then, I say, they are a thousand times more justified, when it is to save fathers, mothers, wives and children from the slave-coffle and the auction-block, and to restore to them their God-given rights." Garrison reiterated his stance as a "non-resistant" who opposed violence for any reason but admitted that in the interest of peace, "I am prepared to say, 'Success to every slave insurrection at the South, and in every slave country.'" The assembly exploded. With the audience under his spell, Garrison admitted that he was weary of watching enslaved people "wearing their chains in a cowardly and servile spirit"; therefore, he preferred to see them—like the nation's revolutionary founders—smash their shackles across the tyrant's head. "Give me, as a non-resistant, Bunker Hill, and Lexington and Concord, rather than the cowardice and servility of a Southern slave plantation."[60]

To defend Brown against the charge of being a "traitor" to his nation, Garrison continued to invoke the language and symbols of American freedom. "*Who* instigated John Brown?" It was Patrick Henry who cried out, "*Give me liberty, or give me death!*" It was Thomas Jefferson, who insisted that the enslaved Americans had far more reason to rebel than the Founding Fathers and in the Declaration of Independence proclaimed it "a SELF-EVIDENT TRUTH, that all men are created equal, and endowed by their Creator with AN INALIENABLE RIGHT TO LIBERTY." It was the Commonwealth of Virginia, whose militant motto, "*Sic semper tyrannis,*" asserted the right of oppressed people to "trample their oppressors" under their feet and, if necessary, "consign them to a bloody grave!" Still, more than anything else, it was the American people, whose national motto was, "Resistance to tyrants is obedience to God"—and whose exulting talk is of Bunker Hill and Yorktown, and the deeds of their REVOLUTIONARY sires!" Inspired by the crowd's enthusiasm, Garrison entreated listeners to "spare no effort" to help the United States fulfill its radical promise of freedom for all people.[61]

While the rafters at Tremont Temple shook in support of John Brown, several of the Harpers Ferry raiders remained in a Virginia jail awaiting execution. Among them was John Anthony Copeland, one of the five African Americans who had participated in the raid.[62] In a published letter written from his cell, the college-educated carpenter expressed no regret for having helped Brown strike a blow for freedom. To the contrary, he was proud for acting as an American patriot who offered his life for the nation and its people. At Harpers Ferry, Copeland did exactly "what George Washington, the so-called father of this great but slavery-cursed country, was made a hero for doing." Now, however, "for having lent my aid to a General no less brave, and engaged in a cause no less honorable and glorious, I am to suffer death."[63] The hypocrisy was astounding.

Even so, Copeland still believed in the United States because of the sacrifices of the patriots before him. "Washington entered the field to fight for the freedom of the American people—not for the white man alone, but for both black and white." Indeed, the American Revolution was a multiracial struggle for freedom, as "The blood of black men flowed as freely as that of white men." Referring to Crispus Attucks, the fugitive slave who had lost his life in the Boston Massacre, Copeland continued, "Yes, the *very first* blood that was spilt was that of a negro." Not long ago, "black men did an equal share of the fighting for American Independence, and they were assured by the whites that they should share equal benefits for so doing." Though White Americans had failed to fulfill their promise of equality to their Black compatriots, Copeland believed that he could not die in a nobler cause.[64] Just prior to his execution, he declared in words reminiscent of Henry Highland Garnet's address to enslaved Americans, "I had rather die than be a slave."[65]

By invoking Crispus Attucks, Copeland amplified the contemporary efforts of free African Americans to resurrect and perpetuate the memory of the Boston Massacre's first victim. In 1851, just months after the Fugitive Slave Act took effect, William C. Nell and six other Black Bostonians petitioned the Massachusetts State Legislature to erect a monument in memory of "the first martyr of the American Revolution."[66] The rejection of the proposal failed to deter its supporters, who continued to fight to memorialize Attucks and secure his status as a Revolutionary War icon. "In Boston and across the North," historian Mitch Kachun writes in his analysis of Attucks's life and legacy, "African Americans invoked Attucks's memory in their arguments for citizenship rights and racial justice."[67] After Harpers Ferry, they also appropriated it to justify revolutionary resistance to slavery.

An address given by the African American activist, doctor, and dentist John Rock on the anniversary of the Boston Massacre demonstrates. Before a predominately Black assembly inside Tremont Temple, the doctor questioned Attucks's willingness to pay the ultimate sacrifice for a new nation whose government subsequently "used every means in its power to outrage and degrade his race and posterity." Rock confessed a strong attachment to the United States, but he believed the only national anniversaries worth commemorating, besides the organization of the American Anti-Slavery Society, were the slave insurrections led by Nat Turner and John Brown. The crowd applauded in agreement.[68]

As to the best way to destroy slavery, Rock knew only one path forward. "John Brown was, and is, the sword, which proposes to settle at once the relation between master and slave—peaceably if it can, forcibly if it must." Though the method was severe, "Slavery has taken up the sword, and it is but just that it should perish by it. (Applause.)" Just as Attucks had launched the first American Revolution in Boston, Brown had undoubtedly unleashed the "second Revolution" at Harpers Ferry. Though preferring peace, Rock now expected—and welcomed—violence.

Copying Henry Highland Garnet's famous line verbatim, he proclaimed, "My motto has always been, 'Better die freemen than live to be slaves.'"[69]

Abolitionists' embracement of the revolutionary nationalism inspired by the Harpers Ferry raid reached its zenith at a Fourth of July celebration at John Brown's North Elba, New York, home in the summer of 1860. An estimated one thousand abolitionists met near the Brown family farmhouse to observe both Brown's death and the birth of the nation. The assembly mobilized around a massive granite boulder and an adjacent tombstone that marked the graves of Brown, his three sons who lost their lives at Harpers Ferry, and his grandfather, Captain John Brown, a Revolutionary War veteran "who died at New York, Sept. ye 3, 1776, in ye 48 year of his age."[70] After the appointment of officers, a reading of the Declaration of Independence, and the adoption of several resolutions, Richard Hinton read several letters that had been sent by important individuals who were unable to attend the event.

While all the communications celebrated the efforts of Brown and the Harpers Ferry raiders to destroy slavery, James Redpath's stood out for its call for revolution. The writer expressed his regret at being unable to attend the celebration and thus publicly reaffirm his faith in both the doctrines of the Declaration of Independence "and in the expediency of the agency of physical force for the liberation of the slaves in our Southern States." Referring to southern plantations as "the Achilles heel of slavery" and the nation's capital as its throat, he entreated enslaved people and their allies to strike at these places simultaneously. Toward that end, Redpath announced that he would stop disseminating the "*doctrines* of the Declaration" and instead encourage revolutionary resistance to slavery. With Bunker Hill and Harpers Ferry as his watchwords, he would devote himself to securing abolition by any means—even if it meant taking "the field" as Brown's successor.[71]

After reading Redpath's letter, Hinton informed the audience that they were in the presence of a modern-day Crispus Attucks. Referring to the Harpers Ferry raid he explained, "We have with us to-day one who bravely acted his part on that memorable occasion, and who, wearing that history as the proud mark of manhood, is worthy to stand on this rock and speak for his race." At that, Osborne Anderson, the only remaining Black survivor of the Harpers Ferry raid, moved forward. Upon taking the platform, he remarked that this was the first time in his life that he felt right about observing the Fourth of July. "That day to him had hitherto been a lie and a juggle," but things had changed. Brown's life and death taught Anderson that the Declaration of Independence represented much more than the "glittering generalities" suggested by slavery's defenders. Though the Harpers Ferry raid came at great cost, Anderson believed the sacrifice "would yet amply be repaid."[72]

Notwithstanding Osborne's stirring words, the most memorable remarks made at the Fourth of July memorial for John Brown came from the "Orator of the Day" Reverend Luther Lee.[73] Though largely forgotten today, this proud son of a Revolutionary War soldier was a prominent religious leader widely regarded for his brave and courageous work on the Underground Railroad. A popular antislavery lecturer across the North, Lee later recalled of the speech he delivered at John Brown's grave, "That was the oration of my life, the most radical and, probably, the most able I ever delivered."[74]

The address drew three conclusions based on Lee's understanding of the Declaration of Independence. First, individuals had a natural right to resist oppressive governments by force. In a proslavery republic like the United States with no source of peaceful redress, "revolution must come, and war and blood must do it." Though regrettable, it was "the legitimate consequence of the Declaration of American Independence, which has given to this national day all its interest and glory." Second, the inalienable rights detailed in that historic document extended to all Americans. If enslaved people seized their liberty forcefully, "the Declaration of Independence, with the practical comment upon the same, would justify them in so doing." Third, any Americans who fought for their freedom had every expectation to receive assistance from their allies, just as the Founding Fathers had from France during the American Revolution. "So sure as the name of La-Fayette is held sacred by this nation, so sure does the nation believe it right to help the oppressed in their struggle for liberty."[75]

For Lee, the Harpers Ferry raid was not only justified but sanctified. "Upon the ground of the Declaration of American Independence," he determined, "John Brown had a right to invade Virginia for the purpose of helping the slaves to obtain their liberty." Still, his work would not be complete "until the fetter is rent from human limbs, until the slave is free, and the nation is redeemed." For this to occur, the American people needed to take inspiration from Brown's actions "until it shall rouse the nation, and the slumbering spirit of Seventy-Six shall be waked up and burn in the hearts of the millions," like it once burned on the battlefields of Lexington, Concord, Monmouth, Saratoga, and Yorktown. When this happened, the rallying cry would again ring out, "Give me liberty, or give me death!"[76]

Like so many of Brown's allies, Lee's self-described "radical and revolutionary" turn was neither sudden nor unexpected.[77] Instead, it embodied the evolution of abolitionism over the course of several decades. Where movement leaders and followers once advocated peaceful resistance to slavery and the Slave Power, they now openly encouraged war. Though dramatic, the change in tactics and strategies was predictable given slavery's survival in a nation with a proud revolutionary tradition.

In the early United States, the language and symbols of freedom inspired forceful and even violent resistance to tyranny and oppression. Accordingly, the emergence of a figure like John Brown was all but assured. When in the aftermath of Harpers Ferry northerners hailed him as a martyr, White southerners' fear about the future of their peculiar institution escalated exponentially. A year later, South Carolina, Mississippi, Florida, Alabama, Georgia, Louisiana, and Texas declared their independence from the United States and formed the Confederate States of America. At last, the long-anticipated impasse over slavery arrived, and it remained for the Civil War to determine the fate of both the nation and freedom.

EPILOGUE

Fighting for Old Glory

On July 18, 1863, the Fifty-Fourth Massachusetts Volunteer Regiment stormed the Confederate battery at Fort Wagner, South Carolina, and changed the course of history. Organized by Massachusetts Governor John Andrews and other prominent abolitionists in the aftermath of President Abraham Lincoln's Emancipation Proclamation, which formally accepted African Americans into the US Armed Forces, the regiment consisted of White commissioned officers and more than one thousand Black enlistees, the majority of whom were formerly enslaved. The Fifty-Fourth was not the only racially integrated northern regiment during the Civil War. It was, however, the most celebrated.

Among the Fifty-Fourth's volunteers was William H. Carney. Born enslaved in Norfolk, Virginia, in 1840, he managed to join his father and the rest of his family in New Bedford, Massachusetts, where they lived as free people. Whether Carney escaped captivity on the Underground Railroad or had his freedom purchased by his father is unclear. Either way, he learned how to read and write while living in Massachusetts and by his early twenties decided to trade in his life at sea for one in the clergy—but fate intervened. When the call for volunteers for the regiment came forth in February 1863, Carney thought he could best serve God "by serving my country and my oppressed brothers."[1]

Five months later, Carney counted among the battalion of Black and White soldiers of the Fifty-Fourth who in the face of heavy fire raced up a sandy embankment on Morris Island, South Carolina, toward the

Confederate Fort Wagner. The troops took heavy casualties as they approached the parapet, which stood some thirty feet above the beach below. Hundreds of the regiment's men, including Colonel Robert Gould Shaw, succumbed to the hail of "shot, shell, and canister" as they attempted to scale the steep slope. When a bullet pierced the body of Sergeant John Wall, the color-bearer collapsed into a ditch taking the large American flag that he held in his hands with him.[2]

Despite suffering two gunshot wounds himself, Carney sprang into action. Discarding his own weapon, he "caught the colors, carried them forward, and was the first man to plant the Stars and Stripes upon Fort Wagner." When the Confederate's superior firepower forced Carney and his compatriots to retreat, "he brought the colors off, creeping on his knees, pressing his wound with one hand and with the other holding upon the emblem of freedom." His appearance at the temporary regimental hospital minutes later produced an emotional response from those inside the infirmary. "With the flag still in his possession, his wounded companions, both black and white, rose from the straw upon which they were lying, and cheered him until exhausted they could shout no longer." Unaffected by the frenzy, Carney remarked calmly, "Boys, I but did my duty; the dear old flag never touched the ground."[3]

Besides Carney's own words and a plethora of published eyewitness accounts, an iconic photograph taken months after the Battle of Fort Wagner made his efforts to save the American flag part of the Civil War's popular culture. In the palm-sized black-and-white *carte-de-visite*, Carney stands proudly in a uniform of the US Army that displays the three-striped chevron of a sergeant on its sleeve.[4] His upper torso tilts toward the right, where his right arm and hand lean on a sturdy walking stick, which suggests his recovery from the injuries suffered in South Carolina was incomplete. Carney's body disappears behind the famous rescued standard that stretches diagonally across the foreground. The top of the flag is furled and extends out of view, while its tattered edges fall to Carney's knees, stopping just inches above the ground.

FIGURE E.I. Sergeant William H. Carney holding the Flag of the United States, from John Ritchie, *Carte-de-visite Album of the 54th Massachusetts Infantry Regiment* (circa 1864). Courtesy of the Collection of the Smithsonian National Museum of African American History and Culture, Gift of the Garrison Family in memory of George Thompson Garrison.

The grainy photograph of a former slave who was willing to fight and die for his country and its flag resonated across the North. It was, like other popular illustrations of African Americans published during the war, "A remarkable, symbolic linkage of Black soldiers with American nationhood."[5] Still, the photograph remained in the public consciousness long after the war had ended. In 1891, when Captain Luis F. Emilio published *A Brave Black Regiment*, the first regimental history written by one of the Fifty Fourth's officers, he copied the Carney photograph on the book's frontispiece. The book was a commercial success, prompting the author to publish a second edition only three years later.

At the same time that readers were consuming Emilio's account of the Fifty-Fourth Regiment, another image of Carney emerged that almost immediately became the quintessential illustration of the regiment and its heroic flag bearer. Included in a collection of colored lithographs published by the Chicago firm of Louis Kurz and Alexander Allison, "Storming Fort Wagner" improves upon a print first issued by New York's renowned lithographers Nathaniel Currier and James Merritt Ives in 1863 and then again in 1888 on the battle's twenty-fifth anniversary. Offering a stunning visualization of the regiment's failed assault, the Kurz and Allison illustration depicts dozens of Black and White Union soldiers in blue jackets engaged in deadly hand-to-hand combat with an equal number of gray-coated Confederates, while smoke from rifles, cannons, and ships fill the air.

The scene is pure chaos, yet the viewer's eyes are drawn to the events transpiring at the center of the illustration. Here, atop the fort's ramparts, Colonel Shaw receives a fatal bullet to his chest as he leads the Fifty-Fourth forward. Beside him, Sergeant Carney, who, in the face of immense and immediate gunfire, charges forward with the Stars and Stripes held firmly in both hands. Though taking artistic license, the image reveals the extraordinary bravery of the racially integrated regiment, and in particular Shaw and Carney. The lithograph, "which strongly suggested that patriotism was now a commodity to which both races could aspire," held a place in popular American culture for generations.[6]

FIGURE E.2. *Storming Fort Wagner* (Chicago: Kurz & Allison, 1890). Courtesy of the Library of Congress.

A century later, the Academy Award-winning motion picture *Glory*, which told the story of the Fifty-Fourth Regiment and the complicated relationship between its White officers and Black soldiers, brought the illustration to life. In the film's climactic scene, Colonel Shaw, played by Matthew Broderick, leads the regiment toward Fort Wagner until enemy gunfire cuts him down. With orchestral music rising in the background, the regiment's enlistees watch in disbelief as their leader dies in the sand alongside the regimental flag that lies crumpled beside him. Though the fictional Sergeant Silas Trip, a composite character portrayed by Denzel Washington, had refused to carry the flag prior to the battle, he now retrieves the standard from the ground and lunges forward until a bullet pierces his chest. When Trip's lifeless body collapses in a heap, another Black soldier hoists the colors into the air and charges headlong into the battle. Carney's name is unmentioned, yet he inspires the entire scene.

Popular representations of William Carney and the Fifty-Fourth Regiments serve as a reminder that as long as there has been a United States, there have been African Americans who were willing to fight and die for it. From the battles of Lexington and Concord in the eighteenth century to the wars in Iraq and Afghanistan in the twenty-first, Black people have repeatedly given their lives for the republic. That they have often done this while being denied freedom and equality represents one of the great paradoxes of American history.

Despite the willingness of African Americans to sacrifice their lives for their nation, the idea that they are less patriotic than European Americans persists. So too does the idea that Americans of African descent are not really Americans at all. In recent years, with protests against police brutality and other forms of racial injustice occurring nationwide, these ideas have found new life. The result has been a concerted effort to undo decades of progress made in the areas of civil rights and social justice. It is a deeply disturbing development.

Yet there is comfort in knowing that in a nation dedicated to freedom, there have always been people willing to resist oppression and oppressors by any and all means. In the antebellum era, enslaved people and their allies fought for liberty and equality in innumerable ways. When they did so forcefully, they often took inspiration from the language and symbols of American freedom. Mindful of the sacrifices of the nation's founders, they demonstrated a fierce commitment to the revolutionary ideas and traditions of the republic. Waging a long and difficult war against both slavery and racism, they not only fought for their own freedom but that of the nation as well.

ACKNOWLEDGMENTS

In the process of researching and writing *Symbols of Freedom*, I incurred a great number of debts to people and institutions who have generously given me their time, energy, and encouragement. It is a joy to thank them here.

I would like to thank the University of Houston's College of Liberal Arts and Social Sciences for their support. A Faculty Development Leave Grant and Research Progress Grant gave me time and resources to complete this book. I also want to thank the staffs and librarians at the Library of Congress, the Maryland Center for History and Culture, the Maryland State Archives, the New York Public Library, and the University of Houston's MD Anderson Library. Judith Andrews at the National Museum of African American History merits a specific mention for her assistance in acquiring a rare illustration.

I am especially fortunate for having the opportunity to present portions of this book at two prestigious symposiums. My gratitude goes to Martha Jones and Lauren Feldman for allowing me to speak at Hard Histories at Hopkins at Johns Hopkins University, and Andra Gillespie, Rhonda Patrick, and Antoinette Burrell for inviting me to participate in the Race and Difference Colloquium Series at the James Weldon Johnston Institute for the Study of Race and Difference at Emory University. I also presented an early excerpt from this book at the 37th Annual Meeting of the Society of Historians of the Early American Republic, where Benjamin Carp, Kay Wright Lewis, Kellie Carter Jackson, and Walter Rucker were among those who offered helpful comments and critiques. I thank all of these people for their support.

Two individuals deserve a special note of thanks. First, while in his capacity as editor of the *Journal of the Early Republic*, David Waldstreicher made important critiques on multiple drafts of an article manuscript that I had submitted for publication. His suggestions not only helped me produce a publishable essay but informed this entire project. I owe a debt of gratitude to him and the anonymous reviewers at the *Journal of the Early Republic*, where a version of chapter 5, "Disciples," appeared as "'Disciples of the Declaration': American Freedom and the Fugitive-Slave Rebellion at Rockville," *Journal of the Early Republic* 41, no. 2 (Summer 2021): 239–266. Copyright © 2021 Society for Historians of the Early American Republic. Second, Kirsten Hilson won a Summer Undergraduate Research Fellow Grant at the University of Houston in 2019, and in this capacity performed vital research for this study. I am very fortunate to have benefitted from Kirsten's enthusiasm and expertise, skills that will serve her well as she embarks on her graduate career in history.

At New York University Press, Clara Platter has repeatedly proven herself an ardent and enthusiastic supporter of my scholarship. I truly hope that this book is worthy of the confidence she continues to show in me. Robert Birdwell's insightful and meticulous editing, along with Ainee Jeong's professional guidance, saved me from committing numerous embarrassing errors, so to them I am deeply grateful.

Last and most importantly, I want to thank my wife Gladys and our three children, Maddie, Joey, and Josh for their love and support. They have no idea how important it is.

NOTES

Introduction

1 Jesse Torrey, *A Portraiture of Domestic Slavery, in the United States* (Philadelphia: Jesse Torrey, 1817), 39–40. Torrey copied the account of the incident five years later in a slightly revised version of his book published in Great Britain, *American Slave Trade* (London: J. M. Cobbett, 1822), 64.

2 SLAVE MARKET OF AMERICA (New York: American Anti-Slavery Society, 1836), www.loc.gov.

3 "PAMPHLETS," *Liberator*, September 3, 1836, 4.

4 Anthony S. Pitch, *The Burning of Washington: The British Invasion of 1814* (Annapolis: Naval Institute Press, 1998).

5 W. T. R. Saffell, *Hail Columbia, the Flag, and Yankee Doodle Dandy* (Baltimore: T. Newton Kurtz, 1864), 54 (first and second quotations), 55 (third quotation), 56 (fourth quotation).

6 Benedict Anderson, *Imagined Communities: Reflections of the Origin and Spread of Nationalism* (New York: Verso, 1991). See also Jürgen Habermas, *The Structural Transformation of the Public Sphere: An Inquiry into a Category of Bourgeois Society* (Cambridge: Massachusetts Institute of Technology Press, 1991).

7 The phrase originated in Benjamin Russell's *Boston Columbian Centinel* on July 12, 1817, following the New England leg of President James Monroe's national tour. The expression then spread nationally. See, for example, "ERA OF GOOD FEELINGS," *Washington National Intelligencer*, July 19, 1817, 2. See also Patricia L. Dooley, ed., *The Early Republic: Primary Documents on Events from 1799–1820* (Westport, CT: Greenwood Press, 2004), 296–299.

8 For general studies of United States nationalism from the American Revolution to the Civil War, see Carol Berkin, *A Sovereign People: The Crisis of the 1790s and the Birth of American Nationalism* (New York: Basic Books, 2017); Robert G. Parkinson, *The Common Cause: Creating Race and Nation in the American Revolution* (Chapel Hill: University of North Carolina Press, 2016); Carroll Smith-Rosenberg, *This Violent Empire: The Birth of an American National Identity* (Chapel Hill: University of North Carolina Press, 2020); Alexander Tsesis, *For Liberty and Equality: The Life and Times of the Declaration of Independence* (New York: Oxford University Press, 2012); François Furstenberg, *In the Name of the*

Father: Washington's Legacy, Slavery, and the Making of a Nation (New York, 2006);
Alfred F. Young, *The Shoemaker and the Tea Party: Memory and the American
Revolution* (Boston: Beacon Press, 2000); Sarah Purcell, *Sealed with Blood: War,
Sacrifice, and Memory in Revolutionary America* (Philadelphia: University of
Pennsylvania Press, 2002); Pauline Maier, *American Scripture: Making the
Declaration of Independence* (New York: Knopf, 1997); Simon P. Newman, *Parades
and the Politics of the Street: Festive Culture in the Early American Republic*
(Philadelphia: University of Pennsylvania Press, 1997); Len Travers, *Celebrating
the Fourth: Independence Day and the Rites of Nationalism in the Early Republic*
(Amherst: University of Massachusetts Press, 1997); David Waldstreicher, *In the
Midst of Perpetual Fetes: The Making of American Nationalism, 1776–1820* (Chapel
Hill: University of North Carolina Press, 1997); Susan G. Davis, *Parades and
Power: Street Theatre in Nineteenth-Century Philadelphia* (Philadelphia: Temple
University Press, 1986); George Dangerfield, *The Awakening of American
Nationalism: 1815–1828* (New York: Harper & Row, 1965); Carl Lotus Becker, *The
Declaration of Independence: A Study in the History of Political Ideas* (New York,
1922).

9   For the rise of Washington, DC, see Adam Constanzo, *George Washington's
Washington: Visions for the National Capital in the Early American Republic*
(Athens: University of Georgia Press, 2018); Robert J. Kapsch, *Building
Washington: Engineering and Construction of the New Federal City, 1790–1840*
(Baltimore: Johns Hopkins University Press, 2018); Fergus Bordewich, *The First
Congress: How James Madison, George Washington, and a Group of Extraordinary
Men Invented the Government* (New York: Simon & Schuster, 2016); Catherine
Allgor, *Parlor Politics: In Which the Ladies of Washington Help Build a City and a
Government* (Charlottesville: University Press of Virginia, 2002); Donald R.
Kennon, ed., *A Republic for the Ages: The United States Capitol and the Political
Culture of the Early Republic* (Charlottesville: University Press of Virginia, 1999);
Pamela Scott, *Temple of Liberty: Building the Capitol for a New Nation* (New York:
Oxford University Press, 1995).

10 While much of the literature on the contested nature of early American
nationalism addresses sectionalism, the role of slavery and White supremacy is
understated. Notable exceptions include Michael F. Conlin, *One Nation Divided
by Slavery: Remembering the American Revolution While Marching to the Civil War*
(Kent, OH: Kent State University Press, 2015); Furstenberg, *In the Name of the
Father*; and Waldstreicher, *In the Midst of Perpetual Fetes*.

11 Rosemarie Zagarri, "The Significance of the 'Global Turn' for the Early
American Republic: Globalization in the Age of Nation-Building," *Journal of the
Early Republic* 31, no. 1 (Spring 2011): 1–37.

12 This study draws especially from Jill Lepore's essay, *This America: The Case for the
Nation* (New York: Liveright, 2019). For nationalism generally see Anderson,
Imagined Communities; Eric J. Hobsbawm, *Nations and Nationalism since 1780:*

Programme, Myth, Reality (Cambridge: Cambridge University Press, 1992); Ernest Gellner, *Nations and Nationalism* (Ithaca: Cornell University Press, 1983).

13 Yuval Noah Harari, *Sapiens: A Brief History of Humankind* (New York: HarperCollins, 2015), 243.

14 George L. Mosse, "Racism and Nationalism," *Nations and Nationalism* 1 (1995): 168.

15 The quotation is from Kay Wright Lewis, *A Curse upon the Nation: Race, Freedom, and Extermination in America and the Atlantic World* (Athens: University of Georgia Press, 2017). For a sampling of the expansive historiography, see Padraic Scanlan, *Slave Empire: How Slavery Built Modern Britain* (New York: Little, Brown, 2020); Howard W. French, *Born in Blackness: Africa, Africans, and the Making of the Modern World, 1471 to the Second World War* (New York: Liveright, 2021); Robin Blackburn, *The American Crucible: Slavery, Emancipation, and Human Rights* (New York: Verso, 2011); Paul Gilroy, *The Black Atlantic: Modernity and Double Consciousness* (Cambridge: Harvard University Press, 1993); Edmund Morgan, *American Slavery, American Freedom: The Ordeal of Colonial Virginia* (New York: W. W. Norton, 1975); Eric Eustace Williams, *Capitalism & Slavery* (New York: Capricorn Books, 1966).

16 Olaudah Equiano, *The Interesting Narrative of the Life of Olaudah Equiano: Written by Himself with Related Documents*, ed. Robert J. Allison (Boston: Bedford/St. Martin's, 2016), 74. See also Vincent Carretta, *Equiano, the African: Biography of a Self-Made Man* (Athens: University of Georgia Press, 2005); and Jocelyn Stitt, "Olaudah Equiano, Englishness, and the Negotiations of Raced Gender," *Michigan Feminist Studies* 14 (1999–2000): 107–122.

17 Anthony W. Marx, *Making Race and Nation: A Comparison of South Africa, the United States, and Brazil* (Cambridge: Cambridge University Press, 1998), 20.

18 Nelson Mandela, *Long Walk to Freedom* (Boston: Little, Brown, 1994), 144 (first quotation), 468 (second quotation). See also, Marx, *Making Race and Nation*, 21.

19 Carroll Smith-Rosenberg, *This Violent Empire: The Birth of an American National Identity* (Chapel Hill: University of North Carolina Press, 2010).

20 Carl N. Degler, "In Pursuit of an American History," *American Historical Review* 92, no. 1 (February 1987): 6 (first and second quotations), 12 (third quotation).

21 The entry for *nation* begins, "A body of people inhabiting the same country, or united under the same sovereign or government." Noah Webster, *An American Dictionary of the English Language* (New York: S. Converse, 1828), vol. 2.

22 Berkin, *A Sovereign People*, 6.

23 The classic account is Sterling Stuckey, *Slave Culture: Nationalist Theory and the Foundations of Black America* (New York: Oxford University Press, 1988). See also Walter C. Rucker, *The River Flows On: Black Resistance, Culture, and Identity Formation in Early America* (Baton Rouge: Louisiana State University Press, 2005).

24 Matthew J. Clavin, *The Battle of Negro Fort: The Rise and Fall of a Fugitive Slave Community* (New York: New York University Press, 2019); Clavin,

Toussaint Louverture and the American Civil War: The Promise and Peril of a Second Haitian Revolution (Philadelphia: University of Pennsylvania Press, 2010); Alan Taylor, *The Internal Enemy: Slavery and War in Virginia, 1772–1832* (New York: W.W. Norton, 2013); Gerald Horne, *Negro Comrades of the Crown: African Americans and the British Empire Fight the U.S. before Emancipation* (New York: New York University Press, 2012); Rucker, *The River Flows On*; Jeffrey R. Kerr-Ritchie, *Rites of August First: Emancipation Day in the Black Atlantic World* (Baton Rouge: Louisiana State University Press, 2007); Douglas R. Egerton, *He Shall Go Out Free: The Lives of Denmark Vesey* (Lanham, MD: Rowman & Littlefield, 2004); Egerton, *Gabriel's Rebellion: The Virginia Slave Conspiracies of 1800 and 1802* (Chapel Hill: University of North Carolina Press, 1993); James Sidbury, *Ploughshares into Swords: Race, Rebellion, and Identity in Gabriel's Virginia, 1730–1810* (New York: Cambridge University Press, 1997). These studies rely on the pioneering works on slave revolts, including Eugene D. Genovese, *From Rebellion to Revolution: Afro-American Slave Revolts in the Making of the Modern World* (Baton Rouge: Louisiana State University Press, 1979); and Herbert Aptheker, *American Negro Slave Revolts* (New York: Columbia University Press, 1943).

25 Martha J. Cutter, *The Illustrated Slave: Empathy, Graphic Narrative, and the Visual Culture of the Transatlantic Abolition Movement, 1800–1852* (Athens: University of Georgia Press, 2017); Manisha Sinha, *The Slave's Cause: A History of Abolition* (New Haven: Yale University Press, 2016); W. Caleb McDaniel, *The Problem of Democracy in the Age of Slavery: Garrisonian Abolitionists and Transatlantic Reform, c. 1787–1820* (Baton Rouge: Louisiana State University Press, 2013); J. R. Oldfield, *Transatlantic Abolitionism in the Age of Revolution: An International History of Anti-Slavery* (Cambridge: Cambridge University Press, 2013); David Brion Davis, *Inhuman Bondage: The Rise and Fall of Slavery in the New World* (New York: Oxford University Press, 2008); Kathryn Kish Sklar and James Brewer Stewart, eds., *Women's Rights and Transatlantic Antislavery in the Era of Emancipation* (New Haven: Yale University Press, 2007); Richard J. M. Blackett, *Building an Antislavery Wall: Black Americans in the Atlantic Abolitionist Movement, 1830–1860* (Baton Rouge: Louisiana State University Press, 2002); Alan Rice and Martin Crawford, eds, *Liberating Sojourn: Frederick Douglass and Transatlantic Reform* (Athens: University of Georgia Press, 1999).

26 McDaniel, *The Problem of Democracy in the Age of Slavery*, 14.

27 Teresa A. Goddu, *Selling Antislavery: Abolition and Mass Media in Antebellum America* (Philadelphia: University of Pennsylvania Press, 2020); John L Brooke, *"There is a North": Fugitive Slaves, Political Crisis, and Cultural Transformation in the Coming of the Civil War* (Amherst: University of Massachusetts Press, 2019); Susan-Mary Grant, *North Over South: Northern Nationalism and American Identity in the Antebellum Era* (Lawrence: University Press of Kansas, 2000);

Harlow W. Sheidley, *Sectional Nationalism: Massachusetts Conservative Leaders and the Transformation of America, 1815–1836* (Boston: Northeastern University Press, 1998).

28 W. E. Burghardt Du Bois, *The Souls of Black Folk: Essays and Sketches* (Chicago: A. C. McClurg, 1903), 3.

29 Patrick Rael, *Black Identity & Black Protest in the Antebellum North* (Chapel Hill: University of North Carolina Press, 2002), 239.

30 For the central and unique role of Black men and women in the antebellum abolitionist movement and their militancy, see Kellie Carter Jackson, *Force and Freedom: Black Abolitionists and the Politics of Violence* (Philadelphia: University of Pennsylvania Press, 2019); Eric Foner, *Gateway to Freedom: The Hidden History of the Underground Railroad* (New York: W. W. Norton, 2016); Sinha, *The Slave's Cause*; Graham Russell Gao Hodges, *David Ruggles: A Radical Black Abolitionist and the Underground Railroad in New York City* (Chapel Hill: University of North Carolina Press, 2012); Blackett, *Building an Antislavery Wall*; Benjamin Quarles, *Black Abolitionists* (New York: Oxford University Press, 1969). The essential scholarship of the birth of Black nationalism among leading African American abolitionists includes Stuckey, *Slave Culture*; Cyril E. Griffith, *The African Dream: Martin R. Delany and the Emergence of Pan-African Thought* (University Park: Pennsylvania State University Press, 1975); Victor Ullman, *Martin R. Delany: The Beginnings of Black Nationalism* (Boston: Beacon Press, 1971); Floyd J. Miller "The Father of Black Nationalism," *Civil War History* 27, no. 4 (December 1971): 310–319.

31 Jacqueline Bacon, *Freedom's Journal: The First African-American Newspaper* (Lanham, MD: Lexington Books, 2007), 23. Important analyses of the civil rights struggles of African Americans in the nineteenth-century United States include Kate Masur, *Until Justice Be Done: America's First Civil Rights Movement, from the Revolution to Reconstruction* (New York: W. W. Norton & Company, 2021); Martha S. Jones, *Birthright Citizens: A History of Race and Rights in Antebellum America* (Cambridge: Cambridge University Press, 2018); Stephen Kantrowitz, *More Than Freedom: Fighting for Black Citizenship in a White Republic, 1829–1889* (New York: Penguin Books, 2013). For anti-colonization and the Colored Conventions movement, see: P. Gabrielle Foreman, Jim Casey, and Sarah Lynn Patterson, eds., *The Colored Conventions Movement: Black Organizing in the Nineteenth Century* (Chapel Hill: University of North Carolina Press, 2021); Beverly C. Tomek and Matthew J. Hetrick, eds., *New Directions in the Study of African American Recolonization* (Gainesville: University Press of Florida, 2017); Tomek, *Colonization and Its Discontents: Emancipation, Emigration, and Antislavery in Antebellum Pennsylvania* (New York: New York University Press, 2011); Eric Burin, *Slavery and the Peculiar Solution: A History of the American Colonization Society* (Gainesville: University Press of Florida, 2005).

1. The Flag

1 For a discussion of the American flag and the historical significance of flags generally, see Tim Marshall, *A Flag Worth Dying For: The Power and Politics of National Symbols* (New York: Scribner, 2016); Marc Leepson, *Flag: An American Biography* (New York: Thomas Dunne Books, 2005); Boleslaw Mastai and Marie-Louise D'Otrange Mastai, *The Stars and Stripes: The American Flag as Art and as History from the Birth of the Republic to the Present* (New York: Knopf, 1973); George Henry Preble, *History of the Flag of the United States of America* (Boston: Houghton, Mifflin and Company, 1894). A recent and reliable appraisal of the history and memory of "The Star-Spangled Banner" is Mark Clague, *O Say Can You Hear? A Cultural Biography of "The Star-Spangled Banner"* (New York: W. W. Norton, 2022).

2 After first appearing in the *Baltimore Patriot*, the poem "Defence of Fort McHenry" appeared in newspapers nationwide. This discussion relies on the version published in the *Daily National Intelligencer* (Washington, DC), September 26, 1814, 2.

3 "The Star-Spangled Banner," *Liberator*, September 13, 1844, 4.

4 *An Act to Establish the Flag of the United* States, 15th Cong., 1st sess., April 4, 1818, Chapter XXXIV, 415.

5 For a sampling of this work, see Aston Gonzalez, *Visualizing Equality: African American Rights and Visual Culture in the Nineteenth Century* (Chapel Hill: University of North Carolina Press, 2020); Martha J. Cutter, *The Illustrated Slave: Empathy, Graphic Narrative, and the Visual Culture of the Transatlantic Abolition Movement, 1800–1852* (Athens: University of Georgia Press, 2017), 8; Jasmine Nichole Cobb, *Picture Freedom: Remaking Black Visuality in the Early Nineteenth Century* (New York: New York University Press, 2015); Maurie D. McInnis, *Slaves Waiting for Sale: Abolitionist Art and the American Slave* (Chicago: University of Chicago Press, 2011); Marcus Wood, *Blind Memory: Visual Representations of Slavery in England and America, 1780–1865* (New York: Routledge, 2000).

6 More recent scholarship includes Teresa A. Goddu, *Selling Antislavery: Abolition and Mass Media in Antebellum America* (Philadelphia: University of Pennsylvania Press, 2020); John L Brooke, *"There is a North": Fugitive Slaves, Political Crisis, and Cultural Transformation in the Coming of the Civil War* (Amherst: University of Massachusetts Press, 2019); Susan-Mary Grant, *North Over South: Northern Nationalism and American Identity in the Antebellum Era* (Lawrence: University Press of Kansas, 2000).

7 John Rankin, *Letters on American Slavery, Addressed to Mr. Thomas Rankin* (Boston: Isaac Knapp, 1838), 42.

8 Theodore Dwight Weld, *American Slavery as It Is: Testimony of a Thousand Witnesses* (New York: American Anti-Slavery Society, 1839), 128. In his important antislavery history, David Brion Davis referred to Dickey as one of the important "southern antislavery refugees." *The Problem of Slavery in the Age of Revolution,*

1770–1823 (New York: Oxford University Press, 1999), 201. See also Thomas
Ebenezer Thomas, *Correspondence of Thomas Ebenezer Thomas: Mainly Relating to
the Anti-Slavery Conflict in Ohio, Especially in the Presbyterian Church* (Oxford,
OH: The Centennial of Miami University, 1909), 78–79; Dwight Lowell
Dumond, *Antislavery: The Crusade for Freedom in America* (Ann Arbor: University
of Michigan, 1961), 91–92; R. C. Galbraith, *The History of the Chillicothe Presbytery,
from its Organization in 1799 to 1889* (Chillicothe, OH: Scioto Gazette Book and
Job Office, 1889), 66–85, 139–140.

9   "From the Western Citizen," *Genius of Universal Emancipation* (October 1822):
11–12.

10   According to Manisha Sinha, the paper was "the preeminent abolitionist newspa-
per in the United States in the 1820s." *The Slave's Cause: A History of Abolition*
(New Haven: Yale University Press, 2016), 177. For a brief history of the paper,
consult Asa Earl Martin, "Pioneer Anti-Slavery Press," *Mississippi Valley
Historical Review* 2, no. 4 (March 1916), 509–528. A fuller account can be found in
Lundy's own, *The Life, Travels and Opinions of Benjamin Lundy, Including his
Journeys to Texas and Mexico; with a Sketch of Contemporary Events, and a Notice of
the Revolution in Hayti* (Philadelphia: William D. Parrish, 1847).

11   "Muses' Bower," *Genius of Universal Emancipation* (December 1822): 16. For the
letter, see "From the Western Citizen."

12   "United States' Internal Slave Trade," *Genius of Universal
Emancipation* (January 1823): 1.

13   Ibid. See also "Muses' Bower." Lundy copied the caption from a poem written by a
young Ohio abolitionist named James Lawton, who wrote under the pseudonym
"Icilius." H. Z. Williams & Bro., *History of Washington County, Ohio, with
Illustrations and Biographical Sketches* (Cleveland: W. W. Williams, 1881), 428–429.

14   "United States' Internal Slave Trade."

15   "A Picture Which Kings Might Laugh At!" *Genius of Universal Emancipation*
(November 1823): 1. Lundy's description of the incident included several new and
unsubstantiated claims, such as the enslaved people were brought to Washington
after being "kidnapped in or near Philadelphia." Years later, other accounts also
embellished the story without offering any evidence. One widely circulated
article even suggested that after the soloist performed the anthem, "The voice
and action, so appropriately timed and affectingly performed, drew tears from the
eyes of many; and to their honor be it said, they immediately *bought and freed
him*." "Original Anecdote," *New York Telescope*, February 25, 1826, 3. For
abolitionists' strategic use of visual imagery, see Gonzalez, *Visualizing Equality*;
Goddu, *Selling Antislavery*; Cutter, *The Illustrated Slave*; Cobb, *Picture Freedom*;
McInnis, *Slaves Waiting for Sale*; John Stauffer, "Creating an Image in Black: The
Power of Abolition Pictures," in Timothy Patrick McCarthy and John Stauffer,
eds., *Prophets of Protest: Reconsidering the History of American Abolitionism* (New
York: New Press, 2006), 256–267; Phillip Lapsansky, "Graphic Discord:

Abolitionist and Antiabolitionist Images," in Jean Fagan Yellin and John C. Wan Horne, eds., *The Abolitionist Sisterhood: Women's Political Culture in Antebellum America* (Ithaca: Cornell University Press, 1994), 201–230.

16 *Anti-Slavery Record*, February 1835, 1. The image appeared in at least two other AASS publications: *The Narrative of Amos Dresser, with Stone's Letters from Natchez,—An Obituary Notice of the Writer, and Two Letters from Tallahassee, Relating to the Treatment of Slaves* (New York: New York Anti-Slavery Society, 1836), 7; and Julius Rubens Ames and Benjamin Lundy, *The Legion of Liberty! and Force of Truth, Containing the Thoughts, Words, and Deeds, of some Prominent Apostles, Champions and Martyrs: Pictures and Poetry* (New York: American Anti-Slavery Society, 1857), 141. The image likely served as a model for an even more realistic depiction of the Paris slave coffle, which appeared in George Washington Carleton's *The Suppressed Book about Slavery!* (New York: Carleton, 1864). Though created in 1857, its 1864 publication puts it beyond the parameters of this study. For an instructive analysis of this and other engravings by Carleton, see Maurie D. McInnis, *Slaves Waiting for Sale*, 152–153.

17 David Lee Child, *The Despotism of Freedom; or the Tyranny and Cruelty of American Republican Slave-Masters, Shown to be the Worst in the World; in a Speech delivered at the First Anniversary of the New England Anti-Slavery Society, 1833* (Boston: Boston Young Men's Anti-Slavery Association, 1833), 51.

18 "*Slave Trade of the United States,*" *Boston Recorder* in *Washington, D.C., United States' Telegraph*, March 26, 1833, 3. For the accomplished service record of Danforth's father, Jonathan Danforth, see F. E. Goodrich, "FOUR DAUGHTERS WHOSE FATHERS SERVED IN THE REVOLUTION," *American Monthly Magazine* 2, no. 2 (February 1893): 189–191.

19 Elias Nason and Thomas Russell, *The Life and Public Services of Henry Wilson, Late Vice-President of the United States* (Boston: B. B. Russell, 1876), 31.

20 William Slade, *Speech of Mr. Slade, of Vermont, on the Subject of the Abolition of Slavery and the Slave Trade within the District of Columbia. Delivered in the House of Representatives, December 23, 1835* (Washington, DC: National Intelligencer Office, 1836), 3 (first quotation), 5 (second, third, fourth, and fifth quotations).

21 George Washington Julian, *The Life of Joshua R. Giddings* (Chicago: A. C. McClurg and Company, 1892), 64.

22 The definitive study of the gag rule is William Lee Miller, *Arguing about Slavery: John Quincy Adams and the Great Battle in the United States Congress* (New York: Vintage Books, 1998).

23 "District of Columbia," *Boston Courier*, February 11, 1839, 3. Slave coffles were routinely spotted throughout Washington. Among the largest was the one that appeared in 1847: "We were informed, as our paper was about to go to press, that last Saturday afternoon a coffle of slaves, to the number of one hundred, was marched over the Long Bridge, across the Potomac, in broad daylight, in full

view of the President's House." *National Era* in *National Anti-Slavery Standard*, August 19, 1847, 2.

24 Joshua R. Giddings, *The Rights of the Free States Subverted, or, an Enumeration of Some of the Most Prominent Instances in which the Federal Constitution has been violated by our National Government, for the Benefit of Slavery* (Washington, DC?: 1844), 13. An engraving of the scene described by Giddings appeared on both the front cover and opening page of William Harned, *Slavery and the Slave Trade at the Nation's Capital* (New York: American and Foreign Anti-Slavery Society, 1846).

25 For the full speech, see "Speech of Mr. Giddings of Ohio, on His Motion to Reconsider the Vote Taken Upon the Final Passage of the 'Bill for the Relief of the Owners of Slaves Lost from on Board the Comet and Encomium,'" *Boston Emancipator and Free American*, March 16, 1843, 1 and 4 (quotations on 1). James Brewer Stewart details the impact of daily witnessing slavery and the slave trade on Giddings while the congressman resided in the District of Columbia in "Christian Statesmanship, Codes of Honor, and Congressional Violence: The Antislavery Travails and Triumphs of Joshua Giddings," in Paul Finkelman and Donald R. Kennon, eds., *In the Shadow of Freedom: The Politics of Slavery in the National Capital* (Athens: Ohio University Press, 2011), 36–57; and "Joshua Giddings, Antislavery Violence, and Congressional Politics of Honor," in John R. McKivigan and Stanley Harrold, eds., *Antislavery Violence: Sectional, Racial, and Cultural Conflict in Antebellum America* (Knoxville: University of Tennessee Press, 1999), 167–192.

26 Jeff Forret, *The Williams' Gang: A Notorious Slave Trader and His Cargo of Black Convicts* (Cambridge: Cambridge University Press, 2020), 48. For a brief early study of the district's slave pens, see Walter C. Clephane, "The Local Aspect of Slavery in the District of Columbia," *Records of the Historical Society, Washington, D.C.* 3 (Washington, DC: 1900): 3:238–240.

27 "The Outrages at Washington," *Boston Emancipator*, May 3, 1848, 2.

28 J. M. M'Kim, *A Sketch of the Slave Trade in the District of Columbia, Contained in Two Letters* (Pittsburgh: Pittsburgh and Allegheny Anti-Slavery Society, 1838), 5 (first quotation), 6 (second quotation), 8 (third and fourth quotations).

29 "Editorial Notes and Gleanings," *National Magazine* (February 1854): 181.

30 Solomon Northup, *Twelve Years a Slave: Narrative of Solomon Northup, a Citizen of New-York, Kidnapped in Washington City in 1841, and Rescued in 1853, from a Cotton Plantation near the Red River, in Louisiana* (Auburn, NY: Derby and Miller, 1853), 42.

31 "The Twelfth National Anti-Slavery Bazaar," *Liberator*, January 23, 1846, 2. For additional information on this highly successful event, see "The Twelfth Massachusetts Anti-Slavery Fair, to be Held in Faneuil Hall, at the Close of the Year," *Liberator*, September 12, 1845, 3; and "The National Anti-Slavery Bazaar, Faneuil Hall, Will Open Dec. 23," *Liberator*, December 12, 1845, 3. For the AASS's

official adoption of the motto, see "Address to the Friends of Freedom and Emancipation in the United States," *Liberator*, May 31, 1844, 1.

32 "The Twelfth Massachusetts Anti-Slavery Fair, to be Held in Faneuil Hall, at the Close of the Year."

33 Lee Chambers-Schiller, "'A Good Work among the People': The Political Culture of the Boston Antislavery Fair," in Jean Fagan Yellin and John C. Han Horne, eds., *The Abolitionist Sisterhood: Women's Political Culture in Antebellum America* (Ithaca: Cornell University Press, 1994), 252. See also Goddu, *Selling Antislavery*, 85–138; Julie Roy Jeffrey, *The Great Silent Army of Abolitionism: Ordinary Women in the Antislavery Movement* (Chapel Hill: University of North Carolina Press, 1998); Nancy Hewitt, "Women's Antislavery Activism in Rochester, New York," in Hewitt, ed., *Women, Families, and Communities, Readings in American History*, 2 vols. (Glenview, IL: Scott, Foresman, and Company, 1990) I: 139–153; Beverly Gordon, *Bazaars and Fair Ladies: The History of the American Fundraising Fair* (Knoxville: University of Tennessee Press, 1998).

34 "For the Colored American," *Colored American*, July 21, 1838, 3. The event brought together members associated with the Sunday schools of the First Colored Presbyterian Church and the Chatham Street Chapel. For the latter's integration, see "REMOVAL OF SABBATH SCHOOL," *Colored American*, July 1, 1837, 3; and Jeanne Halgren Kilde, *When Church Became Theatre: The Transformation of Evangelical Architecture* (New York: Oxford University Press, 2002), 37. A glimpse of the New York abolitionist community's respect for Johnson can be found in Henry Highland Garnet, *A Memorial Discourse; by Rev. Henry Highland Garnet, Delivered in the Hall of the House of Representatives, Washington, D.C., on Sabbath, February 12, 1865* (Philadelphia: Joseph M. Wilson, 1865), 42.

35 Marcus Wood, *The Poetry of Slavery: An Anglo-American Anthology, 1764–1865* (Oxford: Oxford University Press, 2003), 237.

36 Lydia Maria Child, *An Appeal in Favor of That Class of Americans Called Africans* (Boston: Allen and Ticknor, 1833), 34. In addition to Moore's memorable lines, Child also invoked other familiar nationalist imagery when comparing American slavery unfavorably with ancient Roman slavery: "We have no Saturnalia here—unless we choose thus to designate a coffle of slaves, on the fourth of July, rattling their chains to the sound of a violin, and carrying the banner of freedom in hands loaded with irons," 43. For the public's reaction to Child's *Appeal*, see Carolyn L. Karcher, *The First Woman of the Republic: A Cultural Biography of Lydia Maria Child* (Durham, NC: Duke University Press, 1994), 183–194.

37 "Poetical Rebuke," *Liberator*, January 4, 1839, 3. See also "Address: Delivered before the Boston Anti-Slavery Society, in Chardon Chapel, July 4, 1839," *Liberator*, August 2, 1839, 1.

38 "BY THOMAS CAMPBELL," *Christian Reflector*, March 8, 1839, 3.

39 To be sure, Britons had a tradition dating back to the American Revolution of exposing the hypocrisy of slavery in the United States. In 1775, Samuel Johnson asked famously, "How is it that we hear the loudest yelps for liberty among the drivers of negroes?" The following year, Thomas Day declared, "If there be an object truly ridiculous in nature, it is an American patriot, signing resolutions of independency with the one hand, and with the other brandishing a whip over his affrighted slaves." *The Works of Samuel Johnson, LL.D., a New Edition, in Twelve Volumes* (London: Luke Hansard, 1801), 8: 203; Thomas Day, *Fragment of an Original Letter on the Slavery of the Negroes, Written in the Year 1776* (Boston: Garrison and Knapp, 1831), 10.

40 "Cork Anti-Slavery Society," *London Anti-Slavery Monthly Reporter* 5, no. 3 (October 1829): 94.

41 "LONDON MISSIONARY SOCIETY," *Boston Christian Watchman*, July 4, 1834, 2.

42 Review of "A Letter to Lord Brougham, on the Subject of American Slavery. By an American," *Evangelical Magazine and Missionary Chronicle* 14 (February 1836): 57.

43 "LONDON MISSIONARY SOCIETY."

44 James Brown, *American Slavery, in its Moral and Political Aspects, Comprehensively Examined, to Which is Subjoined an Epitome of Ecclesiastical History Shewing the Mutilated State of Modern Christianity* (Oswego, NY: George Henry, 1840), 17–18.

45 John G. Whittier, "POETRY," *Liberator*, January 10, 1840, 4.

46 Francis Gillette, *Speech of Hon. Francis Gillette, of Connecticut, in the Senate of the United States, February 23, 1855* (Washington, DC: Buell & Blanchard, 1855), 8.

47 "PRESENTATION OF THE STANDARD," *Liberator*, August 16, 1844, 2.

48 The reverse read, "'Immediate and Unconditional Emancipation'—American Anti-Slavery Society—formed December 6, 1833.—This Banner presented May 31st, 1844.—No UNION WITH SLAVEHOLDERS!" "DESCRIPTION OF THE BANNER," *Liberator*, June 7, 1844, 3.

49 "'No Union with Slaveholders'—how it works. Presentation of a Banner," *Liberator*, August 16, 1844, 3.

50 *The American Anti-Slavery Almanac, for 1843. Being Bissextile or Leap Year; and Until July 4th, the Sixty-Seventh of the Independence of the United States* (New York: American Anti-Slavery Society, 1843).

51 Ibid. The almanac revised Madden's original mention of "two million slaves" to "three million slaves" to reflect the more recent census statistics. Richard Robert Madden, *A Twelvemonth's Residence in the West Indies, During the Transition from Slavery to Apprenticeship; with Incidental Notices of the State of Society, Prospects, and Natural Resources of Jamaica and Other Island* (London: James Cochrane and Company, 1835), 2: 343. The image also appeared on the front page of the almanac's 1844 edition sans Madden's poem. *The American Anti-Slavery Almanac, for 1844. Being Bissextile or Leap Year; and Until July 4th, the Sixty-Eighth of the Independence of the United States* (New York: American Anti-Slavery Society, 1844).

52 *The American Anti-Slavery Almanac, for 1843*. The image also appeared on the almanac's back cover the following year. *The American Anti-Slavery Almanac, for 1844*. The 1844 back cover replaces Campbell's lines with excerpts of "FOURTH OF JULY," a poem written by William Lloyd Garrison more than a decade earlier. Responding to the continued celebration of the victory over Britain in the Revolutionary War, the verses entreat the American people to lower their flag and refrain from the other displays of false patriotism until all people were free. Garrison first published the poem on June 4, 1831, on the *Liberator*'s front page.

53 "The American Anti-Slavery Almanac for 1843," *Liberator*, September 9, 1843, 3.

54 For Garrison's life see Henry Mayer, *All on Fire: William Lloyd Garrison and the Abolition of Slavery* (New York: W. W. Norton & Company, 1998).

55 "The New Head to the Liberator," *Liberator*, May 31, 1850, 2.

56 Ibid.

57 "*Great Anti-Colonization Meeting in Exeter Hall, London*," *Liberator*, November 9, 1833, 2. Garrison's children denied their father crafted the slogan from Paine's pamphlet, but it seems unlikely. Wendell Phillips Garrison and Francis Jackson Garrison, *William Lloyd Garrison, 1805–1879: The Story of His Life Told by His Children* (New York: The Century Co., 1885), 219.

58 Given Garrison's harsh critiques of his country, it is understandable that historians have questioned his patriotism. Anthony Kaye, for example, has argued that Garrison's patriotism began as "ambivalent" but later became a "staunch repudiation." "Nationalism and Abolitionist Politics in Great Britain and the United States," *Review (Fernand Braudel Center)* 35, no. 2 (2012): 147.

59 "*Great Anti-Colonization Meeting in Exeter Hall, London*," *Liberator*, November 9, 1833, 2. In one of his earliest published addresses, Garrison expressed a genuine belief in American exceptionalism and the United States' depiction as a city on a hill, pronouncing, "Yes! that torch, which was first lit by our progenitors on this mighty day,—and which burns as high, as clear, and unsullied, now as it did then,—has illuminated, electrified, and warmed the world!—Other realms are basking in its lofty beams—other empires hail from it from afar, as a prophetic omen of their deliverance from bondage. The icy-fetters of old despotism melt before its powerful blaze; and the flowers of liberty spring up in places once blasted and withered, in wild luxuriance, and flight their odours on every passing zephyr. Such are its magic rays, that, while they consume the seeds of oppression, they nourish those of equality." [William Lloyd Garrison], *An Address, Delivered Before the Members of the Franklin Debating Club, on the Morning of the 5th July, 1824, being the Forty-Eight Anniversary of American Independence* (Newburyport, MA: Herald Office, 1824), 5.

60 "Anti-Slavery Celebration of Independence Day," *Liberator*, July 9, 1858, 2.

61 Ibid.

2. The Fourth

1 "Fourth of July," *Republican, and Savannah Evening Ledger*, July 6, 1815, 3.

2 "Independence," *Republican, and Savannah Evening Ledger*, July 8, 1815, 3.

3 "Continuation of Mr. Child's Speech, delivered at the Annual Meeting of the New-England Anti-Slavery Society, in support of the following resolution," *Liberator*, February 2, 1833, 2. See also L'AMIE, "Slavery and Nullification," *Liberator*, January 5, 1833, 3.

4 Michael Conlin, *One Nation Divided by Slavery: Remembering the American Revolution While Marching toward the Civil War* (Kent, OH: Kent State University Press, 2015), 26.

5 John Adams to Abigail Adam, July 3, 1776, in Charles Francis Adams, ed., *Familiar Letters of John Adams and His Wife Abigail Adams, During the Revolution, with a Memoir of Mrs. Adams* (New York: Hurd and Houghton, 1876), 193 (first quotation), 194 (second quotation).

6 Frederick Dalcho, *Practical Considerations Founded on the Scriptures, Relative to the Slave Population of South Carolina. By a South Carolinian* (Charleston: A. E. Miller, 1823), 33.

7 Len Travers, *Celebrating the Fourth: Independence Day and the Rites of Nationalism in the Early Republic* (Amherst: University of Massachusetts Press, 1997), 146.

8 "*Amusement of* Negroes," *American Cotton Planter* 4, no. 8 (August 1860): 367–368. For the journal's influence, see Weymouth T. Jordan, "Noah B. Cloud and the *American Cotton Planter*," *Agricultural History* 31 (October 1957): 44–49.

9 Louis Hughes, *Thirty Years a Slave: From Bondage to Freedom* (Milwaukee: South Side Printing Company, 1897), 46–47 (first quotation); 50 (second quotation); 51 (third and fourth quotations).

10 For the use of the WPA interviews as primary sources, see Ellen Hampton, "'Lawdy! I was sho' happy when I was a slave!': Manipulative editing in the WPA Former-Slave Narratives from Mississippi," *L'Ordinaire des Amériques* 215 (2013): 522; Lynda M. Hill, "Ex-Slave Narratives: The WPA Federal Writers' Project Reconsidered," *Oral History* 26, no. 1, *Talking and Writing* (Spring 1998): 64–72; Norman R. Yetman, "Ex-Slave Interviews and the Historiography of Slavery," *American Quarterly* 36, no. 2 (Summer 1984): 181–210; Yetman, "The Background of the Slave Narrative Collection," *American Quarterly* 19, no. 3 (September 1967): 534–553.

11 *Slave Narratives: A Folk History of Slavery in the United States from Interviews with Former Slaves, Georgia Narratives*, Part I (Washington: The Federal Writers' Project, 1941), 4: 267 [3].

12 Ibid., *North Carolina Narratives*, Part I, 11: 105 [2].

13 Ibid., *Florida Narratives*, 3: 257 [1] (first, second, and third quotations); 258 [2] (fourth and fifth quotations).

14 Ibid., *Georgia Narratives*, Part I, 4: 206 [5].

15 Ibid., *Mississippi Narratives*, 9: 6 [6].

16 Holland Nimmons McTyeire, "Master and Servant," in *Duties of Masters to Servants: Three Premium Essays* (Charleston, SC: Southern Baptist Publication Society, 1851), 20–21.

17 "Fourth of July among the Slaves," *New York Daily Tribune*, July 31, 1858, 3. The article appeared in newspapers nationwide. The *Tribune* most likely erred when citing the *"Auburn (Georgia) Gazette,"* as no such paper existed. The article most likely originated in the *Auburn Alabama Gazette*.

18 Anne C. Bailey, *The Weeping Time: Memory and the Largest Slave Auction in American History* (Cambridge: Cambridge University Press, 2017), 22.

19 Charles Ball, *Slavery in the United States: A Narrative of the Life and Adventures of Charles Ball, A Black Man* (New York: John S. Taylor, 1837), 123 (first quotation), 124 (second quotation).

20 Ibid., 124–125 (first quotation), 125 (second and third quotations).

21 Ibid., 126 (first), 127 (second quotation), 129 (third quotation).

22 David James McCord, "Art. VII.—Life of a Negro Slave," *Southern Quarterly Review* 7, no. 13 (January 1853): 206 (first quotation), 210 (second and third quotations). McCord's comments were in direct response to an abridged version of Ball's autobiography that appeared in *Chambers's Miscellany*. For the popularity of Ball's narrative, see Yuval Taylor, ed., *I Was Born a Slave: An Anthology of Classic Slave Narratives, Volume I, 1771–1849* (Chicago: Lawrence Hill Books, 1999), xx, 260–262. Historians have also asserted that Fourth of July slave auctions did not exist. Travers, *Celebrating the Fourth*, 150.

23 "NOTICE," *Savannah Georgian*, June 27, 1826, 3.

24 "AGREEABLY," *Milledgeville (Georgia) Journal*, June 26, 1816, 4.

25 "NOTICE," *Lynchburg Virginia*, June 17, 1833, 3.

26 "Negro for Sale," "Trust Sale of Negroes," and "Sale of Negroes &c.," *Winchester (Tennessee) Home Journal*, June 30, 1859, 1 (first quotation), 3, and 4 (second quotation).

27 "ADMINISTRATOR'S SALE," *Columbus Enquirer*, May 2, 1854, 4.

28 "SOUTHERN DEMANDS," *Washington National Era*, August 23, 1855, 2. Toombs denied making the remark, though his Senate colleagues insisted otherwise. Mark Scroggins, *The Civil Wars of a United States Senator and Confederate General* (Jefferson, NC: McFarland & Company, 2011), 94–95. For Toombs's life, see also William C. Davis, *The Union that Shaped the Confederacy: Robert Toombs and Alexander H. Stephens* (Lawrence: University Press of Kansas, 2001); and William Y. Thompson, *Robert Toombs of Georgia* (Baton Rouge: Louisiana State University Press, 1966).

29 Robert Toombs, "SLAVERY: ITS CONSTITUTIONAL STATUS, AND ITS INFLUENCE ON SOCIETY AND THE COLORED RACE," *De Bow's Review* 20 (May 1856): 582.

30 Pauline Maier, *American Scripture: Making the Declaration of Independence* (New York: Vintage Books, 1997).

31 David Armitage, *The Declaration of Independence: A Global History* (Cambridge: Harvard University Press, 2007).

32 Alexander Tsesis writes that in the aftermath of the War of 1812, Americans generally did not discuss or debate the Declaration's principles, but that "this changed drastically at the end of that decade, when a controversy over whether Missouri would enter the Union as a slave or free state returned the Declaration of Independence's statements about liberal equality to the heart of contemporary issues." Tsesis, *For Liberty and Equality: The Life and Times of the Declaration of Independence* (New York: Oxford University Press, 2012), 59. See also Philip F. Detweiler, "The Changing Reputation of the Declaration of Independence: The First Fifty Years," *William and Mary Quarterly* 19, no. 4 (October 1962): 557–574. The best one-volume study of the Missouri Compromise is Robert Pierce Forbes, *The Missouri Compromise and Its Aftermath: Slavery and the Meaning of America* (Chapel Hill: University of North Carolina Press, 2009).

33 *Annals of Congress*, House of Representatives, 15th Cong., 2nd sess., 1819: 1210–1211.

34 Ibid., 16th Cong., 1st sess., 1820: 1153.

35 William Darlington, *Desultory Remarks on the Question of Extending Slavery into Missouri: As Enunciated during the First Session of the Sixteenth Congress, by the Representative from Chester Country, State of Pennsylvania* (West Chester, PA: Lewis Marshall, 1856), 24

36 Aaron Scott Crawford, "John Randolph of Roanoke and the Politics of Doom: Slavery, Sectionalism, and Self-Deception, 1773–1821" (Ph.D. diss., University of Tennessee, Knoxville, 2012), 275. See also John Quincy Adams, *Memoirs of John Quincy Adams, Comprising Portions of His Diary from 1795 to 1848* (Philadelphia: J. B. Lippincott, & Co., 1875), 4: 532–533.

37 Multiple versions of Calhoun's speech exist. The quotations here are from the most extensive version: "SPEECH OF MR. CALHOUN, OF SOUTH CAROLINA, On the bill to establish a Government in Oregon," *Daily National Intelligencer*, July 12, 1848, 2. For comparison, see "INTERESTING DEBATES IN CONGRESS, SPEECH OF HON. JOHN. C. CALHOUN," *New York Herald*, June 28, 1848, 2; and Richard K. Crallé, *Speeches of John C. Calhoun, Delivered in the House of Representatives, and in the Senate of the United States* (New York: D. Appleton and Company, 1883), 479–512.

38 Matthew Dennis, *Red, White, and Blue Letter Days: An American Calendar* (Ithaca, NY: Cornell University Press, 2002), 22–23.

39 Paul Quigley, "Independence Day Dilemmas in the American South, 1848–1865," *Journal of Southern History* 75, no. 2 (2009): 239. See also Daniel Liestman, "'The Day We Used to Celebrate': The Fourth of July as a National Day in the South, 1860–1865," *Southern Studies* 22, no. 1 (Spring/Summer 2015): 45–71; Kimberly R. Kellison, "Men, Women, and the Marriage of the Union: Fourth of July Celebrations in Antebellum Georgia," *Georgia Historical Quarterly* 98, no. 3 (Fall 2014): 129–154; and A. V. Huff, Jr., "The Eagle and the Vulture: Changing

Attitudes toward Nationalism in Fourth of July Orations Delivered in Charleston, 1778–1860," *South Atlantic Quarterly* 73, no. 1 (Winter 1974): 10–22.

40 John Dixon Long, *Pictures of Slavery in Church and State* (Philadelphia: John Dixon Long, 1857), 351–352.

41 Ibid., 852.

42 David Waldstreicher, *In the Midst of Perpetual Fetes: The Making of American Nationalism, 1776–1820* (Chapel Hill: University of North Carolina Press, 1997), 311.

43 David Brion Davis, *From Homicide to Slavery: Studies in American Culture* (New York: Oxford University Press, 1986), 301.

44 "Fourth of July," *Genius of Universal Emancipation*, July 4, 1821, 4.

45 "Fourth of July," *Genius of Universal Emancipation*, July 8, 1826, 5 (first quotation), 6 (second, third, and fourth quotations).

46 William Lloyd Garrison, *Selections from the Writings and Speeches of William Lloyd Garrison* (Boston: R. F. Wallcut, 1852), 46 (first quotation), 49 (second quotation), 53 (third quotation).

47 Archibald H. Grimke, *William Lloyd Garrison: The Abolitionist* (New York: Funk & Wagnalls, 1891), 61 (first quotation), 68 (second quotation).

48 Henry Mayer, *All on Fire: William Lloyd Garrison and the Abolition of Slavery* (New York: W. W. Norton & Company, 1998), 67.

49 Wendell Phillips Garrison and Francis Jackson Garrison, *William Lloyd Garrison, 1805–1879: The Story of His Life Told by His Children* (New York: The Century Co., 1885), 124–127. Garrison normally avoided militia duty because of his short-sightedness. See also "A Noble Example," *Genius of Universal Emancipation*, September 16, 1829, 6.

50 Denis Brennan, *The Making of an Abolitionist: William Lloyd Garrison's Path to Publishing the Liberator* (Jefferson, NC: McFarland & Company, 2014), 110. See also *William Lloyd Garrison, 1805–1879*, I: 138.

51 "Letters From a Man of Colour, on a late Bill before the Senate of Pennsylvania, Letter IV," *Freedom's Journal*, March 14, 1828, 2. See also, "Letters from a Man of Colour, on a late Bill before the Senate of Pennsylvania. Letter I," *Freedom's Journal*, February 22, 1827, 2.

52 "Fourth of July in New York." See also "Constitution of the American Anti-Slavery Society," *Liberator*, January 11, 1834, 1.

53 Linda K. Kerber, "Abolitionists and Amalgamators: The New York City Race Riots of 1834," *New York History* 48, no. 1 (January 1967): 28–39. Prior to the meeting, anti-abolitionists posted a notice near the Chapel reading, "Notice. The friends of the Union and of the South are requested to attend the Anti-Slavery Meeting at Chatham Street Chapel, at 11 o'clock this morning. Remember, freemen, what this Society aim at—The Disunion of the STATES. Many Friends of the Country, July 4, 1834." "Fourth of July in New York," *New York Emancipator*, July 8, 1834, 2.

54 "The Grand Instigators of the New-York Riots," *Liberator*, July 26, 1834, 3.

55 "*Negro Riot*," Washington, D.C., *United States' Telegraph*, July 11, 1834, 1.

56 "A Real Row," *New York Journal of Commerce*, in the *Liberator*, July 12, 1834, 2.

57 Philip Hone, *The Diary of Philip Hone 1828–1851*, ed. Bayard Tuckerman (New York: Dodd, Mead, and Company, 1889), 109.

58 "Riots in New York," *Washington, D.C., Daily National Intelligencer*, July 14, 1834, 2; "Riots in New York," *Christian Advocate and Journal*, July 18, 1834, 3.

59 "New York Mobs," *New York Commercial Advertiser*, in *Niles' Weekly Register*, July 19, 1834, 13.

60 "More Riots: The Riots Suppressed—The Character of the City Redeemed," *New York The Man*, July 14, 1834, 2.

61 Edwin G. Burros and Mike Wallace, *Gotham: A History of New York City to 1898* (New York: Oxford University Press, 1999), 558.

62 Ray Allen Billington, ed., *The Journal of Charlotte L. Forten: A Young Black Woman's Reactions to the White World of the Civil War Era* (New York: W. W. Norton, 1981), 103 (first quotation), 122 (second, third, and fourth quotations).

63 Dennis, *Red, White, and Blue Letter Days*, 26.

64 "For the Freedom's Journal. Serious Thoughts," *Freedom's Journal*, June 29, 1827, 2.

65 "For the Freedom's Journal," *Freedom's Journal*, June 29, 1827, 3.

66 "Freedom's Journal," *Freedom's Journal*, June 22, 1827, 2.

67 Henry Highland Garnet, *A Memorial Discourse; by Rev. Henry Highland Garnet, Delivered in the Hall of the House of Representatives, Washington, D.C., on Sabbath, February 12, 1865. With an Introduction, by James McCune Smith, M.D.* (Philadelphia: Joseph M. Wilson, 1865), 24.

68 Jeffrey R. Kerr-Ritchie, *Rites of August First: Emancipation Day in the Black Atlantic World* (Baton Rouge: Louisiana State University Press, 2007), 2. William B. Gravely, Benjamin Quarles, and Leonard I. Sweet first described the holiday's special significance for African Americans. See Gravely, "The Dialectic of Double-Consciousness in Black American Freedom Celebrations, 1808–1863," *Journal of Negro History* 67, no. 4 (Winter 1982): 302–317; Quarles, *Black Abolitionists* (New York: Oxford University Press, 1969), 116–142; and Sweet, "The Fourth of July and Black American in the Nineteenth Century: Northern Leadership Opinion within the Context of the Black Experience," *Journal of Negro History* 61, no. 3 (July 1976): 270–271.

69 Samuel Cornish, Thomas Downing, Henry Sipkins, Theodore Wright, and Thomas Van Ransalaer [Rensselaer], "Address in Commemoration of the Great Jubilee, of the 1st of August, 1834," (n.p.: 1836), 2 (first and second quotations), 2–3 (third quotation), 3 (fourth quotation).

70 Samuel E. Cornish, "First of August," *Freedom's Journal*, July 29, 1837, 3.

71 "First of August," *Liberator*, August 20, 1841, 2. For Black and White antislavery and abolitionist celebrations in the antebellum era, see Edward B. Rugemer, "Emancipation Day Tradition in the Anglo-Atlantic World" in Gad Heuman and Trevor Burnard, eds., *The Routledge History of Slavery* (London: Routledge, 2011), 314–330; W. Caleb McDaniel, "The Fourth and the First: Abolitionist Holidays, Respectability, and Radical Interracial Reform," *American Quarterly* 57, no. 1 (March 2005): 129–151; Mitch Kachun, *Festivals of Freedom: Memory and Meaning in African American Emancipation Celebrations, 1808–1915* (Amherst: University of Massachusetts Press, 2003); Len Travers, *Celebrating the Fourth: Independence Day and the Rites of Nationalism in the Early Republic* (Amherst: University of Massachusetts Press, 1997), 141–145; Shane White, "'It was a Proud Day': African Americans, Festivals, and Parades in the North, 1711–1834," *Journal of American History* 81, no. 13 (June 1994): 13–50; Leonard I. Sweet, "The Fourth of July and Black Americans in the Nineteenth Century: Northern Leadership Opinion within the Context of the Black Experience," *Journal of Negro History* 61, no. 3 (1976): 266–175.

72 Samuel J. May, "The First of August," *Monthly Offering* 2, no. 7 (July 1842): 101. See also, "The First of August," *Liberator*, June 24, 1842, 3.

73 W. Caleb McDaniel, "The Fourth and the First: Abolitionist Holidays, Respectability, and Radical Interracial Reform," *American Quarterly* 57, no. 1 (March 2005): 130.

74 John A. Collins, "The Offering," *The Monthly Offering* 2, no. 5 (May 1842): 67 (first and second quotations), 68 (third quotation). See also, "The First of August," *Liberator*, June 24, 1842, 3.

75 "Pic-Nics for the First of August," *Liberator*, June 11, 1845, 2.

76 "First of August in Boston," *Liberator*, August 8, 1845, 3.

77 "The First of August," *Liberator*, July 4, 1845, 3.

78 An estimated three hundred Black and White men, women, and children attended the daylong event. "First of August in Boston." For Allen's family and a brief biographical sketch, see Lois Brown, *Pauline Elizabeth Hopkins: Black Daughter of the Revolution* (Chapel Hill: University of North Carolina Press, 2008), 229–230.

79 "Emancipation Meeting in Tremont Temple," *New York Emancipator and Free American*, August 6, 1845, 2. Written by the Reverend Abel G. Duncan of Hanover, Massachusetts, the song appeared two year earlier in Jairus Lincoln's songbook, *Anti-Slavery Melodies: For the Friends of Freedom* (Hingham, MA: Elijah B. Gill, 1843), 28–29.

80 For the history of Oberlin College and its egalitarian efforts, see Gary J. Kornblith and Carol Lasser, *Elusive Utopia: The Struggle for Racial Equality in Oberlin, Ohio* (Baton Rouge: Louisiana State University Press, 2018).

81 "The First of August—Colored People," *Oberlin Evangelist*, August 17, 1842. See also Robert Samuel Fletcher, *A History of Oberlin College from its Foundation through the Civil War* (Oberlin, OH: 1943), I: 249–250.

82 "The First of August—Colored People."

83 "The First of August at Oberlin," *Boston Emancipator and Free American*, October 6, 1842, 3. See also Fletcher, *A History of Oberlin College*, I: 249–250.

84 "The Philadelphia Riots," *Liberator*, August 12, 1842, 2.

85 Ibid.

86 "Riot in Philadelphia," *The Age and Lancaster and Chester County Weekly Gazette*, August 6, 1842, 2.

87 "The Philadelphia Riots," *Liberator*, August 12, 1842, 2. See also, "States of the Union. Pennsylvania," *Niles' National Register*, August 6, 1842, 4; and "More Riots—Bloodshed," *Cincinnati Philanthropist*, August 20, 1842, 1.

88 Despite his patriotic sacrifices, Black "never received a pension." "Affliction of our Colored Population," *Liberator*, September 9, 1842, 2. See also Eric Johnson, "'Amongst My Best Men,'" *Lake Erie Ledger* 28, no. 3 (October 2015): 4.

89 February 20, 1854, Appendix to the Congressional Globe, 33rd, Cong., 1st Sess., Senate, 214.

90 Rufus Choate to E. W. Farley, August 9, 1856, in Samuel Gilman Brown, *The Works of Rufus Choate with a Memoir of His Life* (Boston: Little, Brown and Company, 1862), I: 215.

91 H. M. Flint, *Life of Stephen A. Douglas to Which are Added His Speeches and Reports* (Philadelphia: John E. Potter and Company, 1863), 173–174.

92 "Dred Scott v. Sandford (1857)," www.archives.gov.

3. The Fifth

1 "Anti-Slavery Convention," *Liberator*, August 20, 1 841, 3.

2 Parker Pillsbury, *Acts of the Anti-Slavery Apostles* (Rochester: Claque, Wegman, Schlicht, and Company, 1883), 327. Several weeks later, the *Liberator* summarized the subject of Douglass's earliest orations thusly: "He states his history and the working of slavery upon his own mind with great eloquence," *Liberator*, August 27, 1841, 2.

3 Frederick Douglass, *My Bondage and My Freedom* (New York: Miller, Orton & Mulligan, 1855), 357–358 (quotation on 357). See also Douglass, *Narrative of the Life of Frederick Douglass, an American Slave* (Boston: American Anti-Slavery Society, 1845), 117; and Douglass, *Life and Times of Frederick Douglass Written by Himself* (Hartford: Park Publishing, 1881), 216–217.

4 Douglass, *Narrative*, 117.

5 Ibid.

6 Reliable studies of American exceptionalism include Godfrey Hodgson, *The Myth of American Exceptionalism* (New Haven, CT: Yale University Press, 2009);

Deborah L. Madsen, *American Exceptionalism* (Jackson: University Press of Mississippi, 1998); Seymour Martin Lipset, *American Exceptionalism* (New York: W. W. Norton & Company, 1997).

7 Lucy Williams, "Blasting Reproach and All-Pervading Light: Frederick Douglass's Aspirational American Exceptionalism," *American Political Thought: A Journal of Ideas, Institutions, and Culture* 9, no., 3 (Summer 2020): 370. For Douglass as an American exceptionalist thinker, see also Jason Frank, *Constituent Moments: Enacting the People in Postrevolutionary America* (Durham, NC: Duke University Press, 2010), 218; Julie Husband, "Multicultural American Exceptionalism in the Speeches of Frederick Douglass and Barack Obama," *Howard Journal of Communications* 29, no. 3 (2018): 225–242.

8 Douglass, *My Bondage and My Freedom*, 52.

9 David W. Blight, "Editor's Introduction: The Peculiar Dialogue Between Caleb Bingham and Frederick Douglass," in Caleb Bingham, *The Columbian Orator Containing a Variety of Original and Selected Pieces Together With Rules, Which Are Calculated to Improve Youth and Others, in the Ornamental and Useful Art of Eloquence,* ed. David W. Blight (New York: New York University Press, 1998), xviii.

10 Douglass, *My Bondage and My Freedom*, 159.

11 Douglass, *Narrative of the Life of Frederick Douglass*, 246–247.

12 *U.S. Statutes at Large*, 4th Cong., 1st. Sess., ch. 36 (1798), 477.

13 Gene Allen Smith, *The Slaves' Gamble: Choosing Sides in the War of 1812* (Boston: St. Martin's, 2013), 54.

14 Douglass, *Life and Times*, 199.

15 David W. Blight, *Frederick Douglass: Prophet of Freedom* (New York: Simon & Schuster, 2018), 11.

16 Jesse Washington, "Washington: The 'Blackest Name' in America," February 21, 2011, www.nbcnews.com.

17 Booker T. Washington, *Up From Slavery: An Autobiography* (New York: Doubleday, 1901), 34.

18 Douglass, *Narrative of the Life of Frederick Douglass*, 111–112.

19 James Matlack, "The Autobiographies of Frederick Douglass," *Phylon* 40, no. 1 (1979): 15.

20 Ukawsaw Gronniosaw, *A Narrative of the Most Remarkable Particulars in the Life of James Albert Ukawsaw Gronniosaw, an African Prince* (Bath, England: W. Gye, 1770); Olaudah Equiano, *The Interesting Narrative and the Life of "Olaudah Equiano," or Gustavus Vassa, the African* (London: Olaudah Equiano, 1789); Venture Smith, *A Narrative of the Life and Adventures of Venture, a Native of Africa: But Resident Above Sixty Years in the United States of America* (New London, CT: C. Holt, 1798); John Jea, *The Life, History, and Unparalleled Sufferings of John Jea, the African Preacher* (Plymouth, England: John Jea, 1811).

21 William Grimes, *Life of William Grimes, the Runaway Slave* (New York: n.p., 1825); Solomon Bayley, *A Narrative of Some Remarkable Incidents in the Life of*

Solomon Bayley, Formerly a Slave in the State of Delaware, North America (London: Harvey and Darton, 1825); Charles Ball, *Slavery in the United States: A Narrative of the Life and Adventures of Charles Ball, A Black Man* (Lewiston, PA: John W. Shugert, 1836).

22 Douglass, *Narrative of the Life of Frederick Douglass*, 84 (first quotation), 85–86 (second quotation), 86 (third quotation).

23 Ibid., 118 (first quotation), 123 (second quotation).

24 Blight, *Frederick Douglass*, 229.

25 John W. Blassingame, ed., *The Frederick Douglass Papers, Series One: Speeches, Debates, and Interviews* (New Haven: Yale University Press, 1979–1982), I: 185.

26 Ibid., II: 21.

27 Ibid., II: 39.

28 Ibid., II: 45 (first quotation), 51 (second and third quotations).

29 "AMERICAN ANTI-SLAVERY SOCIETY," *New York Observer*, in the *Liberator*, May 21, 1847, 2.

30 Blassingame, *The Frederick Douglass Papers*, II: 59.

31 Ibid., II: 60.

32 For example, see "THE ANNIVERSARIES," *Courier and Enquirer*, in *National Anti-Slavery Standard*, May 27, 1847, 1; "ANNIVERSARY WEEK IN NEW YORK," *New York Herald*, May 13, 1847, 2; "EDITOR'S CORRESPONDENCE," *Raleigh Register, and North-Carolina Gazette*, May 18, 1847, 3; "AMERICAN ANTI-SLAVERY SOCIETY," *New York Observer*, in the *Liberator*, May 21, 1847, 2.

33 Matthew Goodman, *The Sun and the Moon: The Remarkable True Account of Hoaxers, Showmen, Dueling Journalists, and Lunar Man-Bats in Nineteenth-Century New York* (New York: Basic Books, 2008), 12.

34 "Anti Slavery Society," *New York Sun*, May 13, 1847, 2.

35 "LETTER FROM MR. DOUGLASS," *Liberator*, June 4, 1847, 4. For the brief albeit successful history of Hodge's and Van Rensselaer's *New York Ram's Horn*, see Irvine Garland Penn, *The Afro-American Press and Its Editors* (Springfield, MA: Willey & Co., 1891), 61–65.

36 Steven Johnston, *The Truth About Patriotism* (Durham, NC: Duke University Press, 2007), 7.

37 Bernard R. Boxill, "Frederick Douglass's Patriotism," *Journal of Ethics* 13, no. 4 (2009): 314.

38 Leslie Elizabeth Eckel, *Atlantic Citizens: Nineteenth-Century American Writers at Work in the World* (Edinburgh: Edinburgh University Press, 2013), 94. On the topic of nationalism, Eckel adds, "Instead of fighting for 'disunion' and fragmentation of the nation as it stood, as he had in his previous speeches, Douglass began to reinscribe himself with the boundaries of the nation and to renew his belief in its integrity as a democratic construct," 95.

39 Blight, *Frederick Douglass*, 180.

40 Blassingame, *The Frederick Douglass Papers*, II: 102.

41 Ibid., II: 103.

42 Douglass, *My Bondage and My Freedom*, 354.

43 "THE GREAT CRISIS!" *Liberator*, December 29, 1832, 3. See also Henry Mayer, *All on Fire: William Lloyd Garrison and the Abolition of Slavery* (New York: W. W. Norton & Company, 1998).

44 "ELEVENTH ANNUAL MEETING of the MASSACHUSETTS Anti-Slavery Society," *Liberator*, February 3, 1843, 3.

45 For a description of Douglass's break from Garrison and the Garrisonians, see Benjamin Quarles, *Frederick Douglass* (Washington, DC: The Associated Publishers, Inc., 1948), 72–79.

46 "PROCEEDINGS OF THE ANNUAL MEETING OF THE AMERICAN ANTI-SLAVERY SOCIETY," *Liberator*, May 23, 1851, 1. For the inability to secure a meeting place, see "Public Sentiment in New York," *Washington Daily National Intelligencer*, April 14, 1851, 3.

47 "PROCEEDINGS OF THE ANNUAL MEETING," *Liberator*, 2.

48 "The Seventeenth Anniversary of the American Anti-Slavery Society," *North Star*, May 25, 1851, 2.

49 Quarles, *Frederick Douglass*, 72. For Quarles's fascination with Douglass, see August Meier, "Benjamin Quarles and the Historiography of Black America," *Civil War History* 26, no. 2 (June 1980): 102–103.

50 James Oakes, *The Crooked Path to Abolition: Abraham Lincoln and the Antislavery Constitution* (New York: W. W. Norton, 2021), xxii.

51 Samuel May claimed that Douglass's reversal revealed an "unsettled state of mind." The Syracuse remarks were, for those in attendance, "painful to witness," "THE CONSTITUTION," *Liberator*, May 30, 1851, 3.

52 "FOURTH OF JULY ADDRESS," *Frederick Douglass' Paper*, June 26, 1851, 2.

53 Frederick Douglass to Gerrit Smith, May 21, 1851, Gerrit Smith Papers, Syracuse University, reel #5.

54 "ROCHESTER, JULY 24, 1851," *Frederick Douglass' Paper*, July 24, 1851, 2. See also "We regret to learn by his last paper," *Liberator*, July 11, 1851, 3; and Frederick Douglass to Gerrit Smith, July 10, 1851, Gerrit Smith Papers, Syracuse University, reel #5.

55 "Frederick Douglass," *Frederick Douglass' Paper*, July 24, 1851, 3. See also in the same issue, "Complement to Frederick Douglass."

56 Examples include "IS THE UNITED STATES CONSTITUTION FOR OR AGAINST SLAVERY?" *Frederick Douglass' Paper*, July 24, 1851, 2; "EXTRACT FROM SPOONER," *Frederick Douglass' Paper*, July 31, 1851, 3.

57 "THE ANNUAL MEETING OF THE AMERICAN ANTI-SLAVERY SOCIETY," *Frederick Douglass' Paper*, May 20, 1852.

58 "Frederick Douglass proposes," *Frederick Douglass' Paper*, May 13, 1852, 2.

59 Julie Roy Jeffrey, *The Great Silent Army of Abolitionism: Ordinary Women in the Antislavery Movement* (Chapel Hill: University of North Carolina Press, 1998),

2. The group first organized in the 1840s as the Rochester Anti-Slavery Society, but suspended operations for almost two years due to insufficient support in the community. Douglass wrote privately, "A female Antislavery Society has been formed in Rochester from which I am expecting much aid. The Ladies who compose it are persons upon whom I can rely. They are intelligent and sound in our views of Antislavery action." Frederick Douglass to Gerrit Smith, September 2, 1851, Gerrit Smith Papers, Syracuse University, reel #5. See also "Friend Douglass," *Frederick Douglass' Paper*, April 22, 1852, 2; "ROCHESTER LADIES' ANTI-SLAVERY SEWING SOCIETY," *Frederick Douglass' Paper*, September 4, 1851, 2; "THE RECENT ANTI-SLAVERY FESTIVAL AND CONVENTION IN ROCHESTER," *Frederick Douglass' Paper*, March 25, 1852, 2.

60 W. Caleb McDaniel, "The Fourth and the First: Abolitionist Holidays, Respectability, and Radical Interracial Reform," *American Quarterly* 57, no. 1 (March 2005): 130.

61 "The Fourth of July," *North Star*, July 7, 1848, 2.

62 Ibid.

63 "CELEBRATION OF THE NATIONAL ANNIVERSARY," *Frederick Douglass' Paper*, June 17, 1852, 2, and June 24, 1852, 2.

64 "Come to the Celebration, and to the County Convention in Rochester, on the 5th of July," *Frederick Douglass' Paper*, June 17, 1852, 2.

65 "THE CELEBRATION AT CORINTHIAN HALL," *Frederick Douglass' Paper*, July 9, 1852, 2.

66 Frederick Douglas to Gerrit Smith, July 7, 1852, Gerrit Smith Papers, Syracuse University, reel #5.

67 Frederick Douglass, *ORATION, Delivered in Corinthian Hall, Rochester, by Frederick Douglass, July 5th, 1852* (Rochester, NY: Lee, Mann & Co., 1852), 3–4. See also James A. Colaiaco, *Frederick Douglass and the Fourth of July* (New York: Palgrave Macmillan, 2006), 208, fn. 60; and Blassingame, *The Frederick Douglass Papers*, I: xxx.

68 Blight, *Frederick Douglass*, 231.

69 Benjamin Quarles, *Frederick Douglass* (Washington, DC: Associated Publishers, Inc., 1948), 60.

70 James A. Colaiaco writes, "Having riveted the attention of his audience with his exordium, Frederick Douglass moved to the main body of his speech, a narrative of America's revolutionary past, its flawed present, and its ominous future." *Frederick Douglass and the Fourth of July*, 31.

71 Douglass, *ORATION*, 4. Colaiaco counts the use of "you" and phrases including the word "your" 112 times. *Frederick Douglass and the Fourth of July*, 208, fn. 2.

72 Douglass, *ORATION*, 7–9 (quotation on 7).

73 Ibid., 9.

74 Ibid., 10 (first and second quotations), 11 (third quotation).

75 Ibid., 12.

76 Ibid., 14 (first quotation), 15 (second and third quotations).

77 Ibid., 16 (first, second, and third quotations), 16–17 (fourth quotation), 17 (fifth quotation).

78 Ibid., 20 (first and second quotations), 21 (third quotation).

79 Ibid., 25. For the internal slave trade and its economic impact, see Steven Deyle, *Carry Me Back: The Domestic Slave Trade in American Life* (New York: Oxford University Press, 2006); Robert H. Grumstead, *A Troublesome Commerce: The Transformation of the Interstate Slave Trade* (Baton Rouge: Louisiana State University Press, 2003); and Jonathan B. Pritchett, "Quantitative Estimates of the United States Interregional Slave Trade, 1820–1860," *Journal of Economic History* 61, no. 2 (2001): 467–475.

80 Douglass, ORATION, 28 (first and second quotations), 32 (third quotation), 34 (fourth quotation).

81 Ibid., 35 (first quotation), 36 (second quotation), 37 (third quotation).

82 David Blight, *Frederick Douglass' Civil War: Keeping Faith in Jubilee* (Baton Rouge: Louisiana State University Press, 1989), 111.

83 Douglass, ORATION, 37 (first and second quotations), 38 (third quotation).

84 "THE CELEBRATION AT CORINTHIAN HALL," *Frederick Douglass' Paper*, July 9, 1852, 3.

85 "We gratefully acknowledge," *Frederick Douglass' Paper*, July 23, 1852, 2.

86 "Meetings at Dryden, and at McGrawville," *Frederick Douglass' Paper*, July 30, 1852, 2. An indicator of the oration's success was that it earned a mention in Garrison's *Liberator*. In a brief report on the Corinthian Hall gathering, the paper characterized Douglass's effort as "a severe rebuke of the hypocrisy and meanness of the American people, for celebrating their own independence, while they keep four millions of blacks in bondage." As could be expected, Douglass's defense of the Constitution as an antislavery instrument went unmentioned. "The National Anniversary," *Liberator*, July 23, 1852, 3.

87 Douglass, *My Bondage and My Freedom*, 441–445.

88 For examples, see "A National Watch Meeting—A Novelty for Troy—Among the Veterans," *Troy (New York) Northern Budget*, July 8, 1894, 2; "A GREAT MAN," *Portsmouth (Ohio) Daily Times*, February 27, 1895, 3; Peter Thomas Stanford, *The Tragedy of the Negro in America: A Condensed History of the Enslavement, Sufferings, Emancipation, Present Condition and Progress of the Negro Race in the United States of America* (Boston: Charles A. Wasto, 1897); James Monroe Gregory, *Frederick Douglass the Orator, Containing an Account of His Life; His Eminent Public Services; His Brilliant Career as Orator; Selections from His Speeches and Writings* (Springfield: Wiley & Co., 1893), 103–106; and Alice Moore Dunbar, ed., *Masterpieces of Negro Eloquence: The Best Speeches Delivered by the Negro From the Days of Slavery to the Present Time* (New York: The Bookery Publishing Company, 1914), 41–48.

89 William S. McFeely, *Frederick Douglass* (New York: Norton, 1991), 173; Blight, *Frederick Douglass: Prophet of Freedom*, 230.

90 Colaiaco, *Frederick Douglass and the Fourth of July*, 34.

4. Rebels

1 "Sumterville, S.C. July 12," *Washington Daily National Intelligencer*, July 20, 1832, 3.

2 Ibid.

3 "We learn from an extra," *Charleston Courier* in *Macon Telegraph*, July 25, 1832, 3. The defiant acts of enslaved people on the Fourth of July were common to many South Carolinians. Though falling beyond the scope of this study, historian Len Travers catalogs a spate of arson cases purportedly perpetrated by enslaved Charlestonians at the turn of the nineteenth century. *Celebrating the Fourth: Independence Day and the Rites of Nationalism in the Early Republic* (Amherst: University of Massachusetts Press, 1997), 148.

4 "POISONING!" *Rochester (N.Y.) Observer* in *Hudson (OH) Observer and Telegraph*, August 2, 1832, 2.

5 Even the classic studies of slave resistance fail to fully recognize the influence of domestic ideas on slave resistance. In *From Rebellion to Revolution*, Eugene Genovese argued that after the Age of Revolutions, slave revolts and other collectives acts of slave resistance across the Americas were global "bourgeois-democratic" movements that challenged the "world capitalist system." Winthrop Jordan, by contrast, insisted in his study of an insurrectionary plot in Civil War Mississippi that "the ideology of natural rights" was, for enslaved people, "a foreign tradition belonging to their enemies, not to them." *From Rebellion to Revolution: Afro-American Slave Revolts in the Making of the Modern World* (Baton Rouge: Louisiana State University Press, 1979), xxi; Winthrop D. Jordan, *Tumult and Silence at Second Creek: An Inquiry into a Civil War Slave Conspiracy* (Baton Rouge: Louisiana State University Press, 1995), 199. Herbert Aptheker found that the ideology of American freedom fueled violent slave resistance but only during the American Revolution. He writes, "Here it is likely that the spirit and philosophy of that movement were important in arousing organized displays of discontent amongst the Negroes." Herbert Aptheker, *American Negro Slave Revolts* (New York: International Publishers, 1987), 87.

6 Demonstrating this hold requires a revision of the historiography of nineteenth-century American nationalism, which focuses largely on White elites, or, in the case of free and enslaved Black people, the emergence of a shared racial identity that transcended national boundaries. Studies of nationalism that allow for a variety of distinct and inclusive nationalisms directly influence this study. Eric Hobsbawm's "revolutionary-democratic" nationalism, Louis Snyder's "egalitarian nationalism," and Yael Tamir's "pluralistic nationalism," are among the important concepts. Eric Hobsbawm, *Nations and Nationalism since 1780* (Cambridge: Cambridge University Press,

1990), 22; Louis L. Snyder, *The New Nationalism* (London: Routledge, 2017), 258; Yael Tamir, *Liberal Nationalism* (Princeton: Princeton University Press, 1995), 90. Among the standard treatments of American nationalism in the nineteenth century are Benjamin E. Park, *American Nationalisms: Imagining Union in the Age of Revolutions, 1783–1833* (Cambridge: Cambridge University Press, 2018); Robert E. Bonner, *Mastering America: Southern Slaveholders and the Crisis of American Nationhood* (Cambridge: Cambridge University Press, 2009); Peter J. Kastor, *The Nation's Crucible: The Louisiana Purchase and the Creation of America* (New Haven: Yale University Press, 2004); Susan-Mary Grant, *North Over South: Northern Nationalism and American Identity in the Antebellum Era* (Lexington: University Press of Kentucky, 2000); Harlow W. Sheidley, *Sectional Nationalism: Massachusetts Conservative Leaders and the Transformation of America, 1815–1836* (Boston: Northeastern University Press, 1998); Anne Norton, *Alternative Americas: A Reading of Antebellum Political Culture* (Chicago: University of Chicago Press, 1986); William R. Taylor, *Cavalier and Yankee: The Old South and American National Character* (Cambridge: Harvard University Press, 1979); George Dangerfield, *The Awakening of American Nationalism: 1815–1828* (New York: Harper & Row, 1965). Important studies of Black nationalism in the United States include Dean E. Robinson, *Black Nationalism in American Politics and Thought* (Cambridge: Cambridge University Press, 2001); Wilson Jeremiah Moses, *The Golden Age of Black Nationalism, 1850–1925* (New York: Oxford University Press, 1988); Sterling Stuckey, *Slave Culture: Nationalist Theory and the Foundations of Black America* (New York: Oxford University Press, 1988); Rodney Carlisle, *The Roots of Black Nationalism* (Port Washington, NY: Kennikat Press, 1975). An exception to the standard treatment of Black nationalism is Tunde Adeleke, *UnAfrican Americans: Nineteenth-Century Black Nationalists and the Civilizing Mission* (Lexington: University Press of Kentucky, 1998).

7   François Furstenberg, *In the Name of the Father: Washington's Legacy, Slavery, and the Making of a Nation* (New York: Penguin Press, 2006), 199.

8   Ibid., 195.

9   "Extract of a letter from a Gentleman in Camden, S.C. to his friend in Philadelphia, dated July 4, 1816," *New York Herald*, July 20, 1816, 2.

10   South-Carolinian [Edwin C. Holland], *A Refutation of the Calumnies Circulated Against the Southern & Western States, Respecting the Institution and Existence of Slavery among Them.* (Charleston: A. E. Miller, 1822), 75. See also H. M. Henry, *The Police Control of the Slave in South Carolina* (Emory, VA: H. M. Henry, 1914), 151–152.

11   Thomas J. Kirkland and Robert M. Kennedy, *Historic Camden, Part Two: Nineteenth Century* (Columbia, SC: The State Company, 1926), 189. See also [Holland], *A Refutation of the Calumnies*, 75–77; and Harvey Toliver Cook, *The Life and Legacy of David Rogerson Williams* (New York: n.p., 1916), 131.

12 [Holland], *A Refutation of the Calumnies*, 76 (first, second, and third quotations), 77 (fourth quotation).

13 *"To the Editor of the Camden Gazette,"* *Camden Gazette*, December 19, 1816, 1. The metaphor of a "slumbering volcano" permeated antebellum American print culture. An early use in the context of American slave revolts came in the wake of Nat Turner's rebellion: "Legislative Debate—Continued," *Enquirer* (Richmond), February 16, 1832. For historians' use of the imagery in popular and scholarly works, see Albert Marrin, *A Volcano Beneath the Snow: John Brown's War Against Slavery* (New York: Knopf, 2014); Maggie Montesinos Sale, *The Slumbering Volcano: American Slave Ship Revolts and the Production of Rebellious Masculinity* (Durham, NC: Duke University Press, 1997); and Alfred N. Hunt, *Haiti's Influence on Antebellum America: Slumbering Volcano in the Caribbean* (Baton Rouge: Louisiana State University Press, 1987).

14 Thomas R. Gray, *The Confessions of Nat Turner, the Leader of the Late Insurrection in Southampton, VA* (Richmond: Thomas R. Gray, 1832), 10. For a sampling of the extensive literature on Nat Turner, see Patrick H. Breen, *The Land Shall be Deluged in Blood: A New History of the Nat Turner Revolt* (New York: Oxford University Press, 2015): David F. Allmendinger, *Nat Turner and the Rising in Southampton County* (Baltimore: Johns Hopkins University Press, 2014); Kenneth S. Greenberg, *Nat Turner: A Slave Rebellion in History and Memory* (New York: Oxford University Press, 2003); and Stephen B. Oates, *The Fires of Jubilee: Nat Turner's Fierce Rebellion* (New York: Harper & Row, 1990).

15 Only after the abolition of slavery during the Civil War did White southerners openly acknowledge Turner's intention to revolt on Independence Day. In a small literary journal published in Virginia, William H. Parker expressed his indignation that the most sacred patriotic holiday "of a proud and chivalrous people was to be devoted to the midnight assassination, the wholesale massacre of the entire white race of mankind." The Fourth of July, "hallowed as a day of liberty and peace, consecrated to the memories of the brave, patriotic heroes of the Revolution, was to be set apart for the complete destruction of the lives of their sons and their property by a band of ferocious miscreants." Given the significance of the national anniversary, it was difficult to fathom how any people, including those held in bondage, could "pervert that sacred day and stain it with gory deeds!" Rather than slavery, Parker concluded the only explanation could be race. "How the complexion affects reason!" he exclaimed. William H. Parker, "The Nat Turner Insurrection," *Ole Virginny Yarns* (January 1893): 17–18.

16 For the Murrell conspiracy, see Joshua D. Rothman, *Flush Times and Fever Dreams: A Story of Capitalism and Slavery in the Age of Jackson* (Athens: University of Georgia Press, 2012); Thomas Ruys Smith, "Independence Day, 1835: The John A. Murrell Conspiracy and the Lynching of the Vicksburg Gamblers in Literature," *Mississippi Quarterly* 59, nos. 1/2 (Winter 2005/Spring 2006): 129–160; James Lal Penick, Jr., *The Great Western Land Pirate: John*

Murrell in History and Memory (Columbia: University of Missouri Press, 1981); Christopher Morris, "An Event in Community Organization: The Mississippi Slave Insurrection Scare of 1835," *Journal of Social History* 22, no. 1 (1988): 93–111; and Augustus Q. Walton [Virgil A. Stewart], *A History of the Detection, Conviction, Life and Designs of John A. Murel, the Great Western Land Pirate. Together with His System of Villany, and Plan of Exciting a Negro Rebellion. And a Catalogue of the Names of Four-Hundred and Forty-Five of His Mystic Clan, Fellows and Followers, and Their Efforts for the Destruction of Mr. Virgil A. Stewart, the Young Man Who Detected Him. To Which is Added a Biographical Sketch of Mr. Virgil A. Stewart* (Athens, TN: George White, 1835).

17 For frontier slave stealers generally, see S. Charles Bolton, *Fugitivism: Escaping Slavery in the Lower Mississippi Valley, 1820–1860* (Fayetteville: University of Arkansas Press, 2019); Rothman, *Flush Times and Fever Dreams*, and Matthew J. Clavin, *Aiming for Pensacola: Fugitive Slaves on the Atlantic and Southern Frontiers* (Cambridge: Harvard University Press, 2015).

18 While the Black people targeted by slave stealers were usually abducted and sold against their will, some were not. Rather than victims, they were criminal accomplices seeking freedom or financial gain by conspiring with their White captors.

19 Smith, "Independence Day, 1835," 131.

20 [Stewart], *A History of the Detection, Conviction, Life and Designs of John A. Murel*, 22.

21 For example, see *"Insurrection in Mississippi—Necessity for Vigilance,"* Richmond *Whig & Public Advertiser*, August 4, 1835, 1. An article first published in Nashville, Tennessee, which declared, "The massacre was to have commenced on the fourth of July," appeared in dozens of newspapers across the country shortly after its publication. "INSURRECTION OF SLAVES IN MISSISSIPPI," *Nashville Banner and Nashville Whig*, July 15, 1835, 3.

22 *Proceedings of the Citizens of Madison County, Mississippi, at Livingston in July 1835, in Relation to the Trial and Punishment of Several Individuals Implicated in a Certain Insurrection in This State*, in H. R. Howard [Virgil A. Stewart], *The History of Virgil A. Stewart, and His Adventure in Capturing and Exposing the Great 'Western Land Pirate' and His Gang, in Connexion with the Evidence* (New York: Harper & Brothers, 1836), 227.

23 Rothman, *Flush Times and Fever Dreams*, 19–27 (quotation on 27).

24 The classic statement on the impact of abolitionists' propaganda war on the Murrell conspiracy belongs to James Lal Penick, Jr.: "As it happened, northern abolitionists chose this summer to launch a vigorous effort to distribute antislavery literature in the region and slaveholders responded wrathfully. Violent incidents occurred all over the South. The 'Murel conspiracy' and abolitionism were merged, and of this portentous union was born the legend of John. A. Murrell." Penick, Jr., *The Great Western Land Pirate*, 3–4.

25 "SERVILE INSURRECTION," *Virginia Free Press*, August 6, 1835, 2.

26 "50 DOLLARS REWARD," *Washington Daily National Intelligencer*, July 18, 1814, 2.

27 "$100 REWARD," *Tuscaloosa Alabama State Intelligencer*, September 17, 1831, 3.

28 "Two HUNDRED DOLLARS REWARD," *Columbus (MS) Southern Argus*, July 24, 1838, 2.

29 "FIFTY DOLLARS REWARD," *Easton (Maryland) Republican Star*, August 29, 1815, 4.

30 "FLAPDODDLE WITH COMMENTS," *Liberator*, October 8, 1858, 2.

31 "$25 REWARD," *Montgomery (Alabama) Journal*, in *National Anti-Slavery Standard*, August 8, 1842, 3.

32 Josephine Brown, *Biography of an American Bondman, by His Daughter* (Boston: R. F. Wallcut, 1856), 15–16. See also William Wells Brown, *Narrative of William W. Brown, a Fugitive Slave. Written by Himself* (Boston: The Anti-Slavery Office, 1847); Ezra Greenspan, *William Wells Brown: An African American Life* (New York: W. W. Norton, 2014).

33 William and Ellen Craft, *Running a Thousand Miles for Freedom; or, the Escape of William and Ellen Craft from Slavery* (London: William Tweedie, 1860), iii.

34 Ibid., 89 (first quotation), 91 (second quotation).

35 For an early version of what is believed to be the full text of Henry's speech, see William Wirt, *Sketches of the Life and Character of Patrick Henry* (Philadelphia: James Webster, 1817), 119–123 (quotations on 120 and 123). Eyewitness accounts of the speech are found in H. W., "GREAT AMERICANS AND WHY (Patrick Henry) Born May 29, 1736," *American Catholic Quarterly Review* 48, no. 192 (October 1923): 280–282. See also Jon Kukla, *Patrick Henry: Champion of Liberty* (New York: Simon and Schuster, 2017); Harlow Giles Unger, *Lion of Liberty: Patrick Henry and the Call to a New Nation* (Cambridge, MA: De Capo Press, 2010); and Henry Mayer, *A Son of Thunder: Patrick Henry and the American Republic* (New York: Grove Press, 1991).

36 "Negro Revolt and Loss of Life," *New Orleans Daily Delta*, February 15, 1846, 2. This article mistakenly reports the death of the unnamed Black driver, when in fact the only fatality appears to have been Lewis. See "We, the undersigned Jury of Planters," *New-Orleans Bee*, February 18, 1846, 1.

37 "We, the undersigned Jury of Planters."

38 "Negro Revolt and Loss of Life."

39 Ibid.

40 "We, the undersigned Jury of Planters."

41 "Negro Revolt and Loss of Life.

42 "Not So," *New-Orleans Bee*, February 16, 1846, 1. Similarly, the *New Orleans Tropic* called the revolt a "gross exaggeration," in the *Liberator*, March 13, 1846, 3.

43 "LETTER FROM J. W. LOGUEN," *Frederick Douglass' Paper*, April 6, 1855, 1.

44 Israel Campbell, *An Autobiography. Bond and Free: or, Yearnings for Freedom, from My Green Brier House* (Philadelphia: Israel Campbell, 1861), 172.

45 William Still, *Still's Underground Rail Road Records. Revised Edition* (Philadelphia: William Still, 1886), 191 (first, second, and third quotations), 192 (fourth quotation).

46 "A SHORT HISTORY OF THE HERO CHARLES BROWN," *Indiana (PA) Clarion of Freedom*, in *National Anti-Slavery Standard*, August 17, 1848, 1. See also William J. Switala, *Underground Railroad in Pennsylvania* (Mechanicsburg, PA: Stackpole Books, 2001), 50. More than two years after first escaping from the smokehouse, a gang of southern slave catchers joined by a local sheriff tried to capture Brown, Jared Harris, Anthony Hollingsworth, and two other escaped slaves in the log cabin home these fugitives shared near Indiana. Harris and Hollingsworth avoided arrest by hiding and escaping from the intruders. The two anonymous fugitives surrendered without putting up a fight, "but Charlie Brown, true to his nature, fought like a demon." Eventually captured, rope tied, and bound to a horse, Brown bellowed, "I have tasted the sweets of liberty and I will never live my life in slavery." True to his word, he somehow managed to free himself and "was never heard of more." The attempted capture and rendition of the twelve-year-old Hollingsworth later resulted in one of the most famous fugitive slave trials in the history of antebellum America. In the end, Judge Thomas White, on the precedent of the famous Somerset Case in Great Britain, "discharged" the prisoner. Having won his freedom at least temporarily, Hollingsworth successfully fled with Harris to Windsor, Canada. Sarah R. Christy, "Fugitive Slaves in Indiana County," *Western Pennsylvania Historical Magazine* 18, no. 4 (December 1935): 278–288 (quotations on 284–285). See also J. T. Stewart, *Indiana County Pennsylvania: Her People, Past and Present* (Chicago: J. H. Beers & Co., 1913), 1: 577–578.

47 "Fugitive Slave Meeting in Faneuil Hall," *North Star*, October 24, 1850, 3.

48 Anthony Bearse, *Reminiscences of Fugitive-Slave Law Day in Boston* (Boston: Warren Richardson, 1880), 31. See also "Fugitive Slave Meeting in Faneuil Hall"; "THRILLING SCENE," *Salem (OH) Anti-Slavery Bugle*, February 16, 1850, 1; "Remarkable Escape of a Slave," *Liberator*, January 11, 1850, 3.

49 John Hope Franklin and Loren Schweninger, *Runaway Slaves: Rebels on the Plantation* (New York: Oxford University Press, 1999), 210 (first quotation), 212 (second quotation). For the growing body of research on female slave resistance, see Karen Cook Bell, *Running from Bondage: Enslaved Women and Their Remarkable Fight for Freedom in Revolutionary America* (Cambridge: Cambridge University Press, 2021); Vanessa M. Holden, *Surviving Southampton: African American Women and Resistance in Nat Turner's Community* (Champaign: University of Illinois Press, 2021); Thavolia Glymph, *The Women's Fight: The Civil War's Battles for Home, Freedom, and Nation* (Chapel Hill: University of North Carolina Press, 2019); Erica Armstrong Dunbar, *Never Caught: The Washington's Relentless Pursuit of Their Runaway Slave, Ona Judge* (New York: 37Ink, 2017); Stephanie Camp, *Closer to Freedom: Enslaved Women and Everyday Resistance in*

the Plantation South (Chapel Hill: University of North Carolina Press, 2004); Deborah Gray White, *Ar'n't I a Woman? Female Slaves in the Plantation South*, rev. edition (New York: W. W. Norton, 1999 [1985]); Amrita Chakrabarti Myers, "'Sisters in Arms': Slave Women's Resistance to Slavery in the United States," *Past Imperfect* 5 (1996): 141–174; and Darlene Clark Hine, "Female Slave Resistance: The Economics of Sex," in Hine, *Hine Sight: Black Women and the Re-Construction of American History* (New York: Clarkson, 1994): 27–36.

50 Sarah H. Bradford, *Scenes in the Life of Harriet Tubman* (Auburn, NY: W. J. Moses, 1869), 25. For Tubman's biography and the estimated number of return expeditions to the South, see Kate Clifford Larson, *Bound for the Promised Land: Harriet Tubman, Portrait of an American Hero* (New York: One World, 2004); Catherine Clinton, *Harriet Tubman: The Road to Freedom* (New York: Little, Brown and Company, 2004).

51 Bradford, *Scenes in the Life of Harriet Tubman*, 21.

52 Sarah H. Bradford, *Harriet, the Moses of Her People* (New York: George R. Lockwood and Son, 1886).

53 Thomas Southerne, *Oroonoko: A Tragedy. As it was Acted at the Theatre Royal, by His Majesty's Servants, In the Year 1699*, in *The Works of Mr. Thomas Southerne. Volume the Second* (London: Jacob Tonson, 1713), 229; For the original story, see Aphra Behn, *Oroonoko: or, the Royal Slave. A True History* (London: William Canning, 1688).

54 H. W. Flournoy, *Calendar of Virginia State Papers and Other Manuscripts from January 1, 1799, to December 31, 1807; Preserved in the Capitol, at Richmond* (Richmond: H. W. Flournoy, 1890), 165.

55 Douglas R. Egerton, *Death or Liberty: African Americans and Revolutionary America* (New York: Oxford University Press, 2009), 279. For Gabriel's revolt generally, see Michael L. Nicholls, *Whispers of Rebellion: Narrating Gabriel's Conspiracy* (Charlottesville: University of Virginia Press, 2012); and Douglas R. Egerton, *Gabriel's Rebellion: The Virginia Slave Conspiracies of 1800 and 1802* (Chapel Hill: University of North Carolina Press, 1993). The legacy of the conspiracy is covered in Alan Taylor, *The Internal Enemy: Slavery and War in Virginia, 1772–1832* (New York: W. W. Norton & Company, 2013); and James Sidbury, *Ploughshares into Swords: Race, Rebellion, and Identity in Gabriel's Virginia, 1730–1810* (Cambridge: Cambridge University Press, 1997).

56 Austin Steward, *Twenty-Two Years a Slave, and Forty Years a Freeman; Embracing a Correspondence of Several Years, While President of Wilberforce Colony, London, Canada, West* (Rochester, NY: Allings & Cory, 1859), 143.

57 Diane Miller Sommerville, *Aberration of Mind: Suicide and Suffering in the Civil War-Era South* (Chapel Hill: University of North Carolina Press, 2018), 94 (first quotation), 119 (second quotation). Sommerville's determination rests in part on her reading of abolitionist texts. In response to slave owners and their supporters who claimed that there were no reasons for enslaved people to kill themselves,

abolitionists "cast suicide as a logical, rational response of desperate men and women to unspeakable suffering" (94).

58 For scholarship that interprets slave suicide as a form of resistance, see David Silkenat, *Moments of Despair: Suicide, Divorce, and Debt in Civil War Era North Carolina* (Chapel Hill: University of North Carolina Press, 2011), 17–18; Terri L. Snyder, *The Power to Die: Slavery and Suicide in British North America* (Chicago: University of Chicago Press, 2015); Michael A. Gomez, *Exchanging our Country Marks: The Transformation of African Identities in the Colonial and Antebellum South* (Chapel Hill: University of North Carolina Press, 1998); and Kenneth M. Stampp, *The Peculiar Institution: Slavery in the Antebellum South* (New York: Vintage Books, 1956).

59 Richard Bell, *We Shall Be No More: Suicide and Self-Government in the Newly United States* (Cambridge: Harvard University Press, 2012), 241.

60 "'Give me Liberty, or give me Death,'" *Liberator*, August 2, 1844, 3.

61 "Liberty or Death," *Pittsburgh Mystery*, in the *Liberator*, October 20, 1843, 1.

62 "Liberty or Death," *Boston Emancipator and Free American*, May 25, 1843, 4.

63 "Liberty or Death," *Washington (D.C.) National Era*, June 15, 1848, 4.

64 "Liberty of Death," *National Anti-Slavery Standard*, October 11, 1849, 2.

65 "Give me Liberty or give me Death," *Cincinnati Philanthropist*, May 6, 1836, 4. See also "LIBERTY OR DEATH," *Ohio State and Columbus Gazette*, in the *Liberator*, February 25, 1832, 2. For the original account of the suicide printed in the *Dayton Journal*, see Henry Howe, *Historical Collections of Ohio in Three Volumes* (Columbus: Henry Howe & Son, 1891), 2: 544–545.

66 "Give me Liberty or give me Death," *Cincinnati Philanthropist*, 4.

67 "Another Suicide by a Slave," *New-York Daily Tribune*, July 21, 1846, 1.

5. Disciples

1 "Rockville, MD" and "Fourth of July," *Rockville Maryland Journal*, July 9, 1845, 2–3.

2 Few accounts of the incident exist. Brief but reliable exceptions are Stanley Harrold, *Border War: Fighting over Slavery before the Civil War* (Chapel Hill: University of North Carolina Press, 2010), 129–130; and Herbert Aptheker, *American Negro Slave Revolts* (New York: International Publishers, 1987), 337.

3 For the contested meaning of the Declaration of Independence and the Fourth of July among African Americans and their abolitionist allies in the antebellum era, see W. Caleb McDaniel, "The Fourth and the First: Abolitionist Holidays, Respectability, and Radical Interracial Reform," *American Quarterly* 57, no. 1 (March 2005), 129–151; Mitch Kachun, *Festivals of Freedom: Memory and Meaning in African American Emancipation Celebrations, 1808–1915* (Amherst: University of Massachusetts Press, 2003); Shane White, "'It Was a Proud Day,' African Americans, Festivals, and Parades in the North, 1741–1834," *Journal of American History* 81, no. 1 (June 1994), 13–50; Benjamin Quarles, "Antebellum Free Blacks and the 'Spirit of '76,'" *Journal of Negro History* 61, no. 3 (July 1976), 229–242; and

Leonard I. Sweet, "The Fourth of July and Black Americans in the Nineteenth Century: Northern Leadership Opinion Within the Context of the Black Experience," *Journal of Negro History* 61, no. 3 (July 1976), 256–275.

4   Following the lead of Manisha Sinha in her award-winning study of the abolitionist movement, this chapter uses the term "fugitive slave rebellion" to describe the events that occurred over the Fourth of July weekend in July 1845. *The Slave's Cause: A History of Abolition* (New Haven, CT: Yale University Press, 2016), 500, 508–527. Herbert Aptheker defined a slave rebellion, "or insurrection," as any armed uprising involving at least ten slaves and thus included the Rockville rebellion in his landmark work, *American Negro Slave Revolts*, 162, 337. For an early use of the term "fugitive slave rebellion," in reference to a violent clash between large numbers of fugitive slaves and their potential slave catchers, see Jonathan Katz, *Resistance at Christiana: The Fugitive Slave Rebellion, Christiana, Pennsylvania, September 11, 1851: A Documentary Account* (New York: Thomas Y. Crowell, 1974). By the middle of the nineteenth century, slavery's supporters coined a new term to describe the phenomenon of fugitive slaves in the border states escaping in large numbers, "stampede," a word usually reserved for animals. Given the racist undertones of this word, historians tend to prefer alternative terms, such as "mass slave escapes" and "large-scale escapes," to describe the flight of large groups of slaves. Like "elopement," however, these labels ignore the violence inherent in fugitive slave rebellions. For historians' terminology, see Harrold, *Border War*, 118, 212. R. J. M. Blackett, *The Captive's Quest for Freedom: Fugitive Slaves, the 1850 Fugitive Slave Law, and the Politics of Slavery* (New York: Cambridge University Press, 2018), 321; Bridget Ford, *Bonds of Union: Religion, Race, and Politics in a Civil War Borderland* (Chapel Hill: University of North Carolina Press, 2016), 233; and J. Blaine Hudson, *Fugitive Slaves and the Underground Railroad in the Kentucky Borderland* (Jefferson, NC: McFarland & Co., 2002), 35. The idea of "self-liberation" derives from Aline Helg, *Slave No More: Self-Liberation before Abolitionism in the Americas* (Chapel Hill: University of North Carolina Press, 2019).

5   This article builds on Sinha's assertion on the first page of her nearly 800-page tome: "Slave resistance . . . lay at the heart of the abolition movement." *The Slave's Cause*, 1. See also Edward B. Rugemer, "Slave Rebels and Abolitionists: The Black Atlantic and the Coming of the Civil War," *Journal of the Civil War Era* 2, no. 2 (June 2012): 179–202; Stanley Harrold, *The Abolitionists and the South, 1831–1861* (Lexington: University Press of Kentucky, 1995); Merton L. Dillon, *Slavery Attacked: Southern Slaves and Their Allies, 1619–1865* (Baton Rouge: Louisiana State University Press, 1990); and Howard Jones, *Mutiny on the Amistad: The Saga of a Slave Revolt and Its Impact on American Abolition, Law, and Diplomacy* (New York: Oxford University Press, 1987).

6   Jason T. Sharples, *The World That Fear Made: Slave Revolts and Conspiracy Scares in Early America* (Philadelphia: University of Pennsylvania Press, 2020); Edward

B. Rugemer, *Slave Law and the Politics of Resistance in the Early Atlantic World* (Cambridge, MA: Harvard University Press, 2018); Kay Wright Lewis, *A Curse upon the Nation: Race, Freedom, and Extermination in America and the Atlantic World* (Athens: University of Georgia Press, 2017); Carl Lawrence Paulus, *The Slaveholding Crisis: Fear of Insurrection and the Coming of the Civil War* (Baton Rouge: Louisiana State University Press, 2017): Matthew Karp, *This Vast Southern Empire: Slaveholders at the Helm of American Foreign Policy* (Cambridge, MA: Harvard University Press, 2016).

7   In 1840, there were 10,001 African Americans (9,182 slaves and 819 free people of color) and 6,022 European Americans in Charles County. *Compendium of the Enumeration of the Inhabitants and Statistics of the United States; as Obtained at the Department of State, from the Returns of the Sixth Census* (Washington, DC: 1841), 28–31. See also *Report from the Select Committee, to Whom Was Referred the Subject of the Removal of the Free Colored Population from Charles County* (Annapolis, MD, 1844), 9.

8   "On the morning of the Fourth of July," *Port Tobacco Times*, June 26, 1845, 2.

9   "Baltimore, July 10, 1845," *New York Herald*, July 11, 1845, 4.

10 "Elopement of a Large Gang of Runaway Negroes," *Washington Daily Union*, July 8, 1845, 2.

11 Biographical information derives from the following: "Notice," *Rockville Maryland Journal*, July 9, 1845, 3; "Great Excitement—*Runaway Slaves*," *Baltimore Sun*, July 12, 1845, 1; "Miscellaneous," *Liberator*, October 3, 1845. For Benjamin Contee's career, see John Thomas Scharf, *History of Maryland from The Earliest Period to the Present Day, 1765–1812* (Hatboro, PA: Tradition Press, 1879), 2: 573; John Chapman's career is described in Henry G. Wheeler, *History of Congress, Biographical and Political* (New York: Harper & Brothers, 1848), 1: 527–545.

12 Maryland Penitentiary Prisoner Record, MSA S275, Mark Caesar, #3921, Maryland Historical Society; Register of Wills (Certificates of Freedom) C655, 1826–1860, Maryland Historical Society, CM972.

13 "Baltimore, July 10, 1845," *New York Herald*. See also "Latest Intelligence," *New York Herald*, July 10, 1845, 3; and "Washington City, July 8, 1845," *Baltimore Sun*, July 9, 1845, 4. For the topography of early Washington, DC, and the history of its earliest bridges, see "Old 'Burnt Bridge,'" *Washington Evening Star*, July 7, 1907, 10; and Robert J. Kapsch, *Building Washington: Engineering and Construction of the New Federal City, 1790–1840* (Baltimore: Johns Hopkins University Press, 2018).

14 Joseph Ellis describes the compromise over the location of the national capital in *Founding Brothers: The Revolutionary Generation* (New York: Vintage, 2002), 48–80.

15 Notwithstanding slavery's precariousness, the national capital was, in the words of historian Don E. Fehrenbacher, "a symbolic stronghold of the slave power in

America." Fehrenbacher offers an excellent overview of the controversy over
slavery and the interstate slave trade in the District of Columbia in *The
Slaveholding Republic: An Account of the United States Government's Relations to
Slavery* (New York: Oxford University Press, 2002), 49–88 (quotation on 88).

16 US Constitution, art 1, sec. 8.

17 The "gag rule" controversy is analyzed at length in William Lee Miller, *Arguing
about Slavery: John Quincy Adams and the Great Battle in the United States Congress*
(New York: Vintage, 1998).

18 James Oakes, *The Scorpion's Sting: Antislavery and the Coming of the Civil War* (New
York: W. W. Norton & Company, 2015), 69. For further discussion, see Paul
Finkelman and Donald R. Kennon, *In the Shadow of Freedom: The Politics of
Slavery in the National Capital* (Athens: Ohio University Press, 2011).

19 Mary Bett Corrigan, "Imaginary Cruelties? A History of the Slave Trade in
Washington, D.C.," *Washington History* 13, no. 2 (Fall/Winter 2001/2002): 5 (first
and second quotations), 6 (third quotation). Examples of this propaganda
includes, Theodore Dwight Weld, *The Power of Congress Over the District of
Columbia* (New York: John F. Throw, 1838); *Slavery and the Slave Trade at the
Nation's Capital* (New York: American and Foreign Anti-Slavery Society, 1846);
and "SLAVERY AND THE SLAVE TRADE IN THE DISTRICT OF
COLUMBIA (Washington, DC: n.d.).

20 *SLAVE MARKET OF AMERICA* (New York: American Anti-Slavery Society, 1836),
www.loc.gov.

21 "The Runaway Negroes," *Baltimore Sun*, July 10, 1845, 4.

22 "LATEST INTELLIGENCE," *New York Herald*.

23 "THE BLOODY AND OPPRESSIVE SOUTH," *Liberator*, July 18, 1845, 2.

24 Sally E. Hadden, *Slave Patrols: Law and Violence in Virginia and the Carolinas*
(Cambridge, MA: Harvard University Press, 2003). 6.

25 "LATEST INTELLIGENCE," *New York Herald*.

26 "The Runaway Negroes," *Baltimore Sun*.

27 "THE BLOODY AND OPPRESSIVE SOUTH."

28 "Capture of Thirty-One of the Runaway Negroes," *Washington Union*, July 9, 1845,
2.

29 "ROCKVILLE, MD," *Rockville Maryland Journal*, July 9, 1845.

30 "Capture of Thirty-One of the Runaway Negroes," *Washington Union*.

31 "RUNAWAY NEGROES," *Washington Daily National Intelligencer*, July 10, 1845, 3.

32 "NOTICE," *Rockville Maryland Journal*.

33 *"The Runaway Negroes," New York Herald*, July 13, 1845, 4.

34 "GREAT EXCITEMENT—*Runaway Slaves*," *Baltimore Sun*.

35 "RUNAWAY NEGROES," *Baltimore Sun*, July 22, 1845, 2.

36 For the numbers of captives and survivors, see also "RUNAWAY NEGROES,"
Washington Daily National Intelligencer, July 10, 1845, 3; "The Runaway Negroes,"
Washington Daily National Intelligencer, July 11, 1845, 3; "The Captured Runaway

Negroes," *Washington Daily National Intelligencer*, July 12, 1845, 3; "Bill Wheeler" and "A Rumor Has Just Reached Us," *Rockville Maryland Journal*, July 16, 1845, 2. For reports of between one and two deaths, see "Washington, July 8, 1845," *American Republican, and Baltimore Clipper*, July 10, 1845, 4; "FRIDAY MORNING," *American Republican, and Baltimore Clipper*, July 25, 1845, 2; and "BY LAST EVENING's MAIL," *New York Herald*, July 12, 1845, 3.

37 "Varieties," *New York Herald*, July 30, 1845, 1.

38 *Boston Emancipator and Weekly Chronicle*, August 6, 1845, 4. The *Baltimore Sun* rejected these reports, despite a lack of evidence, claiming, "Nine fugitive slaves passed through Oswego to Canada, a few days ago. They were, it is said, a portion of the party who escaped from their pursuers, in the recent movement in Maryland. This we think must be incorrect, as all but one or two of them have now been apprehended. "Runaway Slaves," *Baltimore Sun*, July 30, 1845, 1.

39 Jesse Torrey, *A Portraiture of Domestic Slavery, in the United States* (Philadelphia: Jesse Torrey, 1817), 42–44; Torrey, *American Slave Trade* (London: J. M. Cobbett, 1822), 67–70.

40 Torrey, *A Portraiture of Domestic Slavery*, 49.

41 Candy Carter, "'I Did Not Want to Go': An Enslaved Woman's Leap into the Capital's Conscience," in *O Say Can You See: Early Washington, D.C., Law & Family*, edited by William G. Thomas III et al., University of Nebraska-Lincoln, https://earlywashingtondc.org. For more on Anna and the abolitionist response both locally and nationally, see Carter, "What Happened When Anna Jumped from the Window: The Domestic Slave Trade in Antebellum Washington, D.C.," *Tangents* 15 (Summer 2016): 8–14; Richard Bell, *We Shall Be No More: Suicide and Self-Government in the Newly United States* (Cambridge: Harvard University Press, 2012), 217–220; and Robert H. Gudmestad, *A Troublesome Commerce: The Transformation of the Interstate Slave Trade* (Baton Rouge: Louisiana State University Press, 2003), 35–61.

42 Examples include *Proceedings of the New-England Anti-Slavery Convention, Held in Boston on the 27th, 28th and 29th of May, 1834* (Boston: Garrison & Knapp, 1834), 26; Ethan Allen Andrews, *Slavery and the Domestic Slave-Trade in the United States. In a Series of Letters Addressed to the Executive Committee of the American Union for the Relief and Improvement of the Colored Race* (Boston: Light & Stearns, 1836), 112–113, 128–133; and Lydia Maria Child, *Authentic Anecdotes of American Slavery* (Newburyport, MA: Charles Whipple, 1838), 18–19.

43 "For the Genius of Universal Emancipation: TORREY'S PORTRAITURE OF DOMESTIC SLAVERY," *Genius of Universal Emancipation* (March 1832): 8.

44 W. Caleb McDaniel, *The Problem of Democracy in the Age of Slavery: Garrisonian Abolitionists and Transatlantic Reform* (Baton Rouge: Louisiana State University Press, 2013), 30.

45 "THE BLOODY AND OPPRESSIVE SOUTH."

46 "Mr. Editor," *Hartford Daily Courant*, July 25, 1845, 2.

47 "Liberty or Death," *New York Tribune*, July 14, 1845, 2.

48 Ibid.

49 "The Fugitives Taken," *Boston Recorder*, July 17, 1845, 3.

50 Ibid.

51 "THE SLAUGHTERED FUGITIVES," *Boston Courier* in the *Liberator*, July 25, 1845, 3. The abolitionist mantra, "Who would be free, themselves must strike the blow," derives from the British poet–politician Lord Byron's *Childe Harold's Pilgrimage*. Baron George Gordon Byron, *The Poetical Works of Lord Byron: Complete in One Volume* (New York: D. Appleton & Company, 1851), 35. For Lowell's antislavery conversion, see Frederick Douglass, *The Frederick Douglass Papers, Series Three: Correspondence*, ed. John R. McKivigan (New Haven: Yale University Press, 2009), 1:429–430, fn. 9.

52 "THE SLAUGHTERED FUGITIVES."

53 The *Boston Courier, Boston Emancipator and Free American*, the *Liberator*, and the *New Lisbon Anti-Slavery Bugle* (OH) reprinted the poem in 1845. In subsequent decades, all, or excerpts of, the original work appeared in abolitionist pamphlets and became a fixture in anthologies of Lowell's compositions. For examples, see Jonathan Walker, *A Brief View of American Chattelized Humanity* (Boston: Jonathan Walker, 1846), 28; and Lydia Maria Child, *The Duty of Disobedience to the Fugitive Slave Act* (Boston: American Anti-Slavery Society, 1860), 34.

54 Sinha, *The Slave's Cause*, 420. For recent scholarship on these efforts, see Kate Masur, *Until Justice Be Done: America's First Civil Rights Movement, from the Revolution to Reconstruction* (New York: W. W. Norton, 2021); William G. Thomas III, *A Question of Freedom: The Families Who Challenged Slavery from the Nation's Founding to the Civil War* (New Haven: Yale University Press, 2020); Kellie Carter Jackson, *Force and Freedom: Black Abolitionists and the Politics of Violence* (Philadelphia: University of Pennsylvania Press, 2019); Jonathan Daniel Wells, *Blind No More: African American Resistance, Free-Soil Politics, and the Coming of the Civil War* (Athens: University of Georgia Press, 2019); Martha S. Jones, *Birthright Citizens: A History of Race and Rights in Antebellum America* (Cambridge: Cambridge University Press, 2018); Andrew K. Diemer, *The Politics of Black Citizenship: Free African Americans in the Mid-Atlantic Borderland, 1817–1863* (Athens: University of Georgia Press, 2016); and Stephen Kantrowitz, *More Than Freedom: Fighting for Black Citizenship in a White Republic, 1829–1889* (New York: Penguin Press, 2012).

55 "BALTIMORE, July 21, 1845," *New York Herald*, July 22, 1845, 4.

56 "Injustice," *American Republican and Baltimore Clipper*, July 23, 1845, 2.

57 "The Fugitives from Slavery," *Boston Emancipator and Weekly Chronicle*, July 16, 1845, 2.

58 "NEWS BY THE BOAT," *Opelousas St. Landry Whig*, July 24, 1845, 2.

59 "Negro Insurrection in Maryland," *New York Herald*, July 11, 1845, 2.

60 Stanley Harrold, *Subversives: Antislavery Community in Washington, D.C., 1828–1865* (Baton Rouge: Louisiana State University Press, 2003), 64–93. See also Harrold, *Border War*, and E. Fuller Torrey, *The Martyrdom of Abolitionist Charles Torrey* (Baton Rouge: Louisiana State University Press, 2013).

61 Thomas Smallwood, *A Narrative of Thomas Smallwood, (Coloured Man:) Giving an Account of His Birth, the Period He Was Held in Slavery, His Release and Removal to Canada, etc., Together with an Account of the Underground Railroad* (Toronto: J. Stephens, 1851), 33. For the attempted escape of some seventy-seven enslaved people aboard the schooner *Pearl* in 1848, which, unlike the Rockville fugitive slave rebellion, utilized abolitionist assistance, see Harrold, *Subversives*, 116–145; Mary Kay Ricks, *Escape on the Pearl: The Historic Bid for Freedom on the Underground Railroad* (New York: William Morrow, 2007); and Josephine F. Pacheco, *The Pearl: A Failed Slave Escape on the Potomac* (Chapel Hill: University of North Carolina Press, 2005).

62 "SLAVE TOPICS," *Port Tobacco Times* in *Niles' National Register*, July 26, 1845, 12. See also "PUBLIC MEETING" and "To the Editors of the Port Tobacco Times," *Port Tobacco Times*, August 7, 1845, 2; "PORT TOBACCO TIMES" and "SLAVEHOLDERS' MEETING IN ST. MARY'S COUNTY," *Port Tobacco Times*, August 28, 1845, 2.

63 "PUBLIC MEETING."

64 "From the Marlboro' Gazette," *Port Tobacco Times*, August 21, 1845, 3. The metaphor of a "slumbering volcano" reverberated across antebellum American print culture. An early use in the context of American slave revolts came in the wake of Nat Turner's rebellion: "Legislative Debate—Continued," *Richmond Enquirer*, February 16, 1832, 2. For scholarly considerations of the imagery, see Maggie Montesinos Sale, *The Slumbering Volcano: American Slave Ship Revolts and the Production of Rebellious Masculinity* (Durham, NC: Duke University Press, 1997); and Alfred N. Hunt, *Haiti's Influence on Antebellum America: Slumbering Volcano in the Caribbean* (Baton Rouge: Louisiana State University Press, 1988).

65 Barbara Jeanne Fields, *Slavery and Freedom on the Middle Ground: Maryland during the Nineteenth Century* (New Haven, CT: Yale University Press, 1985), 71.

66 "To the Editors of the Port Tobacco Times," *Port Tobacco Times*, August 7, 1845, 2; Walter Johnson, "Clerks All! Or, Slaves with Cash," *Journal of the Early Republic* 26, no. 4 (Winter 2006): 647. For citizens opposed to banishing free Black people from the state, see "Memorial in Behalf of the Colored Population," *Baltimore Sun*, February 26, 1846, 2. See also James M. Wright, *The Free Negro in Maryland, 1634–1860* (New York: Longmans, Green and Company, 1921), 304–305; and Jeffrey R. Brackett, *The Negro in Maryland: A Study of the Institution of Slavery* (Baltimore: N. Murray, 1889), 248. For laws passed to curtail the rights of enslaved and free Black people, refer to *Index to the Laws of Maryland from the Year 1838 to 1845, Inclusive* (Annapolis: Riley & Davis, 1846), 283–284.

67 "An Insurrectionist found Guilty," *Baltimore Patriot* in the *Liberator*, October 10, 1845, 4. For the trials of William Wheeler and Mark Caesar, see "Trial of Negroes," *Baltimore Patriot* in *New York Herald*, September 20, 1845, 2; "Charles County Court," *Port Tobacco Times*, August 28, 2; September 4, 3; September 11, 2; and November 6, 1825, 2.

68 "Charles County Court," September 4, 1845, 3.

69 "Trial of Negroes." There are no extant records of these trials in the Maryland State Archives in Annapolis. Curiously, registers of other 1845 cases, which occurred in the Port Tobacco courthouse both before and after September, do exist.

70 "Charles County Court," September 4, 1845, 3; Maryland Penitentiary Prisoner Record, MSA S275, Mark Caesar, #3921, Maryland Historical Society. See also Joshua E. Kastenberg, *A Confederate in Congress: The Civil War Trial of Benjamin Gwinn Harris* (Jefferson, NC: McFarland & Company, 2016), 17–18.

71 *Annual Message of The Executive to the General Assembly of Maryland. December Session, 1845* (Annapolis: Riley & Davis, 1845), 25–26; "An act to authorise and require the Warden and Keepers of the Penitentiary of Maryland, to receive and keep negro William Wheeler, now under sentence of death into the Penitentiary, in the event of the commutation of his sentence by the Governor," *Laws Made and Passed of the General Assembly of the State of Maryland, at a Session begun and held at Annapolis, on Monday, the 29th day of December, 1845, and Ended on the 10th Day of March, 1846* (Annapolis: William M'Neir, 1846), Chapter 368; Message of Governor Thomas G. Pratt to the Sheriff of Charles County, March 24, 1846, Proceedings of the Governor, January 1845–January 1853, Maryland Historical Society, E.1. Reel 2, 1839–1861.

72 Theodore Dwight Weld, *American Slavery as It Is: Testimony of a Thousand Witnesses* (New York: American Anti-Slavery Society, 1839), 55. For a secondary account of White southerners attempting to suppress information about violence meted out against enslaved people, see Winthrop Jordan, *Tumult and Silence at Second Creek: An Inquiry into a Civil War Slave Conspiracy* (Baton Rouge: Louisiana States University Press, 1993). See also Margaret Nicola Abruzzo, *Polemical Pain: Slavery, Cruelty, and the Rise of Humanitarianism* (Baltimore: Johns Hopkins University Press, 2011); Lacy K. Ford, *Deliver Us from Evil: The Slavery Question in the Old South* (New York: Oxford University Press, 2009); James Oakes, *The Ruling Race: A History of American Slaveholders* (New York: Knopf, 1982); and Dickson D. Bruce, Jr., *Violence and Culture in the Antebellum South* (Austin: University of Texas Press, 1979).

73 "Broke Jail," *Port Tobacco Times*, March 26, 1846, 3.

74 For a similar finding of the effect of slave resistance in the early United States and Jamaica, see Rugemer, *Slave Law and the Politics of Resistance*.

6. Radicals

1 Levi Coffin, *Reminiscences of Levi Coffin, the Reputed President of the Underground Railroad; Being a Brief History of the Labors of a Lifetime in Behalf of the Slave, with the Stories of Numerous Fugitives, Who Gained Their Freedom Through His Instrumentality, and Many Other Incidents* (Cincinnati: Western Tract Society, 1876), 472–474 (quotation on 474).

2 Ibid., 474.

3 The militancy of African Americans continued to impress Blunt. During the Civil War, he wrote of the Black men he fought alongside at the Battle of Honey Springs, Arkansas, "The question that negroes will fight is settled; besides they make better solders in every respect than any troops I have ever had under my command." James G. Blunt, "BATTLE OF HONEY SPRINGS," July 25, 1863, in Frank Moore, ed., *The Rebellion Record: A Diary of American Events, with Documents, Narratives, Illustrative Incidents, Poetry, etc.* (New York: D. Van Nostrand, 1864), 7: 381.

4 Levi Coffin, *Reminiscences of Levi Coffin*, 474. For Blunt's role in Bleeding Kansas and the Civil War, see Robert Collins, *General James G. Blunt: Corrupt Conqueror* (Gretna, LA: Pelican Publishing Company, 2005); Michael J. Forsyth, *The Great Missouri Raid: Sterling Price and the Last Major Confederate Campaign in Northern Territory* (Jefferson, N.C.: McFarland & Company, 2015, 2); and James G. Blunt, "General Blunt's Account of His Civil War Experiences," *Kansas Historical Quarterly* 1, no. 3 (May 1932): 211–265.

5 For the abolitionist movement and its radicalization, see Kellie Carter Jackson, *Force and Freedom: Black Abolitionists and the Politics of Violence* (Philadelphia: University of Pennsylvania Press, 2019); Manisha Sinha, *The Slave's Cause: A History of Abolition* (New Haven: Yale University Press, 2017); Andrew Delbanco, *The Abolitionist Imagination* (Cambridge, MA: Harvard University Press, 2012); John Stauffer, *The Black Hearts of Men: Radical Abolitionists and the Transformation of Race* (Cambridge, MA: Harvard University Press, 2004); Paul Goodman, *Of One Blood: Abolitionism and the Origins of Racial Equality* (Berkeley: University of California Press, 2000); Stanley Harrold and John R. McKivigan, *Antislavery Violence: Sectional, Racial, and Cultural Conflict in Antebellum America* (Knoxville: University of Tennessee Press, 1999); and George A. Levesque, "Black Abolitionists in the Age of Jackson: Catalysts in the Radicalization of American Abolitionism," *Journal of Black Studies* 1, no. 2 (December 1970): 187–201.

6 *DECLARATION OF THE ANTI-SLAVERY CONVENTION* (Philadelphia: Merrihew & Gunn, 1833).

7 Henry Mayer, *All on Fire: William Lloyd Garrison and the Abolition of Slavery* (New York: W. W. Norton & Company, 2008), 175.

8 *DECLARATION OF THE ANTI-SLAVERY CONVENTION*.

9   Henry Highland Garnet, *Walker's Appeal, With a Brief Sketch of His Life, by Henry Highland Garnet, and Also Garnet's Address to the Slaves of the United States of America* (New York: J. H. Tobitt, 1848), 5.

10 For Walker's life and times, see Peter Hinks, *To Awaken My Afflicted Brethren: David Walker and the Problem of Antebellum Slave Resistance* (University Park: Pennsylvania State University Press, 1997), 249.

11 David Walker, *Walker's Appeal, in Four Articles; Together with a Preamble, to the Coloured Citizens of the World, But in Particular, and Very Expressly, to Those of the United States of America* (Boston: David Walker, 1830), 9.

12 Robert S. Levine, *Dislocating Race and Nation: Episodes in Nineteenth-Century American Literary Nationalism* (Chapel Hill: University of North Carolina Press, 2008), 71–86. See Sterling Stuckey, *The Ideological Origins of Black Nationalism* (Boston: Beacon Press, 1972), 9; Stuckey, *Slave Culture: Nationalist Theory and the Foundations of Black America* (New York: Oxford University Press, 1987), 98–137.

13 Walker, *Walker's Appeal*, 22–24.

14 Hinks, *To Awaken My Afflicted Brethren*, 249.

15 Walker, *Walker's Appeal*, 73. See also 62, 75, 77, 79.

16 Ibid., 49.

17 Hinks, *To Awaken My Afflicted Brethren*, 247.

18 Walker, *Walker's Appeal*, 85.

19 Stephen Kantrowitz, *More Than Freedom: Fighting for Black Citizenship in a White Republic, 1829–1889* (New York: Penguin Press, 2012), 29–30.

20 Julie Winch, *A Gentleman of Color: The Life of James Forten* (New York: Oxford University Press, 2002), 245.

21 "Men Must Be Free," *Liberator*, August 20, 1831, 1.

22 Henry Highland Garnet, *A Memorial Discourse; by Rev. Henry Highland Garnet, Delivered in the Hall of the House of Representatives, Washington City, D.C. on Sabbath, February 12, 1865. With an Introduction, by James McCune Smith, M.D.* (Philadelphia: Joseph M. Wilson, 1865), 44–51. This discussion cites Smith's 1865 publication; however, as historian Derrick R. Spires shows, multiple versions of the address appeared in print, and "None of these iterations give direct access to what Garnet read or to his performance in 1843." Spires, "Flights of Fancy: Black Print, Collaboration, and Performance in 'An Address to the Slaves of the United States of America (Rejected by the National Convention, 1843),'" in *The Colored Conventions Movement: Black Organizing in the Nineteenth Century*, ed. P. Gabrielle Foreman, Jim Casey, and Sarah Lynn Patterson (Chapel Hill: University of North Carolina Press, 2021), 126.

23 Garnet, *A Memorial Discourse*, 46 (first, second, and third quotations), 49 (fourth quotation).

24 Ibid., 49 (first and second quotations), 50 (third and fourth quotations), 51 (fifth quotation).

25 "CONVENTION OF COLORED PERSONS," *Buffalo Commercial Advertiser* in *New York Emancipator and Free American*, October 12, 1843, 4.

26 With the convention unwilling to publish the address, Garnet did it himself, though the process took longer than expected. Five years after the Buffalo Convention, the piece finally appeared in print owing to the aid of New York City's John H. Tobitt. Garnet included a copy of David Walker's *Appeal* in the publication, along with an autobiographical sketch of Walker's life. Garnet prayed the "little book" would circulate widely "until the principles it contains shall be understood and adopted by every slave in the Union." Garnet, *Walker's Appeal*. See also, "The Colored Convention," *Liberator*, September 8, 1843, 2.

27 *Minutes of the National Convention of Colored Citizens: Held at Buffalo, On the 15th, 16th, 17th, 18th and 19th of August, 1843. For the Purpose of Considering Their Moral and Political Condition as American Citizens* (New York: Piercy & Reed, 1843), 12–24 (quotation on 13).

28 Howard H. Bell, "National Negro Conventions of the Middle 1840's: Moral Suasion vs. Political Action," *The Journal of Negro History* 42, no. 4 (October 1957): 253. Kellie Carter Jackson shares Bell's surprise, noting that the close vote on the motion proved "the weakening of the moral suasion position." *Force and Freedom*, 39.

29 François Furstenberg, *In the Name of the Father: Washington's Legacy, Slavery, and the Making of a Nation* (New York: Penguin Press, 2006), 195.

30 *Minutes of the State Convention of Colored Citizens, Held at Albany, on the 18th, 19th, and 20th of August, 1840, for the Purpose of Considering Their Political Condition* (New York: Piercy & Reed, 1840), 26 (first quotation), 31 (second quotation), 32 (third and fourth quotations).

31 Jackson writes, "Courting the base of supportive readers was essential for survival, particularly the survival of a press." *Force and Freedom*, 21.

32 Sarah Purcell, *Sealed with Blood: War, Sacrifice, and Memory in Revolutionary America* (Philadelphia: University of Pennsylvania Press, 2002).

33 "THE INSURRECTION," *Liberator*, September 3, 1831, 3.

34 "AN ADDRESS," *Liberator*, July 13, 1838, 1. The motto is credited to the famed British jurist John Bradshaw, who presided over the trial of King Charles I for treason, which resulted in the king's execution. For Thomas Jefferson's use in 1776 of a variation of the phrase, see "Hiding in the Archives—Identifying a Priceless Jefferson Manuscript of 1776," www.monticello.org.

35 "PEACE," *Liberator*, February 13, 1836, 2. For the life of Stebbins's father, Jotham Stebbins, see Hamilton Child, *Gazetteer and Business Directory of Windham County, VT, 1724–1884* (Syracuse: Journal Office, 1884), 160–161; and Elizabeth Gadsby, *Lineage Book: National Society of the Daughters of the American Revolution* (Harrisburg: Telegraph Printing Company, 1909), 27:117.

36 "RIGHT OF SELF-DEFENCE," *Liberator*, December 22, 1837, 3.

37 Andrew Delbanco, *The War Before the War: Fugitive Slaves and the Struggle for America's Soul from the Revolution to the Civil War* (New York: Penguin Press, 2018), 5.

38 "Cazenovia Convention," *North Star*, September 5, 1850, 3.

39 "MEETING OF THE COLORED CITIZENS OF BOSTON," *Liberator*, October 4, 1850, 2.

40 "MEETING OF THE COLORED CITIZENS," *Liberator*, November 8, 1850, 2.

41 "MEETING OF COLORED CITIZENS OF NEW YORK," *North Star*, October 24, 1850, 1. For the number of attendees, see "Denunciation of the Fugitive Slave Bill," *Boston Emancipator & Weekly Republican*, October 10, 1850, 1.

42 "MEETING OF COLORED CITIZENS," *National Anti-Slavery Standard*, December 5, 1850, 2.

43 "Frederick Douglass," *North Star*, October 24, 1850, 2.

44 "MARSHFIELD RESOLUTIONS IN REGARD TO THE FUGITIVE LAW," *Liberator*, March 14, 1851, 2.

45 "ARREST OF WHITE AND COLORED SYMPATHISERS," *National Anti-Slavery Standard*, April 10, 1851, 2. M'Clure's presence is also noted at an antislavery gathering in Boston six years earlier. "NEW-ENGLAND ANTI-SLAVERY CONVENTION," *Liberator*, June 27, 1845, 1. In addition, see Caroline Wells Healey Dall, *Selected Journals of Carolina Healey Dall: 1838–1855* (Boston: Massachusetts Historical Society, 2006), 324.

46 Theodore Parker, *The Rights of Man in America* (Boston: American Unitarian Association, 1911), 151 (first, second, and third quotations), 152 (fourth and fifth quotations). For Parker helping the famous fugitive slave couple William and Ellen Craft, see Weiss, *Life and Correspondence of Theodore Parker*, 2: 95–99, 101–103, 307.

47 John Weiss, *Life and Correspondence of Theodore Parker, Minister of the Twenty-Eighth Congregational Society, Boston* (New York: D. Appleton & Company, 1864), 2: 119–120 (first quotation), 120 (second quotation).

48 Paul E. Teed, "A Brave Man's Child: Theodore Parker and the Memory of the American Revolution," *Historical Journal of Massachusetts* 29, no. 1 (Winter 2001): 181 (first quotation), 182 (second quotation). For the founding of the organization and its membership, see Weiss, *Life and Correspondence of Theodore Parker*, 2: 92–97, 102–110, 116, 133–142. Parker's radicalism and his wider impact on the abolitionist movement are discussed fully in Teed, *A Revolutionary Conscience: Theodore Parker and Antebellum America* (Lanham, MD: University Press of America, 2012). See also Michael Fellman, "Theodore Parker and the Abolitionist Role in the 1850s," *Journal of American History* 61, no. 3 (December 1974): 666–684.

49 Gordon S. Barker, *Fugitive Slaves and the Unfinished American Revolution: Eight Cases, 1848–1856* (Jefferson, NC: McFarland & Company, 2013), 16.

50 For the Battle of Christiana and the rendition of Anthony Burns, see also Jonathan Katz, *Resistance at Christiana: The Fugitive Slave Rebellion, Christiana,*

Pennsylvania, September 11, 1851 (New York: Thomas Y. Crowell, 1974); and Barker, *The Imperfect Revolution: Anthony Burns and the Landscape of Race in Antebellum America* (Kent, OH: Kent State University Press, 2013).

51 "Proceedings of a Meeting Held in Columbus, Ohio, to Sympathise with the VICTORIOUS HEROES at the Battle of Christiana, Penn., held Sept. 22, 1851, *Frederick Douglass' Paper*, November 13, 1851, 1.

52 "PENNSYLVANIA ABOLITIONISM," *Liberator*, October 24, 1851, 2 (first, second, third, fifth, sixth, and seventh quotations); George DeCou, *Burlington, a Provincial Capital: Historical Sketches of Burlington, New Jersey, and Neighborhood* (Philadelphia: Harris and Partridge, 1945), 88 (fourth quotation).

53 "PENNSYLVANIA ABOLITIONISM."

54 The paper mistakenly referred to the well-known antislavery lecturer as "C.M.K. Glen," in "BATTLE AT CHRISTIANA," *Frederick Douglass' Paper*, October 2, 1851.

55 "LETTER FROM ALBRO S. BROWN," *Frederick Douglass' Paper*, October 23, 1851, 3.

56 "For Frederick Douglass' Paper," *Frederick Douglass' Paper*, March 18, 1852, 2.

57 "Little Sodus, July 29, 1852," *Frederick Douglass' Paper*, August 6, 1852, 1.

58 Fergus M. Bordewich, *Bound for Canaan: The Underground Railroad and the War for the Soul of America* (New York: Amistad, 2005), 332. For Douglass's role is aiding Parker, see Frederick Douglass, *Life and Times of Frederick Douglass Written by Himself* (Hartford, CT: Park Publishing, 1881), 287–289.

59 David Blight writes, "Griffiths was perhaps the single most important personal influence in [Douglass's] life" and "certainly his most cherished friend." *Frederick Douglass's Civil War: Keeping Faith in Jubilee* (Baton Rouge: Louisiana State University Press, 1989), 19.

60 "LETTER NO. XIV," *Frederick Douglass' Paper*, October 9, 1851, 2. For the relationship between Griffiths and Douglass, see Janet Douglas, "A Cherished Friendship: Julia Griffiths Crofts and Frederick Douglass," *Slavery and Abolition* 33, no. 2 (2012): 265–274.

61 Julia Griffiths, *Autographs for Freedom* (Boston: John P. Jewett, 1853), 33 (first quotation), 34 (second quotation), 38 (third and fourth quotations). Horatio T. Strother, *The Underground Railroad in Connecticut* (Middletown, CT: Wesleyan University Press, 1962), 82–83, 101, 117–118; Charles Bancroft Gillespie, *An Historic Record and Pictorial Description of the Town of Meriden, Connecticut and Men Who Have Made It* (Meriden, CT: Journal Publishing, 1906), 156–157.

62 "Meeting of Colored Men in Philadelphia," *Frederick Douglass' Paper*, June 23, 1854, 3.

63 A leading opponent of the plan to colonize African Americans beyond their "native land" of the United States, Watkins long dreamed that all Black people would secure their God-given unalienable rights peacefully, "without confused noise, or garments covered in blood." The Fugitive Slave Act convinced him otherwise. "AN ABLE REPLY," *Liberator*, June 4, 1831, 1. See also Bettye J.

Gardner, "William Watkins: Antebellum Black Teacher and Anti-slavery Writer," *Negro History Bulletin* 39 (1976): 623–625; and "Opposition to Emigration, A Selected Letter of William Watkins (The Colored Baltimorean)," *Journal of Negro History* 67.2 (Summer 1982): 155–158.

64 "Meeting of Colored Men in Philadelphia."

65 "The True Remedy for the Fugitive Slave Bill," *Frederick Douglass' Paper*, June 9, 1854, 2.

66 Charlotte Forten, *The Journal of Charlotte L. Forten*, ed. Ray Allen Billington (New York: Dryden Press, 1953), 37.

67 "Is it Right and Wise to Kill a Kidnapper?" *Frederick Douglass' Paper*, June 2, 1854, 2.

68 Ibid.

69 "NEW ENGLAND A.S. CONVENTION," *Liberator*, June 23, 1854, 2.

70 The reaction of the crowd "of almost unprecedented numbers" was mixed. While most shouted approvingly at Garrison's actions, some hissed and howled in disapproval. "THE MEETING AT FRAMINGHAM," *Liberator*, July 7, 1854, 2.

71 Mayer, *All on Fire*, 444.

72 "THE MEETING AT FRAMINGHAM." To explain Garrison's changing outlook, Mayer writes that by the middle of the 1850s, "Garrison's millennial vision became clouded and challenged by a growing determination to apply the militant principles of the First American Revolution to the moral necessity of the Second." Mayer, *All on Fire*, 445.

73 "ANNUAL MEETING OF THE MASSACHUSETTS ANTI-SLAVERY SOCIETY. SKETCHES OF DISCUSSION, CONTINUED," *Liberator*, February 13, 1857, 2. See also "ANNUAL MEETING OF THE MASSACHUSETTS ANTI-SLAVERY SOCIETY," *Liberator*, February 6, 1857, 2.

74 "ANNUAL MEETING," February 13, 1857, 2.

75 "ANNUAL MEETING," February 6, 1857, 23.

76 "ANNUAL MEETING," February 13, 1857, 2.

77 Furstenberg, *In the Name of the Father*, 195.

78 "ANNUAL MEETING," February 13, 1857, 2.

79 "ANNUAL MEETING," February 6, 1857, 2.

7. Revolutionaries

1 Richard J. Hinton, *John Brown and His Men: With Some Account of the Roads They Traveled to Reach Harper's Ferry* (New York: Funk & Wagnalls, 1894), 654. "A friend" of Brown's wrote, "As a boy he was present at Hull's surrender" of Fort Detroit to the British in August 1812. James Redpath, *The Public Life of Capt. John Brown, by James Redpath, with an Auto-Biography of His Childhood and Youth* (Boston: Thayer and Eldridge, 1860), 29.

2 Franklin Benjamin Sanborn, *Memoirs of John Brown, Written for Rev. Samuel Orcutt's History of Torrington, CT, with Memorial Verses, by William Ellery Channing* (Concord, MA: J. Munsell, 1878), 23.

3 Frederick Douglass, *Life and Times of Frederick Douglass Written by Himself* (Hartford, CT: Park Publishing, 1881), 281.

4 Sanborn, *Memoirs of John Brown*, 26.

5 For a recent reappraisal of the context of Brown's actions in Springfield and the militancy of the city's Black community, see Joseph Carvalho, III, "John Brown's Transformation: The Springfield Years, 1846–1849," *Historical Journal of Massachusetts* 48, no. 1 (Winter 2020): 47–95.

6 John Brown, *The Life and Letters of John Brown, Liberator of Kansas, and Martyr of Virginia*, ed. Franklin Benjamin Sanborn (Boston: Roberts Brothers, 1885), 125.

7 Brown, *Life and Letters of John Brown*, 126. Brown's biographers agree that the Agreement and Resolutions demonstrated the loyalty of Brown and his allies to their nation—despite its deficiencies. To Louis DeCaro, Jr., the commitment reflects "John Brown's patriotism—his belief in America and its potential *apart* from the evil of slavery." For David Reynolds, it was "a patriotic gesture, showing that the league was not set *against* the United States but wanted to work *within* it, to help its core values be fully realized on the racial level." Evan Carton argues that "In this invitation to America to be true to its flag and worthy of their love, the Gileadites and their founder were not traitors but patriots." Louis A. DeCaro, Jr., *"Fire from the Midst of You": A Religious Life of John Brown* (New York: New York University Press, 2002), 191; David S. Reynolds, *John Brown, Abolitionist: The Man Who Killed Slavery, Sparked the Civil War, and Seeded Civil Rights* (New York: Alfred A. Knopf, 2005), 124; Evan Carton, *Patriotic Treason: John Brown and the Soul of America* (Lincoln: University of Nebraska Press, 2006), 137.

8 William Wells Brown, "John Brown and the Fugitive Slave Law," *New York Independent*, March 10, 1870, West Virginia Memory Project, John Brown/Boyd B. Stutler Collection Database, BBS Scrpbk4, www.wvculure.org.

9 For Washington's life and work, see Ann M. Shumard, "Augustus Washington: African American Daguerreotypist," *Exposure* 35, no. 2 (2002): 5–16; Shumard, "A Durable Memento: Portraits by Augustus Washington, African American Daguerreotypist," *Smithsonian* 30, no. 2 (1999): 1–24; David O. White, "Augustus Washington, Black Daguerreotypist of Hartford," *Connecticut Historical Society* 39, no. 1 (January 1974): 14–19. While there is some mystery over Washington's ethnicity, the official publication of the American Colonization Society described him "as an unmixed representative of the colored race." *African Repository* 30, no. 6 (June 1854): 187. Named after its French inventor, Louis-Jacques-Mandé Daguerre, the dangerous and complicated process involved the capturing of an image on a silver-plated copper plate using various chemicals, including mercury. See M. Susan Barger and William B. Whit, *The Daguerreotype: Nineteenth-Century Technology and Modern Science* (Baltimore: Johns Hopkins University Press, 1991); and Beaumont Newhall, *The Daguerreotype in America. Third and Revised Edition* (New York: Dover Publications, 1976). For Washington's

biography, see Ann M. Shumard, "Augustus Washington: African American Daguerreotypist," *Exposure* 35, no. 2 (2002): 5–16.

10 For the provenance of the surviving daguerreotypes, see Owen Edwards, "John Brown's Famous Photograph: An 1840s Image Captures an Extremist's Fervor," *Smithsonian Magazine*, September 20, 2009, www.smithsonianmag.com; "Important Long-Lost Quarter Plate Daguerreotype of John Brown, the Abolitionist, by the African-American Daguerreotype Artist, Augustus Washington," December 6, 2007, www.cowanauctions.com.

11 Hinton, *John Brown and His Men*, 27. See also 716–717. Another description of the daguerreotype comes from a March 27, 1885 letter from John Brown's son, John Brown, Jr., to Frank B. Sanborn: "In regard to the daguerreotypes [*sic*] you refer to, I have them both. The one with flag, (which appears to be only of white or light colored cloth of some kind without stars, stripes or emblems of any sort), was taken by a Colored dagueresian [*sic*] artist at Hartford, named Washington. I doubt if you would consider it a good one." West Virginia Memory Project, John Brown/Boyd B. Stutler Collection Database, MS04–0050 A-D, 2021, www.wvculture.org.

12 Oswald Garrison Villard, *John Brown, 1800–1859: A Biography Fifty Years After* (Boston: Houghton Mifflin Company, 1910), 121.

13 For primary sources on the incident, see Hinton, *John Brown and His Men*, 61–92, 688–697. An enlightening secondary account is in Reynolds, *John Brown, Abolitionist*, 138–178.

14 "INTERESTING LETTER FROM KANSAS," *Boston Daily Bee*, in the *Liberator*, July 18, 1856, 3.

15 Redpath, *The Public Life of Capt. John Brown*, 105 (first and second quotations), 114 (third quotation). Redpath's extraordinary life is recounted in John R. McKivigan, *Forgotten Firebrand: James Redpath and the Making of Nineteenth-Century America* (Ithaca: Cornell University Press, 2008).

16 Hinton, *John Brown and His Men*, 721 (first and second quotations), 426–427 (third quotation). See also Redpath, *The Public Life of Capt. John Brown*, 190–192.

17 Franklin Sanborn to Thomas Wentworth Higginson, February 11, 1858, Boston Public Library, Digital Commonwealth: Massachusetts Collections Online, www.digitalcommonwealth.org. Years later, Sanborn clarified his remarks with the following: "What was meant was that treason to negro slavery was to be changed into allegiance to the Union, and anti-slavery was to be recognized as patriotism." Theodore Parker, *Saint Bernard and Other Papers*, ed. Charles W. Wendte (Boston: American Unitarian Association, 1911), 398. For Sanborn's first meeting with Brown and lifelong support of Brown's mission, see R. Blake Gilpin, *John Brown Still Lives! America's Long Reckoning with Violence, Equality, and Change* (Chapel Hill: University of North Carolina Press, 2011), 66–78.

18 Carton, *Patriotic Treason*, ix.

19 Hinton, *John Brown and His Men*, 614 (first and second quotations), 615 (third and fourth quotations).

20 For the history of White supremacy and racial segregation in nineteenth-century Canada, see Robin W. Winks, *The Blacks in Canada: A History*, 2nd ed. (Montreal: McGill-Queen's University Press, 1997), 490; John Boyko, *Last Steps to Freedom: The Evolution of Canadian Racism* (Winnipeg: Watson & Dwyer, 1995).

21 Hinton, *John Brown and His Men*, 32.

22 For the various meetings between Brown and Tubman and their relationship in general, see Jean M. Humez, *Harriet Tubman: The Life and the Life Stories* (Madison: University of Wisconsin Press, 2003), 32–42; Brown, *John Brown and His Men*, 172–173.

23 Frank A. Rollin, *Life and Public Services of Martin R. Delany, Sub-Assistant Commissioner Bureau Relief of Refugees, Freedmen, and of Abandoned Lands, and Late Major 104th U.S. Colored Troops* (Boston: Lee and Shepard, 1883), 86. Martin Delany recalled proudly of his role in organizing the convention: "The convention, when assembled, consisted of Captain John Brown, his son Owen, eleven or twelve of his Kansas followers, all young white men, enthusiastic and able, and probably sixty or seventy colored men, whom I brought together." Hinton, *John Brown and His Men*, 716.

24 Hinton, *John Brown and His Men*, 634–637, 714–718; James Cleland Hamilton, "John Brown in Canada," *Canadian Magazine* 4, no. 2 (December 1894): 124–128.

25 According to Martin Delany, rather than replacing the US government, "it was proposed that an independent community be established within and under the government of the United States, but without the state sovereignty of the compact, similar to the Cherokee nation of Indians, or the Mormons. To these last named, references were made, as parallel cases, at the time. The necessary changes and modifications were made in the constitution, and with such it was printed." Hinton, *John Brown and His Men*, 718.

26 Hinton, *John Brown and His Men*, 619–634 (first quotation on 632, second quotation on 631).

27 Ibid., 619 (first and second quotations), 619–620 (third quotation).

28 Villard, *John Brown*, 321.

29 Frederick Douglass, *Life and Times of Frederick Douglass Written by Himself* (Hartford, CT: Park Publishing, 1881), 276.

30 Villard, *John Brown*, 336

31 Carton, *Patriotic Treason*, 242 (first and second quotations), 263 (third quotation).

32 Reynolds, *John Brown, Abolitionist*, 263.

33 Hinton, *John Brown and His Men*, 633.

34 For Reynolds's biography, see Tom Calarco, *People of the Underground Railroad: A Biographical Dictionary* (Westport, CT: Greenwood Press, 2008), 253–255. For Reynolds's motion to strike Article 46, see Hinton, *John Brown and His Men*, 635.

35 Osborne P. Anderson, *A Voice from Harper's Ferry, a Narrative of Events at Harper's Ferry; with Incidents Prior and Subsequent to Its Capture by Captain Brown and His Men* (Boston: Printed for the Author, 1861), 11 (first quotation); Hinton, *John Brown and His Men*, 180 (second quotation).

36 Hamilton, "John Brown in Canada," 132.

37 Ibid., 133 (first quotation), 134 (second, third, and fourth quotations).

38 Hinton, *John Brown and His Men*, 217–228, 644–646 (quotations on 645). Hamilton, "John Brown in Canada."

39 Hinton, *John Brown and His Men*, 681 (first, second, third, fourth, and fifth quotations), 682 (sixth quotation).

40 Redpath, *The Public Life of Capt. John Brown*, 192–193; Hinton, *John Brown and His Men*, 236–239, 319–320.

41 Sarah H. Bradford, *Harriet, the Moses of Her People* (New York: George R. Lockwood and Son, 1886), 96. See also, Hinton, *John Brown and His Men*, 172–173.

42 Brown, *The Life and Letters of John Brown*, 468 (quotation), 525 (second quotation). See also 452.

43 Hinton, *John Brown and His Men*, 472. For Cook's extraordinary life, see Steven Lubet, *John Brown's Spy: The Adventurous Life and Tragic Confession of John E. Cook* (New Haven, CT: Yale University Press, 2012).

44 Tony Horwitz, *Midnight Rising: John Brown and the Raid That Sparked the Civil War* (New York: Henry Holt and Company, 2011), 122.

45 John Brown, "A Declaration of Liberty by the Representatives of the Slave Population of the United States of America," Preserving American Freedom: The Evolution of American Liberties in Fifty Documents, Historical Society of Pennsylvania, https://digitalhistory.hsp.org. While historians once dismissed the document as the work of a madman, this is no longer the case. David Reynolds explores the text's significance in *John Brown, Abolitionist*, 300–303. For a legal analysis, which refers to Brown as a "fringe constitutionalist," see Robert L. Tsai, "John Brown's Constitution," *Boston College Law Review* 51, no. 1 (2010): 151–207 (quotation on 186).

46 Brown, "A Declaration of Liberty."

47 Louis A. DeCaro, Jr., *The Untold Story of Shields Green: The Life and Death of a Harper's Ferry Raider* (New York: New York University Press, 2020), 71.

48 Brown, "A Declaration of Liberty."

49 François Furstenberg, *In the Name of the Father: Washington's Legacy, Slavery, and the Making of a Nation* (New York: Penguin, 2006), 195.

50 Brown, "A Declaration of Liberty."

51 Ibid.

52 Hinton, *John Brown and His Men*, 283, 293, 297, 329, 468. Scholars have long disagreed over the sword's provenance. For the origins of the historical debate, refer to "The John Brown Letters. Found in the Virginia State Library in 1901,"

Virginia Magazine of History and Biography 10, no. 1 (July 1902): 17–32; and Moncure D. Conway, "Washington and Frederick the Great. With the Story of a Mythical Sword," *Century Magazine* 41, no. 6 (April 1891): 945–948.

53 Select Committee on the Harper's Ferry Invasion, Report, 36th Cong., 1st sess., 1860, S Rep. 278, 14.

54 A. J. Phelps to W. P. Smith, October 17, 1859, *Correspondence Relating to the Insurrection at Harpers Ferry, 17th October, 1859* (Annapolis: B. H. Richardson, 1860), 5–30 (quotation on 5).

55 For the raid generally, see Horwitz, *Midnight Rising*; Reynolds, *John Brown, Abolitionist*; Stephen B. Oates, *To Purge this Land with Blood* (New York: Harper Torchbooks, 1970).

56 Hinton, *John Brown and His Men*, 398.

57 Horwitz, *Midnight Rising*, 256.

58 For some of the speeches and lectures by abolitionists in the weeks after Brown's arrest, see James Redpath, *Echoes of Harper's Ferry* (Boston: Thayer and Eldridge, 1860). For a much broader sample of reactions, refer to John Stauffer and Zoe Trodd, eds., *The Tribunal: Responses to John Brown and the Harpers Ferry Raid* (Cambridge, MA: Harvard University Press, 2012).

59 "Great Meeting in Boston, on the Day of the Execution of Captain John Brown," *Liberator*, December 9, 1859, 2. For the history of Tremont Temple and its capacity, see Anne C. Loveland and Otis B. Wheeler, *From Meetinghouse to Megachurch: A Material and Cultural History* (Columbia: University of Missouri Press, 2003), 28–31; and R. L. Midgley, *Sights in Boston and Suburbs, or Guide to the Stranger* (Boston: John P. Jewett, 1856), chapter VI.

60 "Speech of WM. Lloyd Garrison," *Liberator*, December 16, 1859, 2.

61 Ibid. In his initial remarks on the Harpers Ferry raid, Garrison called the action a "well-intended but sadly misguided effort of Capt. John Brown and his score of confederates." Nevertheless, the history of the American Revolution convinced Garrison to endorse Brown and violent resistance to slavery explicitly: "by the logic of Concord, Lexington and Bunker Hill, and by the principles enforced by this nation in its boasted Declaration of Independence, Capt. Brown was a hero, struggling against fearful odds, not for his own advantage, but to redeem others from a horrible bondage, to be justified in all that he aimed to achieve, however lacking in sound discretion. And by the same logic and the same principles, every slaveholder has forfeited his right to live, if his destruction be necessary to enable his victims to break the yoke of bondage; and they, and all who are disposed to aid them by force and arms, are fully warranted in carrying rebellion to any extent, and securing freedom at whatever cost." "The Tragedy at Harpers Ferry," *Liberator*, October 28, 1859, 2.

62 The other prisoners were John Edwin Cook, Edwin Coppoc, and Shields Green.

63 "Letter from John A. Copeland," *Oberlin Evangelist*, December 21, 1859, 203 [3]. For Copeland's life, see Steven Lubet, *The 'Colored Hero' of Harper's Ferry: John*

Anthony Copeland and the War against Slavery (Cambridge: Cambridge University Press, 2015).

64 "Letter from John A. Copeland."

65 "CHARLESTON, VA., Dec. 17," *Baltimore Sun*, December 19, 1859, 4.

66 William Cooper Nell, *The Colored Patriots of the American Revolution, with Sketches of Several Distinguished Colored Person* (Boston: Robert F. Wallcutt, 1855), 14.

67 Mitch Kachun, *First Martyr of Liberty: Crispus Attucks in American Memory* (Oxford: Oxford University Press, 2017), 51.

68 "SPEECH OF DR. JOHN S. ROCK," *Liberator*, March 16, 1860, 2. For contextualization, see "Speech by John S. Rock," March 5, 1860, *Black Abolitionist Papers*, Document 12, 5: 58–70. For a description of the vestry known as The Menionaon, see Midgley, *Sights in Boston and Suburbs*, 51–53.

69 Ibid.

70 "CELEBRATION AT NORTH ELBA," *Liberator*, July 27, 1860, 2.

71 Ibid., 2 (first and second quotations), 3 (third and fourth quotations).

72 Ibid., 2.

73 Ibid., 1.

74 Luther Lee, *Autobiography of the Rev. Luther, D.D.* (New York: Phillips and Hunt, 1882), 295.

75 "FOURTH OF JULY ORATION," *Liberator*, August 30, 1860, 1.

76 Ibid., 2.

77 Ibid., 1.

Epilogue

1 "Interesting Correspondence," *Liberator*, November 6, 1863, 4.

2 "THE MASS 54TH AT FORT WAGNER," *Liberator*, August 28, 1863, 2.

3 Ibid. Among those inside the hospital was journaler Charlotte Forten, the African American abolitionist from Boston who moved to South Carolina during the war to assist Union troops and the local Black population. She wrote of the gravely injured sergeant, "He is said to be one of the best and bravest men in the regiment." *The Journal of Charlotte L. Forten*, ed. Ray Allen Billington (New York: Dryden Press, 1953), 216.

4 Mike Fitzpatrick, "Union Army Rank Insignia," *Military Images* 22, no. 4 (Jan./Feb. 2001): 25.

5 Alice Fahs, *The Imagined Civil War: Popular Literature of the North & South, 1861–1865* (Chapel Hill: University of North Carolina Press, 2001), 168.

6 Mark E. Neely, Jr., and Harold Holzer, *The Union Image: Popular Prints of the Civil War North* (Chapel Hill: University of North Carolina Press, 2000), caption for Plate 21.

INDEX

Page numbers in italics indicate Figures.

ABOUT THE AUTHOR

MATTHEW J. CLAVIN, Professor of History at the University of Houston, is the author of *The Battle of Negro Fort*, *Aiming for Pensacola*, and *Toussaint Louverture and the American Civil War*.